THE RELIGIONS
OF
THE OPPRESSED

THE
RELIGIONS
OF THE
OPPRESSED

A STUDY OF
MODERN MESSIANIC CULTS

BY

VITTORIO LANTERNARI

TRANSLATED FROM THE ITALIAN BY
LISA SERGIO

1 9   6 3

New York   ALFRED·A·KNOPF

L. C. catalog card number: 62-15568

THIS IS A BORZOI BOOK,

PUBLISHED BY ALFRED A. KNOPF, INC.

FIRST AMERICAN EDITION

Originally published in Italian as *Movimenti religiosi di libertà e di salvezza dei popoli oppressi* by Giangiacomo Feltrinelli Editore. Copyright © 1960 by Giangiacomo Feltrinelli Editore.

PREFACE

THE HISTORY of religious movements can be written from a variety of angles and on the basis of very different criteria. Some prefer to present the facts pertaining to the religious life of a given civilization as viewed from within the closed circle of the subject itself; hence they do not feel the need to relate these particular developments to others of a secular nature, or to the culture from which they originally stem. This type of historian is a *phenomenologist*, who is concerned mainly with discovering and identifying the universal and unchanging religious "structures."

Others, instead, tend to place all religious manifestations, regardless of the cultural level on which they occur, into certain clearly defined categories, grouping them indiscriminately under certain common denominators, such as solar cults, agrarian cults, sky worship, etc., even if they occur against very different historical backgrounds. This is the criterion of the *morphologists*. It is a useful one in so far as it brings about a comparison between various religious movements by putting them side by side; but it is also dangerous in that for the sake of a common heading it tends to obliterate the fundamental differences between movements and minimizes growth.

The present author prefers the historical approach by means of which it is possible to explain the religious phenomenon and therefore to justify it. To justify a religious movement means to explain its nature, its function, and its genesis as well as its internal and external dynamics due, respectively,

v

to factors inherent in the culture and to the impact from other cultures and external forces. My approach is based on the concept that it is not possible to envision an authentic history of religion outside the broad scope of the culture by which it is encompassed. This book is a book of religious history, planned as a study of the relationship between religious and secular life as it develops within the general pattern of a civilization. A religious phenomenon may be explained only in so far as it is possible to trace its historical origin and development and to analyze it systematically in relation to concrete secular conditions. These conditions may be described as the *existential experiences* to which human society is bound at any given historical moment, and which in turn give rise to cultural *exigencies* which apply likewise to that particular moment. These *experiences* and *exigencies* are to be found at the root of every religious manifestation.

The birth of the cults of liberation deriving from a colonial status provide one of the most startling demonstrations of the close tie between religious life and secular, political, and cultural life. The birth of these movements can only be understood in the light of historical conditions relating to the colonial experiences and to the striving of subject peoples to become emancipated. Furthermore, it is not possible to separate the world of the so-called primitive peoples from the world commonly described as historical, be it ancient or modern. There is an unbreakable continuity between these two levels of civilization which must be taken into account in order fully to understand both the primitive and the modern world. Despite the absence of "written history" and of precise evidence testifying to the past of the primitive civilizations, these too are affected by the historical process whereby they are altered and transformed.

The study of these ethnological civilizations, with their

economic and technological backwardness, reveals characteristics found in ancient or in prehistoric cultures which were
also based on primitive ways of life. These ancient and prehistoric cultures are the roots of our present Western civilization, which, despite the growth and progress of centuries, in
many cases has retained some of the early elements found in
folklore, in popular superstitions and taboos.

The prophetic and messianic movements of the "primitive"
world with which this book is concerned cannot be fully
understood unless they are methodically compared to the
prophetic and messianic movements underlying the so-called
historical civilizations. As a matter of fact, it is absurd to
speak of religious ethnology and of religious history as two
separate sciences. They are merely two phases of the same
historical process.

Today, as we watch the so-called savage or backward
peoples come to the fore and take their place on the world
stage, it becomes the cultural, political, and moral duty of
those who belong to a so-called cultured and elite civilization
to recognize the call to freedom and liberation rising from
the mouths of thousands of prophets who speak from the
jungles of the Congo, from the remote islands of Melanesia,
from the atolls of Polynesia, from the forgotten tribes of
continental Asia, and from the Indian reservations of North
America. This call, solemn and powerful because of the
cultural dignity it seeks to express, demands an answer from
the Western world—and the answer must be at once political,
social, and religious. It is the task of governments, churches,
and other bodies to formulate the terms in which the answer
must be couched, but the purpose of this book is merely to
underscore the indictment of Western civilization implicit in
this cry for freedom.

The voice of these countless prophets reminds us of the

boundaries which we have imposed upon our own civilization. The cry for freedom rising from the throats of the oppressed peoples is fraught with lessons for us to learn, for it inherently denounces the contradictions within our own culture, as they appear to the new worlds now beginning to take shape. These new worlds, so very different from ours, are now experiencing a crisis; but their impact upon the West has thrown our civilization into shock, initiating an era of travail which can be fruitful for all mankind if it leads to a broader humanism than the world has ever before known.

The field covered by this book has been deliberately circumscribed to include only the prophetic movements and movements for liberation among peoples still at the ethnological level of development. Even so, this is in no way a complete picture of all religious movements in that field, for our work has been guided by considerations of existing problems rather than by any intention of producing a systematic, documented study.

The modern religious movements that are occurring in the "civilized" world of East and West have been excluded, as have been the great prophetic movements of ancient times. Such major religious phenomena as Buddhism, Taoism, Judaism, Christianity, or Islam appear in this book only where they relate directly to the movements of liberation. Indeed, it is important to remember that each of these great religions began as a prophetic movement of renewal stimulated by certain given cultural and social conditions in a time of crisis.

By comparing these great religious movements with those which now prevail among the so-called primitive peoples, one discovers certain key situations which are common to all of them, including the fact that the striving for religious renewal and liberation arises from the rebellion of the masses against the existing official cults imposed by a ruling caste.

This book, within its clearly defined boundaries, seeks to offer a history of the religious movements among colonial and semicolonial peoples, viewed in relation to the political and social conditions prevailing at a time when the voice of the people demanding change is gradually rising above the din of conservative tradition.

FOREWORD TO
THE ENGLISH-LANGUAGE
EDITION

MANY SIGNIFICANT events in the religious and social history of what was once the colonial world have occurred since the original publication of this book in Italian, in the autumn of 1960. Between then and now the indigenous populations of the Congo, both French and Belgian, of Upper Volta, of Sierra Leone, of the Ivory Coast, of Tanganyika, and of other parts of Africa discussed here, have shaken off the yoke of colonial rule. The newly achieved political independence of these countries has put into tangible form at least a part of the religious promise of liberation and renewal voiced by native prophets during many decades and kept alive by the religious movements they gave rise to.

The fact that these prophetic movements pave the way for political emancipation in Africa is not without precedent; the same sequence of events occurred earlier in the Philippines, in Indonesia, and in Vietnam. In more recent times, however, the promise of liberation has tended to transcend the realm of hopeful expectations; it has entered into that of social and civil realities, sometimes at the cost of violence and upheavals. For the people freed from foreign rule, the attainment of these realities often involves a laborious and even violent process of acculturation.

The question has been raised whether, once independence

has been attained, the religious message of renovation preserves its purpose and meaning; or whether, conversely, it changes purpose and function or, indeed, ceases to exist. It seems to me that if, on the one hand, a major part of the religious message has found social and political implementation through a tangible process of change, on the other hand the religions themselves are now striving to express the need for individual salvation created by the change, while the newly formed independent churches are playing a role which tends to be socially static and conservative. The prophetic messages, being of a strictly religious nature, urge expectation of a complete change in human conditions and an *eschaton* involving the "absolute" end of all evil and the achievement of a "supreme" good. Probably there is no phenomenon which reflects more clearly than do the religious movements among oppressed peoples the contradictory, yet indissoluble, bond between current reality and future goals, between history and eschatology, which lies at the root of almost every major human experience.

A study of these religious movements among so-called primitive peoples is of the utmost importance to modern man, because each of them reveals a final end of its own by interpreting human life in terms of an ultimate goal which is both "supreme" and "absolute." The movements analyzed here are concerned with a bitter and painful present as well as with a radiant future wherein all evil will be erased. Modern Western civilization has the merit of having understood the historical relationship between human goals and human values and of devising an eschatology which is completely humanistic rather than theological, even though the problem of the relationship between history and eschatology has not been solved even for the West. Thus, the Roman Catholic view of history is governed by Providence; for the Calvinists, history is the fulfillment of the Kingdom of God; and an outstanding Protestant thinker, such as Dr. R. Bultman, believes that "every moment is an eschatological moment." Many Western philosophies view history as an evolutionary or dialectical process; the Marxists see it as a dynamic development tending to integrate man in the world around him; and many a "common man" sees the meaning and goal of history summarized in the four freedoms of Franklin D. Roosevelt. Although each history has its own teleology, the important fact is that the drive which motivates man's practical choices and causes him to struggle and suffer for a better future is common to all and rises out of a faith that is absolute. Thus, even while man is aware of the relativity of human values and goals, nonetheless he behaves "as if" the goal were a final one (*eschaton*) and "as if" the values he defends were absolute values. The "as if" approach, which is symbolical and eschatological, is used by modern man even though his symbolism and his final ends are becoming more and more humanistic and less and less theological. Indeed, the movements among primitive peoples, at least in their early phase, also express a humanistic eschatology, in that they promise and expect a world in which man will be fully integrated and free from oppression.

Many books and studies on this subject have appeared since the publication of this book in its original Italian form, and a great number of sociologists, historians, ethnologists, missionaries, and churches are becoming increasingly concerned with these so-called "non-Christian sects." Recent contributions of outstanding importance include *East African Rebels*, by F. B. Welbourn (London, 1961); a new edition of *Bantu Prophets in South Africa*, by B. G. M. Sundkler (London,

1961); W. E. Mülhlmann's sociological and ethnological synthesis called *Chiliasmus und Nativismus* (Berlin, 1961); and the report on the Thirty-first Week of Missiology called *Devant les Sectes Non-Chrétiennes* (Louvain, 1961).

My preface to the Italian edition states that I was not attempting to cover all the available material, for even a survey limited to all ethnological data would have doubled the size of the volume and greatly delayed its publication. My primary concern was not the listing of a vast number of religious movements. Numbers hold less interest for me than the quest for answers to the "whys" arising in each case, and social and historical implications are far more important, affecting, as they do, major trends in Western society. Even in this regard, however, I had to place a limitation on the amount of material I could deal with; much that I was obliged to set aside could be used in a later revised edition.

The choice of such religious movements as I singled out for study was neither subjective nor arbitrary. It was based, rather, on the quality of the material, which abounded in some cases and was scarce in others. There was a great deal to draw from in regard to Africa and America and much less in regard to Asia. Peyotism was treated in great detail, because this movement is amply documented and also because, through a more complete study of it, I could illustrate the full historical setting in which these movements occur.

I have been charged with dealing unfairly with the work of the missions by placing it in an unfavorable light. I therefore wish to make it clear that it was not my purpose to write a history of missionary work, but to analyze the religious reaction of the indigenous peoples to the various manifestations of the white man's cultural policy. Obviously, a historian would have had to show the countless contributions made by the missions, both Protestant and Roman Catholic, often at the price of great abnegation and sacrifice, to the progress of native communities—through the establishment of hospitals and schools, through the teaching of hygiene and other techniques for better living, through the introduction of modern tools and goods, as well as through the study of aboriginal languages and the gathering of vitally important scientific facts. None of this is highlighted in my book, not because I underestimate its significance but because these facts, positive as they are, do not enter into the history of the religious movements as such. The only aspect of missionary work which does affect and concern the native peoples is the preaching of the Gospel, which I have emphasized throughout my book.

The protagonists of these religious movements are the indigenous populations with whom this study is concerned and not, as in many other studies, the ruling minorities which have exposed themselves to the judgment and criticism of the natives seeking liberty and progress. The anti-Western attitude which emerges from this study is not the personal attitude of the author but that of the native peoples expressed through their own ideas and, often, in their own words. Their feeling toward the missions is only one facet of their general stand in regard to the white man. There have been instances of the cruel and violent turn which anti-Western feeling has taken among the natives and, dislike this as one may, it is the duty of the historian to report facts and reactions as they are and to strive to discover their motivations. Indeed, I hold the belief that, in an age of major historical change, when so many populations are coming to the fore and asserting their right to cultural and political independence, it is the duty of the Western world to listen to what these populations are saying, to learn what they are thinking, especially in regard to those who were once their masters and should now be their partners.

One final point should be brought out. Several authors in this field have insisted upon making a distinction between Protestant and Roman Catholic missions; they state that the religious movements and sects which arose among native peoples were the result of Protestant evangelism, whereas, in their view, Roman Catholic preaching did not lead to similar results. This statement is an oversimplification of the facts and largely incorrect, even though it does contain certain elements of reality. It is an undeniable fact that the liberal interpretation of the Bible offered by Protestantism has favored the growth of new religious movements and sects, even as it is true that a majority of these new religions are found in areas where Protestant missions were prevalent. Nonetheless, it cannot be gainsaid that several such movements have stemmed directly from Roman Catholicism. Without overlooking the Lazzaretti movement, the neo-Mosaic movement of San Nicandro, and other modern sects found in Italy and France, it is most important to realize the Roman Catholic influence in the movements started by Kanakuk and Smohalla among the North American Indians, in the prophetic cults of the Tukunas in South America, in the syncretistic movements of Haiti and Brazil, in the neo-Brazilian cults and in those initiated by Solares in Argentina and by Santos Atahuallpa in Peru, in the Antonian movement in the Congo, in the Karoem sect in Dutch New Guinea, and in the Aglipayan church and other nativistic movements in the Philippines. The Kugu Sorta emerged in a Russian Orthodox milieu.

In conclusion, the reasons behind these new religions involve the entire picture of native society and the general conditions of life prevailing within it. Therefore, it is vitally important not to confuse their "determining causes" with the "factors" which favored them, among which Protestantism must certainly be included.

VITTORIO LANTERNARI

March 1962

CONTENTS

Contents

THE RELIGIONS
OF
THE OPPRESSED

CHAPTER

I

NATIVISTIC-RELIGIOUS
MOVEMENTS IN AFRICA

W HEN THE FIRST tremors of rebellion ran through the Belgian Congo, Nyasaland, French Equatorial Africa, Kenya, and West Africa, neither the seasoned observer nor the discerning ethnologist was taken by surprise. These were the inevitable if perturbing manifestations of a religious ferment which had been ripening in Africa for well over fifty years, causing profound disturbances in the patterns of traditional culture. As a matter of fact, premonitory religious movements of revival and transformation usually lie at the origin of every political or military uprising among the native peoples and take the form of messianic cults promising liberation.

Such movements and cults have been growing not only on the African continent, where they have reached from South Africa to Rhodesia and Tanganyika, to Equatorial Africa and the West Coast, to Angola and the Congo, to Uganda and

Kenya; they have flourished likewise in Melanesia, Polynesia, and Indonesia, as well as among the aborigines of the Americas. In Africa, when the clash first occurred between Western culture and the culture of the indigenous populations, new native religious movements quickly began to take shape and soon expanded so powerfully as to command the attention not only of the colonial governments and of the Western churches but of modern civilization as a whole. Far from being the product of outside propaganda, or being instigated by alien forces to serve their own game of power politics, these movements were the spontaneous result of the impact of the white man's presence on native society—an impact which, having generated more and more pressures during two world wars, was inevitably bound to create far-reaching disturbances.

The religious nature of these movements reveals a trait characteristic of native societies. In these societies, if the indigenous way of life has been subjected to misery, persecution, and other adversities, the people seek relief from their frustrations and sufferings in religious ways—in many cases even before attempting to do so by political means. In such a situation all the manifestations of the native culture—economic, social, political, or philosophical—become permeated by a deeply religious spirit. When a people is unable to repel the intruders who have seized its land, as in the case of the Plains Indians in North America or the Maoris in New Zealand, almost invariably a new religious cult springs into being which inspires the natives to express opposition to foreign rule. Thus, by making a display of their religious independence, the people strive to fight the racial segregation, forced acculturation, or destruction of tribal life imposed both by the missionaries and by the colonial administrators.

The native cults are as varied in form as are the problems

4

they attempt to solve. Some of them, intended to meet the need for change awakened in the aboriginal society by its contact with Western culture, even establish a working relationship with the whites. Nonetheless, in their religious aspects these cults always adhere to native tradition and reject Western beliefs, although often adjusting the ancient myth or ritual to the new environment created by alien rule. Whatever the form, the vitality of these movements proves that the dynamic element is strong even in the most primitive groups, thereby refuting a long-held belief that aboriginal culture and religion are completely stagnant and incapable of moving ahead with the times. Actually, the new cults not only express and implement a popular yearning for liberty and a fuller life, but also fulfill, in modern terms, the role of secular leadership which religion is expected to play in a primitive society.

In Africa, the political and social situation which brought on the nativistic religious movements is clearly summarized in the cry of native agitators to the whites: "At first we had the land and you had the Bible. Now we have the Bible and you have the land." These bitter words contain the diagnosis of the ill which has gripped the continent. They also point to the fundamental cause of the conflict between the natives and the predatory ruling minority: the white man's seizure of the land. As a British official once put it, "the Native question *is* the land question." And Dr. Bengt Sundkler, an enlightened Swedish Protestant missionary, added that "even the Separatist church problem is a corollary of the land problem."[1] The increase in the number of Bantu independent churches parallels the tightening squeeze of the natives through drastic land legislation.

[1] B. G. M. Sundkler: *Bantu Prophets in South Africa* (London, 1958), p. 33.

5

The first major clash occurred in South Africa in 1913 when the Natives Land Act made it illegal for Africans to acquire or rent land except within certain zones. In Natal, which in 1921 covered 25,000 square miles of territory and had a European population of 132,000 as against one million Africans, the latter were permitted to hold less than 4,000 square miles of land. In the whole of South Africa, populated by one million whites and five million Africans, the latter, confined to the so-called reservations, had to be content with far less living space than was set aside for the Europeans, who were only one fifth their number.

In Natal, the Act forced the Africans to leave their native province in great numbers and to move into the reservations or crowd into the cities, especially Johannesburg. In 1923 the segregation policy, which had previously applied only to rural areas, came to affect the cities. This resulted from the enforcement of the Urban Act, which made the situation even more tragic for the natives while assuring the white farmers of all the hands they needed on the land. Now the natives had but one or two choices left: to become serfs of the European masters on their soil, or huddle together on the outer rims of the cities. In 1926 the South African Parliament legislatively imposed the "colour-bar" on the mining industries; and as the possibilities of finding employment decreased for the natives, their bitterness mounted like a rising tide, spilling venom all over the Union. The Native Trust and Land Act of 1936 did little or nothing to alleviate these conditions.

The question of color separation—*apartheid*—became of paramount importance from the first encounters between whites and natives. All the social activities of the two groups were governed by three fateful words: *Net Vir Blankes*— "for Europeans only." An incident related by Pastor Sundkler

6

shows to what extent this rule was accepted by even the Christian missionaries. A European woman who worked in the mission at Natal went to visit a missionary center in Durban and, meeting a Zulu pastor in the street, greeted him cordially and stopped to chat with him in a friendly, normal way. A few days later she received a letter from the pastor, thanking her in touching terms for having deigned to treat him as a human being and for honoring him by talking to him in the street. The letter also added that the missionaries did not seem to mind treating the natives as ordinary mortals on the mission compound, but that when they were in a public place or in the street they complied with the accepted rule which regarded the natives as "serfs of their European masters."[2]

Not by chance, then, did the separatist movement penetrate the churches. It was a direct consequence of racial ill feeling and of forced idleness among the indigenous population. In fact, it is symptomatic that the leaders of many independent churches and cults are former land or city workers, deprived of jobs by the various Acts and startled by the contradiction between the white man's behavior toward the natives and the Christian principles he teaches. All of this served to tear the natives away from the mission churches and gave rise to nativistic interpretations of Christianity[3] in the form of prophetic cults which promise liberation and independence to their followers.

THE CONGO, EQUATORIAL AND CENTRAL AFRICA

The region lying between the banks of the Middle and Lower Congo River is a focal center of religious movements from which new cults have been expanding into French Equatorial

[2] Ibid., pp. 32, 35.
[3] Ibid., pp. 34, 36-7.

Africa and the Belgian Congo. From an eighteenth-century chronicle we learn of strange ways in which the impact of Christianity affected the traditional religious beliefs. A Belgian monk, working among the Bakongo tribes, came upon a prophetess known as Beatrice, who, by virtue of dreams and visions and by her memory of deaths and births, claimed to be the reincarnation of Saint Anthony. Announcing that the Day of Judgment was at hand, Beatrice surrounded herself with "angels," and to one of them, named Saint John, she bore a son. Shortly thereafter she founded a movement called Antonian, after the saint she embodied; it attracted a huge following dedicated to the restoration of the native kingdom of San Salvador and to the revival of all customs banished by the missionaries. For her heresies the monk saw to it that she was burned at the stake, but her large following remained united in pursuing the goals set by the martyred prophetess. Thus we see an astonishing example of pagan-Christian syncretism in which a Christian saint, usually portrayed holding the Child Jesus in his arms, is given a pagan connotation as the protector of fecundity and fertility.[4] Hunters among the Bakongo Christians use the crucifix[5] as a fetish for their protection—again showing the extraordinary result of the impact between two cultures totally unprepared to meet or understand each other. The native religions must answer such vital human needs as fecundity, fertility of the soil, and good hunting; whereas Christianity, arising as it did from urban societies in crisis, both in the Middle East and in the West, fulfills spiritual yearnings of a totally different order, and remains obscure and irrelevant to the natives of Africa.

Fetishism—the worship of inanimate objects having specific

[4] J. Cuvelier: *Relation sur le Congo du Père Laurent de Lucques,* 1700–1717 (Brussels, 1953).

[5] R. Wannijn: "Objets anciens en métal du Bas Congo," *Zaïre,* V (1952), pp. 391–4.

8

uses and endowed with magical powers—is a typical religious form in the Congo and has a major role in the new messianic movements,[6] which are basically intended to fulfill two major functions: express hostility to the white man and protect the natives from the effects of sorcery and black magic. The first great prophetic movement in the Congo dates back to 1904 and is both fetishist and xenophobe. Founded by a miracle worker called Epikilipikili, it was dedicated to a fetish of his own creation called *bwanga*, effective against every sort of evil, including black magic, and capable of rendering the native immune to the white man's bullets. This secret sect spread from the Congo to other regions and gained the support of many powerful tribal chiefs.

Epikilipikili established a pattern for many other secret societies (Mani in Boma, Punga or Muana Okanga among the miners of Katanga, Nebili in the Azande) which flourished throughout Central and West Africa and which, although stemming from the traditional association of tribes for mutual protection from sorcery, were mainly anti-Western in purpose. In fact, in the year following the foundation of Epikilipikili's sect, rebellions broke out in the Kasai region on the Sankuru River. Other uprisings, marked by violence and bloodshed, were spurred by the new cult in the Cuango and Lukenie regions. Members were pledged to passive resistance to European rule: boycotting its textiles and other products including salt, refusing to pay taxes or to serve the white man in any capacity whatsoever. Thus the first revolts against imperialism started under cover of religious worship, and when, as in 1905 and thereafter, the white man's bullets killed the rebels, it became easy for the natives to believe that their defeat was due to their own transgressions of their secret

[6] J. Comhaire: "Africa" (1955), p. 55.

9

societies. Hence they lost neither their faith nor their determination to persevere.

In the Kasai region, the Bashilele peoples formed a society called Lukusu or Nkisi Lukoi, founded on the worship of a *nkisi* (panacea), which gave immunity to all diseases and to all the effects of sorcery. Later the Lukusu became the cult of the "talking serpent" or "snake-man" who protected the faithful from all evil, becoming one of the countless sects to worship the man-beast. It is still a major expression of religious belief in Equatorial Africa. The "talking serpent" or "snake-man" of the Bashilele had an unmistakably anti-European intent, for the serpent was expected to bring forth prophets and messiahs to fight the white masters and chase them forever from the land.

According to the cult of the Bashilele, which began to expand in 1933, the advent of a Messiah or liberator was to be preceded by extraordinary events, such as the collective rising of the dead, the eclipse of the sun, the appearance in every village of a black talking-dog, and the coming of a Man, part white and part black. The natives were to acquire invincible power by drinking a special magic potion from special magic cups. Not long after the sect had gained a footing, secret rituals were performed around the ancestral tombs, and the natives actually stopped working in order to wait for the return of the dead bringing them untold riches with which to inaugurate a new era of happiness and well-being.

Here the old belief in the end of the world and in regeneration is merged with a new belief in the expulsion of the white man—this combination being found in many religious cults which prophesy the liberation of the natives from foreign rule. This newfangled creed strives to satisfy the yearning of the natives for autonomy, better conditions of life, and deliverance from oppression and misery while remaining within the framework of such long-accepted beliefs as the rising of the dead, the eclipse of the sun, and the impending appearance of a Man, part white and part black, who will announce the end of the existing order and prepare the way for the Messiah. The familiar beliefs merely provide a foundation for new cults whose ultimate purpose it is to fulfill unprecedented aspirations stimulated in the natives by the presence of the Westerners, with their new instruments of power and the fruits of their new economy.

The Secret Societies, which operated simultaneously against sorcery and the white man's rule, flourished chiefly among the Congolese who had been removed from their tribe after World War I and made to work for foreign masters. On the other hand, the religious movements of messianic character with Christian overtones gained a following largely among the natives who had remained in their own villages.

The year 1921 brought forth the powerful personality of Simon Kimbangu, whose movement, called Kimbangu or Ngunzi (the word *ngunzi* means prophet), found fertile soil wherever Christianity had been preached. Eventually the Ngunzi movement gave rise to several autonomous churches and to a number of well-organized political groups working for national independence. In the Congo this phase of religious development produced such prophets as Kimbangu, André Matswa, Simon Mpadi, and Mavonda Ntangu; Rhodesia had Muana Lesa, who ended on the gallows in 1926. All these native leaders, influenced by the Protestant missions, had committed themselves to Christianity. Their teachings, however, harked back almost entirely to the Old Testament, from which they carefully culled only the passages best suited to furthering their nationalistic and anti-Western goals—a fact which profoundly altered the meaning and values of Christian doctrine.

11

Simon Kimbangu was raised in the British Baptist Mission of Nkamba, a stronghold of Protestantism, and came into further contact with Western culture working as a house servant for a European family at Kinshasa. In 1921, answering the call to evangelism which had come to him through precognizant dreams and visions of the Supreme Being of the ancient Bakongo tradition, now identified in his mind with the Judeo-Christian God, he went forth as a prophet among the people of his native land. The fame of his miracles, including the resurrection of the dead, soon spread far afield, drawing more and more followers in his wake who obeyed his Mosaic injunctions to forsake idolatry and polygamy and to worship a single God. The Biblical passages favored by Kimbangu were chosen for the antiwhite message which they could be made to convey. On one occasion, when the French Resident came from Thysville to see him, the prophet was engaged in explaining the story of David and Goliath to a large crowd of natives and eliciting an enthusiastic response from his audience. The caller's request for an immediate interview merely caused the prophet deliberately to turn his back on him and to continue his inflammatory sermon.[1] Very soon the Congolese were calling Kimbangu "God of the Black Man," in contrast to the God of the White Missionaries; and although his evangelism was Christian in essence and baptism and confession were regularly adopted by his followers, the tone of his preaching was unmistakably nationalistic. Kimbangu prophesied the imminent ousting of the foreign rulers, a new way of life for the Africans, the return of the dead, and the coming of a Golden Age to be awaited in the arms of the native church.[2] He was strongly opposed by the local

[1] E. Andersson: *Messianic Popular Movements in the Lower Congo* (Uppsala, 1958), p. 62; J. van Wing: "Le Kibangisme vu par un témoin," *Zaïre*, XII (1958), p. 568.
[2] G. Balandier: *Sociologie de l'Afrique Noire* (Paris, 1955), p. 428; Andersson: op. cit., p. 63; Van Wing: op. cit., pp. 573–6.

authorities and was finally arrested and deported. After escaping from prison, he returned voluntarily to serve his term and died behind bars at Elisabethville in 1950.[3]

Despite its intransigent opposition to the white man's rule, the Kimbangu movement was highly advanced in a Western sense, even though it placed definite limitations upon the influence which Christian doctrine was permitted to exert over native tradition. Certain basic elements of this tradition, such as the cult of healing and belief in the collective rising of the dead and in a Supreme Being, were reshaped to fit into a new context, thereby creating a renewal rather than a mere revival of religious fervor. On the one hand, the fight against fetishism, derived from the traditional fight of the Secret Societies against sorcery, constituted a break with the older belief in magic;[4] and on the other, the Christian doctrine of the dignity of the individual, learned from the missionaries, was interpreted as God's promise that the natives would soon be delivered from the presence of the white man. The one God of the Judeo-Christian faith was grafted onto the traditional figure of the Supreme Being of the native cults; the Bible, recognized as religious authority, was used to stimulate popular demand for freedom; the struggle of David against Goliath was explained as the struggle of the blacks against the whites; the prophet himself, claiming to reincarnate Moses and Christ, viewed his own persecution as the re-enactment of the sacrifice made of himself by Jesus, for the redemption of mankind. The seeds of religious renewal planted by Kimbangu and nurtured on the hope of autonomy bore fruit only after the prophet had suffered imprisonment and death. For it was the "martyrdom" of the founder, identified with the sufferings of Moses and of Christ, which brought the Africans

[3] Andersson: op. cit., pp. 63–7; Van Wing: op. cit., pp. 578–80.

[4] It is to be noted that fetishism and witchcraft are two very different phenomena: the latter (black magic) is antisocial, whereas the former, turning against witchcraft, seeks to protect society.

13

to a full acceptance of the new faith, now become relevant to their needs.

Kimbangu's call to emancipation was soon to be implemented by his successors; under their guidance the early National Negro Clan became in effect an autonomous native church.[5] The principle of the "native church" is particularly important because it testifies to the impact of Christian thought upon the natives, which awakened them to their own need for a religious regeneration—even though they sought it in ways of their own making, outside and often against those taught by the missionaries. The deportation of Kimbangu did not extinguish or even dim the religious flame he had lighted. His followers carried on their rituals clandestinely in the forest, while new prophets continued to feed the fire, spreading the Kimbangu or Ngunzi[6] doctrine throughout the Congo until, in 1930, another great leader emerged in the person of André Matswa.[7]

Born near Brazzaville, into the Sundi Ladi tribe of Balali people, and raised a Roman Catholic, André Matswa fought in the First World War on the battlefields of France. Later, in Paris, he encountered such political groups as the Union des Travailleurs Nègres (the Negro Workers Union) and the Ligue de la Défense de la Race Nègre (League for the Defense of the Negro Race), and soon became a recognized leader in their midst. Still in France, in 1926, he founded the Amicale Balali (the Friendly Balali Society), later known as Amicalism, designed to induce the French government to seek and find a solution to the Negro problem and even to support the antiwhite resistance of the Africans. His arrest, in 1930 and in 1940, his deportation to the Chad, and his long

[5] Andersson: op. cit., p. 70.
[6] Ibid., pp. 69–95; Van Wing: op. cit., pp. 581–95.
[7] Andersson: op. cit., pp. 96–117.

imprisonment added to his stature as a hero-leader and finally endowed him with the crown of martyrdom. Thus, André Matswa became the successor to Simon Kimbangu; and the manner of his death in 1942, far from attenuating the enthusiasm of his followers, helped to spread the belief that he would soon return as the liberator of his people. Living, André Matswa had been the Messiah; dead, he became the Negro Christ and the people called him Jesus Matswa.[8]

During their lifetime, both André Matswa and Simon Kimbangu had received the title of "King of the Congo" from the natives of all territories under Belgian and French rule, symbolizing the unity and freedom eagerly sought by the indigenous populations. The continuing spiritual presence of these leaders motivated the organization of a strong new church, unswervingly autonomous, polemical in regard to both the missionaries and the government, and founded upon old traditions but receptive to Christian ideas.[9] What Georges Balandier points out in his *Sociologie de l'Afrique Noire* applies to Matswa even more aptly than to Kimbangu: Christianity, offering the example of a Messiah sacrificed to the blind intransigence of public powers no less than to the infamy of his enemies, yet rising triumphant for the redemption of the faithful, awakened in the natives a revolutionary spirit, from which Christianity itself had stemmed, and thereby set the seal of religious approval on the demand for religious and cultural independence and self-determination.

The Christian promise of a "Kingdom" and a "Millennium" for the salvation of all mankind, inherited from the messianic tradition of the Jews, was heeded by the natives as a call against the repressive rule of the colonial powers. Worshipping its own martyrs, Matswa and Kimbangu, and

[8] Balandier: op. cit., pp. 397-416; Andersson: op. cit., pp. 117-25.
[9] Balandier: *Afrique ambiguë* (Paris, 1957), pp. 236-7.

15

guided by its current prophets,[1] the natives' messianic cult was powerfully unified by the Christian promise and by the more tangible reality of a struggle to be won against the European master and his white churches. "Christ is a French God," said the natives, offsetting him with their duel deity of Matswa-Kimbangu. They added: "Christianity is the religion which serves to keep wealth in the white man's hands while hiding from the natives the secret of his power."[2]

The combination of past and present found in the Ngunzi and in the Amicale cults, typical of all native churches in the Congo, is strikingly exemplified in the use of the sign of the cross. Taking the cruciform gesture from Christianity, the natives accompany it with words which vitiate its entire meaning: "In the name of the Father, of Simon Kimbangu, and of André Matswa."[3] This nativistic[4] and heretical trinity[5] shows how the Africans have taken over the scriptural idea of God the Father because of its affinity to the pagan Supreme Being, Nzambi Pungu, flanking it with two aboriginal prophets, whom they identify with the Son and the Holy Spirit, even as the Christian lighting of candles embodies, in their eyes, an ancient pagan ritual.[6] The altar of the native chapel, rising above a platform with steps, is draped in vivid red and fur-

[1] Ibid., p. 237; Balandier: *Sociologie de l'Afrique Noire*, p. 434.

[2] Balandier: *Afrique ambiguë*, p. 219.

[3] Ibid., p. 232.

[4] In regard to the concept of nativism, Linton has this to say: "A nativistic movement is any conscious organized attempt on the part of a society's members to revive or perpetuate selected aspects of its culture." I should like to correct this to the effect that nativism should not be viewed only from its restorative or conservative aspect, but rather in the broader context within which it is at odds with Western culture and seeks to establish a cult for the exclusive use of the aborigines—in other words, a totally *new* cult. R. Linton: "Nativistic Movements," *Am. Anthr.*, XLV (1943), p. 230. See also P. Worsley: *The Trumpet Shall Sound* (London, 1957).

[5] Balandier: *Afrique ambiguë*, p. 226.

[6] Ibid., p. 229.

16

nished with such symbolic objects as a photograph of André Matswa, a dagger of ancient style, a lighted oil lamp, and a huge wooden "V" encasing the cross of Lorraine, symbol of the Free French. The vivid red, traditionally the color of fecundity and fertility, is now identified with the martyrdom of the Congolese saviors and of their disciples; the dagger stands for fealty pledged to the ancestors, while the lamp and the cross express Christianity. But it is the gigantic "V," towering above all else, that gives tangible expression to the natives' faith in rebellion and ultimate victory, so that Winston Churchill's famous symbol of the West's determination to survive and win is now seen in an anti-Western role, as a symbol of the indigenous peoples' triumph over the white man's rule.[7]

The words used by the prophets make it unmistakably clear that theirs is a religion of war and revolt: "The war is now at hand and we have come to announce God's good news to the world." "No member of this church shall ever speak to any person bound to the government, to the mission, or to any Negro who is still lost in darkness." "The time of the red blood is upon us . . . those who rise again shall enter into into the glory of the triumphant kingdom." Again, using Biblical and allegorical terms, they say: "The whites do not yet know that they will meet with death and ruination on other people's land. The buffalo and the elephant are powerful, they are Goliath, but they have not the understanding to build the road they take. . . . The death of the elephant and the buffalo is at hand and their kingdom shall be overthrown."[8]

In 1939 Amicalism took a forward stride under the leadership of Simon Pierre Mpadi, a new apostle and prophet. A

[7] Ibid., pp. 232–4; *Sociologie de l'Afrique Noire*, p. 458.
[8] Balandier: *Afrique ambiguë*, pp. 234–5.

17

native of the Kongo tribe, Mpadi, by his choice of two such names as Simon and Peter, had announced his twofold plan: on the one hand he would expand the movement founded by the first Simon, Kimbangu; and on the other he would build a new Negro church, following the example of Peter, the Apostle of Christ. In fact, Simon Mpadi founded the Mission des Noirs (Mission to the Blacks), later known as the Khaki movement, which had a complex hierarchical structure supporting the Apostolic leader. Its members wore a khaki uniform (hence the name) as a means of expressing the warlike spirit of their sect and their certainty of achieving victory. Traditional forms of ancestor worship were at the core of the Khaki movement, whose followers went collectively into trance, practiced healing by the imposition of hands, and gave new spiritual impetus to the fight against witchcraft by relating it to a new need for physical and material security.[9]

The imprisonment of Simon Mpadi caused the movement to gain as great a sway in the cities as it already had in the villages and paved the way for a new personality, Kufinu Philippe, known to his followers as Mavonda Ntangu.

Although relentlessly persecuted, this prophet from the lower Congo is still engaged in carrying on the teachings of Kimbangu, Matswa, and Mpadi, and is regarded as "the master of the entire land," signifying both the French and the Belgian Congo. The sect established by Mavonda eluded the enemy by worshipping in its own reserved areas (pendele) or upon the tombs of the ancestors. Prayers, chants, and confessions, all taken from Christianity, are combined with healing rituals, vigils at the tombs, and divinatory rites performed by the

---

[9] Balandier: *Sociologie de l'Afrique Noire*, pp. 431–5, 447–63; Andersson: op. cit., pp. 138–50; Van Wing: op. cit., pp. 595–603. It should be noted that the effigy of a rooster, symbol of Simon Pierre Mpadi, is placed on the Khaki altar along with the picture of Matswa. Balandier: *Sociologie de l'Afrique Noire*, p. 458.

prophet and his apostles in a state of ecstasy, amid the epilep-
toid convulsions by which the multitude is collectively seized
in an atmosphere of extreme exaltation and excitement.[1] The
followers of Mavonda believe that the state of ecstasy is engendered in them by the dead about to rise from their tombs;[2]
this traditional belief is combined with Christian elements in
a religious pattern which emphasizes the drive for emancipation and the hatred of the white man typical of Kimbangu's
ministry. The Kingdom will be established, say the Khaki
leaders, interpreting the Gospel to suit their needs, "when
André Matswa and Simon Kimbangu come back. They will
then come with power to take the rule"—and this Kingdom
will be African.

"God of Abraham, God of Isaac, God of Simon Kimbangu, God of André Matswa," runs the prayer of Mavonda
Ntangu, "when shall we receive the blessing and be free?
Thou shalt no more hear the prayers of the whites, for Thou
hast heard them for a long time and they have received blessing enough. Hear us now! Amen."[3]

The arrival of the Salvation Army in the Congo in 1935
produced an extraordinary reaction among the Congolese, due
chiefly to the atmosphere of messianic expectation generated
by the power of Kimbangu's movement and of its offshoots.
The Salvation Army, seeking strictly humanitarian goals, un-
sullied by vested institutional or ecclesiastical interests, opposed to proselytizing, quickly became for the natives a most
attractive substitute for the Christian missions. Whereas these
had antagonized much of the native population with their
coercive systems, their intolerance, and their doctrinal rigors,
the ways of the Salvation Army had a soothing and welcome

[1] Andersson: op. cit., pp. 140 ff., 151 ff., 162–75.
[2] Ibid., p. 174.
[3] Ibid., p. 193.

19

effect. The natives recognized that although these spiritual soldiers worshipped the God of the white missionaries, their way of life was based on religious and moral codes which they could understand and which could truly meet their needs and aspirations.

Instead of the meticulous confession of the missions, the Salvation Army proposed a simple act of contrition flowing directly from the sinner's heart. The uniforms, the ceremonies accompanied by martial hymns conveying an assurance of victory, the rhythm of the drums and the lively sounds of other instruments in their bands, the colorful flags unfurled against the sky—all tended to cast a spell over the natives, who saw in this new religion a beguiling similarity to their own pagan rituals. Soon they had come to believe that the Salvation Army was a European missionary body with ceremonial customs identical with those known to the Africans for all time; and because it made a particular effort to eradicate sorcery, the Congolese accepted it as a new and unsuspected ally in their struggle for liberation and as the embodiment of a deeply beneficent force from on high. Eventually, the idea took root that these white men and women in uniform, so understanding and helpful to the natives, were the reincarnation of the spirit of Simon Kimbangu, their own great savior. The letter S displayed on the Salvation Army uniform was regarded as the badge of their own prophet. Pursuing an eager hope of salvation and protection from the perils which they had perennially faced, ranging all the way from witchcraft to foreign rule, both religious and secular, the natives now began to desert the missions in huge numbers and attach themselves to the Salvation Army. Many natives undertook long and often perilous journeys to participate in the ceremonies, believing that salvation, health, and every good thing could be attained by following these new missionaries, who seemed to have the magical power to make the natives free. Naturally enough, the Salvation Army, whose uniforms inspired Simon Mpadi to prescribe khaki garments for his followers, encountered resistance and rivalry from the Christian missions in the Congo, which regarded the area as their own preserve.[4]

Other interesting episodes marked the development of the Kimbangu movement, some of them, such as the rise of the Mvungi and Tonsi cults, highlighted by a touch of the grotesque. Both these sects arose in 1940, as the Congolese reacted with dramatic suddenness to Hitler's occupation of Belgium— a development which temporarily removed that country from the scene as an active colonial power. The Mvungi movement (*mvungi* means shepherd or pastor) began among the Bayaka people on the banks of the Cuango River, spurred by an American Baptist mission. It had much in common with the Kimbangu cult, although the prophet's name was never invoked; its central deity was Jahve, however, whom Kimbangu also placed at the heart of his worship. Through the intermediary of the Baptist Mvungi, Jahve was to bring a new dispensation, reappearing in all his glory to call back the dead, who would come bearing great riches for their people. The white man would vanish at Jahve's command, said the prophecy, and with him every Bayaka who rejected the new faith; while awaiting the fateful hour of liberation, however, the Bayaka must destroy all their idols and fetishes and baptize every member of their families.

The campaign against fetishism, which the new cult had in common with Kimbangu's doctrine, was implemented to the full, so that not a single amulet or magical object was spared of the countless varieties which the Bayaka possessed. Every connection with the culture of the West was severed

[4] Andersson: op. cit., pp. 126–35; Van Wing: op. cit., pp. 594–5.

21

and all contact with the white man carefully avoided, until every plantation or school and every item of food or medicine introduced from abroad were rejected, while the natives awaited the coming of Jahve in total idleness. The Mvungi had said that the Germans had now taken the natives' land away from the white man, destroying his power so that he could no longer do harm; but when, instead of Jahve, the white man's armies came back to Africa, the fetishes and idols were promptly restored and the Mvungi cult was at an end.[5]

The story of the Tonsi cult is similar. But whereas the Mvungi movement had arisen on the Cuango River, the Tonsi (meaning drop) started in West Angola in 1940 under the name of Tawa. It migrated into the Congolese territories of Thysville, Madimba, and Kimbambi, where the new name was adopted. The ritual consisted of pouring three drops of a consecrated liquid upon the tongue and forehead of the candidate for initiation: the first drop symbolized and replaced the rite of baptism, the second stood for confirmation, and a third, called "drop of blood," enlightened the spirit of the receiver, enabling him to evoke the dead and enter into direct communication with them. The invocation accompanying the threefold ritual addresses the extraordinary trinity of Tata Mupepe (Father Spirit), Tata Kimbangu (Father Kimbangu), and Tata Alamni (German Father), in which the Christian elements of the Trinity itself and of the Divine Father are combined with a political element, the German Father, included as a tribute to the Germans, who had invaded Belgium.

The sect was equally militant against Christianity and against sorcery. In every meeting the followers solemnly abjured the Christian religion along with every form of Black Magic, pledging themselves to absolute secrecy about their associa-

[5] Van Wing: op. cit., pp. 603–6.

tion. The worshippers of this cult, as of most others, gathered after nightfall at the tombs of their forebears, in preparation for the rising of the dead and in the belief that on the Day of Resurrection the white man would perish by fire and water, while the Africans would achieve regeneration by becoming white themselves. The ritual prescribed the destruction of all black animals and objects, and abstention from agricultural labor on Wednesdays, Fridays, and Sundays; it placed a taboo on many foods, rejected any African who did not accept the Tonsi doctrine or who attended a school, a hospital, or a clinic established by a white man.[6]

The idea that the unification of all the African peoples was necessary in order to achieve liberation from foreign rule was diffused throughout the religious movements. Zaccharias Bonzo, a Congolese, made headway in Angola with the cry of "Africa for the Africans!" while Simon Toko in 1949, also in Angola, founded the cult of the "Red Star" based on the concept that God was on the side of the multitude and therefore in Africa was with the Africans. Toko prophesied that God would again send a Messiah in the person of His Son, this time incarnate in a Negro in order to redeem the people with dark skin.[7] The messianic cults become more and more decisively Pan-African, sparking a great deal of religious and political agitation, and leading to the organization of several new movements, such as the Kintwadi and the Dieudonné in the Lower Congo.

The Kintwadi movement, which owes its name to an agricultural co-operative at Kisantu, combined with the word *ntwadi*, which means collective or communal, appeared after 1953, also in the Lower Congo, and expanded rapidly into

[6] Ibid., pp. 606–8.
[7] R. P. Tastevin: "Nouvelles manifestations du prophétisme en Afrique Equatoriale et en Angola," *C. R. Acad.*, XVI, 3 (February 1956), pp. 151–3.

Bangui and Leopoldville. Kintwadi merged the old-line Kimbangu sects with the Brethren of the Negro Church and various dissenting groups. Then, with increasing political as well as religious awareness, it appealed to the government for official recognition on the same footing as the Christian mission churches. Tracts and pamphlets were secretly circulated, reiterating the tenets of the Kimbangu cult: "Kimbangu is our Saviour." "His religion is the religion of all Black people." "He will return to banish the white man from Africa." "The Roman Catholic missions are responsible for every injustice perpetrated by the colonial power against the natives." Until the end of 1956 the movement continued to grow.[8]

Between 1955 and 1956 another movement came to strengthen the Kintwadi in Madimba, Kasangula, and Thysville; it was called Dieudonné, after its founder. It ordered that all fetishes be immediately destroyed and replaced by holy water secured from the missionaries, and enjoined the faithful to carry out the command promptly; much to the horror of the missionaries, it saw that the command was fulfilled. Soon, however, the cult degenerated into an orgy of man-killings which finally compelled the authorities to put an end to it by law and by force in March of 1956.[9]

Aside from these peculiar proliferations, the Kimbangu movement preserved all of its original quality and vigor. In 1956 it felt strong enough to submit a memorandum to the United Nations demanding that an end be put to Belgian and Portuguese rule in Africa, on the grounds that these powers had introduced themselves illegally into the ancient Kingdom of the Congo. The memorandum also proposed that a Kimbangu government be set up to replace the Europeans. On April 18, 1957, twelve Kimbangu leaders addressed a letter

[8] Van Wing: op. cit., pp. 611–12.
[9] Ibid., pp. 612–15.

to Belgian Prime Minister Van Acker, requesting that the vexations inflicted upon the followers of Kimbangu cease immediately and invoking, to this end, the Colonial Charter as well as the United Nations Declaration on Human Rights in respect to religious freedom. The letter, retracing the history of the Kimbangu movement, recited the long list of arrests and deportations made by the colonial authorities and declared that, in order to justify these arrests, the authorities had falsely accused the Kimbangu cult of disrupting law and order and had branded its followers as rabid xenophobes.

The letter maintained that the arrest of the founder in 1921 had been due entirely to the fact that his cult was creating strong competition for the Roman Catholic missions and that, in order to make it appear that the cult had run afoul of the law, both in action and in purpose, the government officials of the time, who were subservient to the Church, had classified it as a "politico-religious movement." Actually, the letter continued, the Roman Catholic missionaries, who brought about the arrest of Kimbangu, made a common and habitual practice of what, in his case, they had defined as a "crime." Who in the Congo, the letter asked, can ignore the fact that these gentlemen of the missions are constantly interfering with matters that are the concern of the civil authorities?[1]

Ever since 1956 the Kimbangu movement has been gathering its local groups into a single force, called *Église de Jésus-Christ sur la Terre par le Prophète Simon Kimbangu* (Church of Jesus Christ on Earth through the Prophet Simon Kimbangu), which closely follows the original ritual and doctrine established by Simon Kimbangu. The Église, as the new body is usually referred to, is prevalent in the Lower Congo, Bakongo, Bangala, Baluba, and in the Republic of the Congo;

[1] Ibid., pp. 615-16.

25

and the populations of Leopoldville[2] and other cities are rapidly coming to swell its ranks.

The doctrine of the Église is based on the acceptance of the Ten Commandments, on the preaching of the Protestant Bible (in the edition published by the Foreign Bible Society of London) freely interpreted, on baptism by immersion as a requirement for admission into the church, performed theoretically in the River Jordan but in practice in a pool near the Nkamba Baptist Center, where Kimbangu was raised. Now the goal of religious pilgrimages, Nkamba had been given the messianic name of Jerusalem by Kimbangu; this name was preserved after his death by his widow and sons, as well as by his disciples. At present the official leader of the Église is a son of Kimbangu, named Kiangan Dialungana Salomon, who resides in Leopoldville. The Église prohibits polygamy and requires the destruction of fetishes and holy drums (*ngoma*). The liturgy consists largely of the singing of austere and solemn hymns, mostly borrowed from the Baptist church, which has greatly influenced the ritual of the Église. This is especially true in regard to baptism by immersion, which the Église accepts as the one certain cure for all physical as well as spiritual ills.

The attribution of magical powers to religious healing is a feature of nearly every new messianic cult rising among people subjected to foreign rule, and, in the Église, represents the strongest link with aboriginal tradition within an otherwise Christian pattern. Genuflections before the "sages" of the church and frenzied ritual dances, performed at night, are other aspects of the ceremonial carried over from native usage. Although the Église openly and officially recognizes the administrative authority of the colonial power and declares

[2] P. Raymaekers: "L'Église de Jésus-Christ sur la terre par le prophète Simon Kimbangu," *Zaïre*, XIII, 7 (1959), pp. 679–82.

itself to be a strictly religious organization, devoid of any political involvement or implication, nonetheless it is quite evident that the movement is deeply concerned with the conflict between natives and whites and in many ways strives to meet the needs and aspirations of its followers by secular means. Indeed, the development of political drives within the religious context is fostered by the intolerant attitude of the Christian missions,[3] as well as by the support given by the Église to the belief that the spirit of Simon Kimbangu was reincarnated in the political figures who led the Congo uprisings of 1959. The articles of faith laid down by the Église declare that "Tata [Father] Simon Kimbangu, after being sent by the government into the Upper Congo [meaning by this his deportation to Elisabethville], died and rose again and now dwells among us in the spirit"; that "Tata Simon Kimbangu is not God, but that God in every age has chosen from each race one man to enlighten his own people." The religious texts used by the Église denounce the oppressive practices of the white man and accuse the authorities of bad faith in rejecting the legitimate request of the natives for religious autonomy. During the 1959 uprisings in Leopoldville, the members of the Église openly raised money for the national Abako party and for the native victims of the battle, and also organized a boycott of all Christian missions which opposed the granting of recognition to the native church.

The Église represents the final phase of a drive for freedom initiated some forty years before, as a clandestine religious movement which has been constantly obliged to shield itself from persecution. It was only when the opposition of the colonial government to all native religious movements began to weaken that the Kimbangu cult emerged from hiding. It then declared itself to be a purely religious movement, free of

[3] Ibid., p. 703.

connections with the political and revolutionary activities of the nationalist parties. In spite of this disclaimer, however, religion and politics are, in fact, closely interlaced within the Eglise, and the principle of independence, rooted in the religious doctrine, is likely to generate political action as long as the colonial powers refuse to recognize the rights of the native churches.[4]

While the messianic cults were being nurtured and fostered in the Congo and in Equatorial Africa by a succession of revolts and repressions, movements of like character were developing in other parts of Africa. In 1925 Romo Nyirenda, a native of Nyasa, proclaimed himself to be Muana Lesa, the Son of God, thus introducing the Kitawala or Kitower cult into the mining areas of Katanga, where clashes between natives and whites were frequent and bitter. Kitawala is an offshoot of the American Watch Tower movement (Kitawala and Kitower are corruptions of the English words), also known as the Jehovah's Witnesses, founded in 1874 by Charles Taze Russell. The Jehovah's Witnesses found their belief on the coming of the millennium after Armageddon, the final battle between God and the Devil, when all believers will be saved, unbelievers cast out, and justice will reign upon the earth. They deny such Christian tenets as the Trinity, the divinity of Christ, the immortality of the soul, and eternal damnation, and are, moreover, antimilitarist and antinationalist by conviction. They condemn both the state and the organized church as works of the devil. To the Africans this version of Christianity appeared to be far more acceptable and

[4] With regard to the doctrinal and ritual nature and the process of development of the Église de Jésus-Christ, see Raymaekers' work, pp. 685–707; with regard to the incidents of 1959, see pp. 682, 693, 703; with regard to its catechism, pp. 737–8; with regard to its controversy with the missions, p. 704.

28

understandable than the doctrine preached and practiced by the missionaries.[5]

The Kitawala, which originated in Africa at the beginning of the twentieth century, was an indigenous interpretation of the doctrines of Russell and, as such, soon spread outward from South and Central Africa. Confronted with the possible disintegration of native culture at the hands of the white man, the preachers of Kitawala, traveling through Rhodesia, Kenya, Nyasa, and Uganda, publicly accused the missionaries of distorting the Bible to suit their own purposes. They maintained, for example, that since polygamy, a cornerstone of African society,[6] had been regarded as a legitimate practice in the Old Testament, the missionaries had no right to insist that under the Christian dispensation it had to be wiped out.

Before long, Muana Lesa, founder of the Kitawala movement, fell into the hands of the colonial authorities, who accused him of having killed "baptized people," by which they meant "white Christians." After a first escape from prison, Muana Lesa was recaptured in Rhodesia and finally sent to the gallows in 1926. His death infused the movement with an even greater determination to survive and caused it to spread into the Belgian colonies and into territories under French and British rule, where it fomented uprisings and attacks upon foreigners. Adhering to the American model, which they sought to follow, Kitawala's preachers prophesied the imminent end of all foreign religious and political bodies and disseminated a Pan-African ideology based on the expectation of a day when justice would prevail in the name of Jesus

---

[5] K. Schlosser: *Propheten in Afrika* (Braunschweig, 1949), pp. 235–9; E. Briem: *Jehovas Vittnen* (Stockholm, 1944); A. Ström: *Religion och Gemenskap* (Uppsala, 1946), pp. 190–203; H. H. Stroup: *The Jehovah's Witnesses* (New York, 1945); W. Watson: *Tribal Cohesion in a Money Economy* (Manchester, 1958), pp. 197 ff.

[6] Andersson: op. cit., p. 249.

Christ.[7] More recently, a Kitawala prophet and agitator in the Congo named Bushir proclaimed himself the Substitute of Jesus, Mulumozi wa Yesu. It is interesting and somewhat surprising to find two religious movements of such similar orientation and motivation as the Kitawala and the Jehovah's Witnesses rising, within the same half-century, in such totally different worlds as colonial Africa and the United States of America. This, however, may be explained by the fact that a cultural and spiritual crisis had developed in both areas, for which a solution was being sought through new religious movements.

The United States affected the Kitawala movement in other ways as well. When World War II came to an end, many Africans expected the American forces to land in their midst as liberators and messengers of God.[8] The Kitawala followers, who already regarded the Americans as their leaders because of the Watch Tower origin of their own religious movement, were particularly eager in their expectation, their hopes having been raised by the arrival of large shipments of American economic aid to African countries. It was only a few years earlier that an American Negro, Marcus Garvey, had organized the Universal Negro Improvement Association, a religious Pan-Negro movement with deep social and political implications. His aim was to unify the entire population of the African continent. From Liberia to the Nile, from Uganda to South Africa, Marcus Garvey visited cities and villages, preaching a gospel which called for the expulsion of the white man from African soil and the establishment of a Negro religion, with a Negro Christ and Negro angels. The Kitawala movement, influenced by Garvey's evangelism, became all the more certain that the coming of the Americans would bring the long-

[7] D. Biebuyck: "La société Kumu face au Kitawala," *Zaïre*, XI, 1 (1957); J. P. Paulus: "Le Kitawala au Congo Belge," *Rev. Inst. Soc.*, II, 3 (1956).
[8] Andersson: op. cit., pp. 250 ff.

30

awaited millennium; it grew stronger than ever and still remains one of the most forceful nativistic religious bodies in Africa.[9] When a group of Kitawala followers organized an anti-British revolt in Uganda in 1942, their cry was: "We are the children of God and therefore not bound by the laws of man. The times have changed; we shall no longer obey the secular laws, for to obey man means to obey Satan."[1]

All these movements, doctrines, and cults point to the fact that when native peoples strive to renovate their religion and their society in the midst of pressures from without and from within, their efforts often take them back to traditional forms and ancient myths. Although their actions are sometimes puerile and confused, they always reflect the instinctive reaction of the native people to the events and experiences caused by these pressures.

SOUTH AFRICA

The messianic cults rose and multiplied in South Africa long before they developed elsewhere on the African continent.[2] The Ethiopian Church founded in 1892 by Mangena M. Mokone set the first example of autonomy, and the most effective one because the founder had been an active member of the Methodist church. Several isolated attempts at secession from established mission churches, poorly organized and scarcely influential, had been made by such earlier leaders as Nehemiah Tile and Kgantlapane. Nehemiah Tile, who left the Methodist missions under attack for his interest in native Tembu nationalism, created a Tembu church as early as

[9] Comhaire: op. cit., pp. 58–9.

[1] Balandier: *Sociologie de l'Afrique Noire* (Paris, 1955), p. 420.

[2] M. Leenhardt: *Le mouvement Ethiopien au sud de l'Afrique de 1896 à 1899* (Cahors, 1902); H. Tracey: "Zulus find the Middle Road," *Natural History*, LXIV, 8 (1955); Jacqueline Eberhardt: "Messianisme en Afrique du Sud," *Arch Soc. Rel.*, IV (1957).

1884. The objective of the Tembu was to oppose the religious control of the Europeans while also adapting the Christian message to native conditions; and since the Queen of England was the head of the Anglican Church, the Tembu maintained that their own Supreme Tribal Chief should be recognized as the bishop of their religious body.

The secession of tribal Chief Kgantlapane from the London Missionary Society at Taung in 1885 stemmed from almost identical motives, which later caused him to found the Independent Congregational Church of Bechuanaland. Secession also produced the Lutheran Bapedi Church, established by a German missionary, the Reverend J. K. Winter, in 1889, and the Church of Africa, founded in Pretoria by Khayame Napo, once an Anglican evangelist. These early efforts attained much greater significance once they reached the region of the Witwatersrand where thousands of Africans worked in the gold mines with many outstanding lay preachers in their midst. One of them was Mokone, who, having struggled in vain against racial segregation in his own church, finally abandoned it to form another, which eventually became the Ethiopian Church.

In Biblical terminology, Ethiopia stands for Africa; hence the new movement, opposing the missions, pursued a policy of independence for all of Africa, taking the Bible for its sole authority and rejecting most of the terminology used by the whites. The main tenet of the church was "Africa for the Africans";[3] the form of worship followed that of the missions, but the sermon was loaded with nationalistic implications: "O Sons of Cush who feed upon suffering and must quench your thirst in tears, your slavery shall not endure much longer!"[4] Christian doctrine was re-interpreted to express the yearning of the natives for liberty.

[3] Sundkler: op. cit., pp. 38-9, 56.
[4] Ibid., pp. 182-3, 190.

Among outstanding leaders of the Ethiopian Church was another former Wesleyan preacher, M. Dwane, who played a major role in the movement by bringing about its affiliation with the African Methodist Episcopal Church of the United States, founded by American Negroes in 1816, as well as by soliciting and gaining its official recognition from the government of the Transvaal. Eventually Dwane carried his movement into Rhodesia, the Zambezi, the Sudan, Egypt, and Abyssinia, after negotiating agreements with them at a high political level. This was the first time that Abyssinia had been taken into account by the Ethiopian movement, for in his day Mokone had never given the slightest indication that he was even aware of that country's existence. However, in 1896, when the Abyssinians defeated the Italians at Aduwa, their banners became symbols of liberty for all Africans; and in 1935, when the Blackshirts of the Italian Fascist regime invaded Haile Selassie's kingdom of Ethiopia, the ideological factors involved struck a responsive chord in the South African natives, who began to flock to the Ethiopian churches in great numbers, and founded new ones where none had existed before. Services were conducted at night to offer special prayers for the sister nation, now re-enacting, in the anguish of its people victimized by European aggression, the anguish of all blacks living under the white man's rule. Some of the newly founded churches purposely took the name of "Abyssinian," the Abyssinian Baptist Church being among the first.[5] Eventually Dwane's rugged individualism caused him to sever his ties with the African Methodist Episcopal Church of America, to whose Pan-Negro goals he still subscribed. He founded instead an Ethiopian Order, separate from his original church, the latter having remained affiliated to the A.M.E.

The stronger influence and prestige of tribal ties in local

[5] Ibid., pp. 40-1, 56-7.

churches than in the broad Pan-African movements is reflected in the multiplication of small groups breaking away from the older major body; some of them are the Zulu Congregational Church (1896), the African Congregational Church (1917), the African Native Healing Church (1938), the Native Primitive Church (1940).[6] The hold of the tribal patterns coupled with the strong personality of most of the church founders caused the Ethiopian churches to take on the hierarchical structure of Bantu society, in which political and religious authority is vested in a single leader, who could well have claimed the title of king. Although the local churches operate independently, they are bound by a common purpose, part messianic and part nationalistic: the expulsion of the white man[7] and the elimination of his social order. This bond was further strengthened when the Constitution of the Union of South Africa gave its blessing to the policy of apartheid.[8]

The South African government[9] favored repression of the autonomous churches long before the Union was created in 1910, its policy having been intolerant in the province of Natal and liberal in the Cape Colony. It is not surprising, therefore, that the Ethiopian preachers had a hand in the Zulu uprisings of 1906 and used the pulpit to incite the people to rebellion. In quick retaliation, the government forbade all native gatherings and barred from the pulpit any minister who belonged to an unrecognized church. After 1910, cautious

[6] Jacqueline Eberhardt, in 1954, noted the existence of 1,286 native churches, with 761,000 members. Op. cit., p. 34.

[7] Leenhardt: op. cit., pp. 22-3; Sundkler: op. cit., pp. 50-2, 80-1, 94, 100, 106 ff.; Schlosser: op. cit., p. 233.

[8] L. Marquard: *Peoples and Policies of South Africa* (London, 1952); E. P. Dvorin: *Racial Separation in South Africa* (Chicago, 1952). Sundkler: op. cit., p. 65.

[9] The "separatist" churches come into being by secession from missionary churches; the "independent" churches were not originally related to missionary churches but tend to find some synthesis between their own tribal religion and Christianity. Sundkler: op. cit., p. 5.

34

efforts were being made to establish throughout the Union a more liberal policy patterned on that obtaining in the Cape Colony, when the government was given a sudden jolt by the "Israelite incident" at Bullboek.

The Israelite church involved in the incident had been founded in the small village of Bullboek, near Queenstown, by a prophet named Enoch Mgijima, whose gospel was similar to that preached in Rhodesia by John Chilembwe, an evangelist for Jehovah's Witnesses. In a vision, Mgijima had seen the symbols of two great colonial powers, which he had identified as the Netherlands and Britain, first engaged in battle with each other and then suddenly being both annihilated by an enormous monkey, which the prophet recognized as representing the African people, destined to destroy their white rulers. Guided by this vision, Mgijima attracted the natives to a new sect called the Israelites; he proclaimed himself its "bishop, prophet and guardian." Rejecting the New Testament as a hoax perpetrated by the missionaries, the Israelites adhered to the Old; they celebrated the Sabbath and other Jewish feasts and regarded themselves as the chosen people of Jehovah, who would not fail to come to their aid when the time was ripe for throwing off the foreign yoke. Before long, the government of South Africa ordered the sect dispersed and the village of Bullboek razed to the ground. The prophet, unperturbed by the order, awaited its enforcement; and when the troops marched in, the fanatical Israelites, galvanized by Mgijima to a high pitch of frenzy, met them with lances and staves. A massacre ensued in which 117 villagers of the 500 who had resisted at Mgijima's side were killed. The incident, appalling as it was, forced the government to retreat from its intransigent position against recognizing[1] the native churches, and to appoint a Native Church

[1] Sundkler: op. cit., pp. 65-72.

35

Commission, which, in 1925, published norms for their official acceptance. Although recognition was strictly limited and controlled, the action of the government had at least revealed a new sense of responsibility and realism toward the growing force of Africa's native religious movements.

The Israelites of Bullboek were not the only natives attracted to a cult which, centering upon a single God and rejecting the New Testament, identified them with the Jews. This same phenomenon occurs in such distant and disparate places as among the Maoris in New Zealand, the aborigines in Polynesia,[2] and the Kikuyus in Kenya (as studied by Jomo Kenyatta). In all of them the impact of the West has awakened an urge to modernize the ancient heritage of myths and rituals without also having to accept the rigid antipagan code of the Christians. It has also aroused them to the need for self-determination and liberation from the oppressive presence of their foreign masters. The Judaic pattern meets these requirements because its doctrine and rituals are sufficiently progressive and yet sufficiently attached to tradition to be comprehensible to the African natives, and also because, down through the ages, the Jews have established themselves as the unparalleled example of a people able to survive all manner of persecution, an image of anguish and successful survival with which the natives wish to be identified.

This identification is strongly shown in South Africa by the religious pattern of Zionist churches rising alongside the Ethiopian movement, differing from it in ritual and doctrine while sharing its messianic motivation and the expectation of the millennium destined to bring freedom from foreign rule. African Zionism is patterned on the Christian Catholic

[2] Caillot: *Les Polynésiens orientaux, au contact de la civilisation* (Paris, 1909), p. 38; Vittorio Lanternari: "Culti profetici polinesiani," *S.M.S.R.*, XXVIII, 2 (1957), pp. 69–77. See chapter 5 and beyond.

Apostolic Church in Zion founded in 1896 at Zion City, Illinois, by John Alexander Dowie and Wilbur Glenn Voliva, using Mount Zion as a symbol of liberation and presaging a New Jerusalem. From the American church the Africans have taken the basic belief that physical and spiritual health are divine gifts to be attained through baptism, performed by a threefold immersion in a stream or pool always called "the New Jordan." In a new guise, this continues the tradition of the southern Bantus, who practiced ritual bathing to attain spiritual as well as physical purification.[3] A symbolic repetition of the baptismal ceremony, used mainly to admit new members to the church, occurs during regular worship services when the celebrant washes the feet of the faithful. The natives are especially attached to this ritual both because it is traditional in their own culture and because it challenges the orthodoxy of the European Christians who no longer practice it.[4] Zionist liturgy also reflects the continuing attachment to exorcism and magic, and culminates in the coming forward of the sick, carried by fellow worshippers if they are unable to walk. Each one in turn is vigorously shaken by the celebrant to expel the demons from the ailing body, after which two other practitioners, having repeated this first ritual, perform aspersions and the imposition of hands on the postulant, while the congregation intones hymns.[5] Healing is part of the oldest Zulu tradition and is so appealing to the natives in these newer forms that a Zionist preacher once described his church as being "more like a hospital than like a chapel." The Swedish missionary, Bengt Sundkler, believes that "the natives are drawn to the Zionist churches chiefly by their eagerness to be healed and when they say 'Before, I was ill;

[3] Sundkler: op. cit., pp. 201–2, 208.
[4] Ibid., pp. 215–16.
[5] Ibid., pp. 186–7, 232.

37

they prayed for me; now I am well,' their motivation is plainly revealed."[6]

The political and social dilemma by which the natives are now beset is partly solved by the Zionist cult, which offers protection against insecurity at the community level and a cure for many individual ills, which are usually as much spiritual as physical or psychological. The natives believe that sickness of the body and sickness of the soul are one and the same thing—caused either by the presence of the devil in the human person or by the evil spell of a sorcerer.[7] By waging vigorous battle against witchcraft, the Zionist church is relieving native society of one of its most painful burdens—the fear of black magic and sorcery. Incantations, chants, and incomprehensible words, with which the Zionist service is replete, satisfy the people's atavistic love of mystery and heighten their faith in the invisible power of God.[8] The use of emetics, which combine ordinary local beverages with imported cathartics, soap, and salts,[1] is an important part of the ritual: the preacher leads the congregation to the edge of the stream, where they drink the potions until they vomit. All of this is accompanied by prayer and singing and finally by a state of trance.[2] The many taboos which govern the lives of the faithful Zionists, as they do the lives of the Ethiopians, affect sexual relations, foods (pork is prohibited to them as it is to the Jews), and all medicines dispensed by the Europeans, which are proscribed as "the work of the devil."[3]

A modern interpretation of pagan traditions is found in the

[6] Ibid., p. 220.
[7] Ibid., p. 255.
[8] Ibid., p. 248.
[1] Ibid., pp. 233, 240.
[2] Ibid., pp. 151–2.
[3] Ibid., pp. 216–20, 226.

worship of the Christian angels and of the Holy Ghost, whom the natives regard as the spirits of the dead. In many pagan cults the living become possessed by the spirit of a deceased person, who acts through them, but in the Zionist doctrine it is the Holy Ghost who works in the believers, thereby carrying on the tradition in modified form. The angels are regarded as guardians, counselors, and comforters, and demand animal sacrifices in return for their aid to humans.[4] Over and above all rituals and beliefs, the Zionist movement assures its followers of God's imminent coming to earth to redeem the faithful.

The principal difference between the Zionist and Ethiopian churches is in the fulfillment of their messianic hopes: the Ethiopians promise a united Christian Africa ruled by the Lion of Judah, King of Kings, whereas the Zionists look to the Judeo-Christian land of Palestine, to which Moses and John the Baptist will lead them.[5] The Ethiopian churches are governed by men who fulfill the traditional role of king in an aristocratic hierarchy, whereas the Zionists, rejecting the concept of aristocracy,[6] choose their religious heads from among preachers, healers, clairvoyants, or sworn enemies of witchcraft.

Isaiah Shembe, founder of the Ama Nazaretha Church, is notable among Zionist leaders.[7] He first became aware of his religious calling in childhood, when visions came to him,

[4] Ibid., pp. 243–4, 249–50.
[5] Ibid., p. 277.
[6] Eberhardt: op. cit.; Tracey: op. cit.; Sundkler: op. cit., pp. 94–5. Praetoria was the cradle of the Ethiopian churches, Johannesburg of the Zionist churches (Sundkler: op. cit., pp. 80–1); but the Zionist cults flourished less in the cities than in the reserves where the prophets made their homes (ibid., p. 93). As to the manifestations of collective possession, they are typical of Khakism, as of a great many other prophetic movements on every continent.
[7] The first founders of Zionist churches in Johannesburg were Daniel Bryant in 1904 and Father Le Roux in 1908 (Sundkler: op. cit., p. 50).

39

always during thunderstorms. These visions continued through adolescence and into manhood, exhorting him to forsake the "immoral life," to leave his mother, wife, sisters, and children to answer the call of the Lord God Jehovah, from whom he would receive the Gift of Healing. After one particularly impressive vision in which he saw his own body dead and decomposed, Shembe obeyed the command and traveled from place to place throughout Natal, preaching in the name of the Holy Ghost and earning fame as a healer and miracle maker. In 1906 he was baptized and ordained in the African Native Baptist Church and, moving to the coastal areas near Durban, baptized others in turn. Five years later, in 1911, he founded the sect of the Nazarenes; then in 1916 he established a center of worship near Ekuphakameni, and at the command of Jehovah built another such place high on Mount Nhlanga-kazi. Both centers remained active, one as the goal of a pilgrimage each July, the other each January.[8] Soon Shembe was being regarded as the Savior of the Zulus, among whom he preached, saying of himself: "I am Shembe, the servant of the Lord, who has come to wipe away the tears of his people. The peace of God be with you. I come among you from afar, sent by the King." Claiming to be the Moses of his people, he also called himself King of the Nazarenes, as Jesus had been called King of the Jews. While he emulated

[8] Sundkler: op. cit., pp. 110–11. The Nazarite church year oscillates between two great festivals, the July festival of the "mecca" of Ekuphakameni, and the January festival of the Nazarites' Holy Mount Nhlangakazi. The July feast lasts three or four weeks and includes healing, dancing, prayers, possession (with hallucinations), and the washing of feet. The January feast lasts two weeks and includes a procession to the top of the mountain and the rituals which also take place in July. The faithful build grass huts, very similar to the tabernacles of the Jews, and heaps of flowers, which are then set alight (ibid., pp. 198–9). Another feast is that of the first fruits, which, under Christian influence, has been moved to December 25. On this occasion the prophet becomes the king consecrating the produce (ibid., pp. 103–4).

Moses as a leader, he undertook to play the role of Jesus:[9] rarely did he speak of Christ in his evangelism, and then only to describe Him as "the One who promised to send the Holy Spirit." Gradually the people began to look upon him as the Black Christ. After his death they buried his body in a great mausoleum and worshipped him as a saint. The mantle of leadership then fell upon Johannes Galilee Shembe, his son, a man of learning educated at Fort National College. Although he lacked the personal magnetism of his father, he was still, in 1957, head of the Nazarene Church.[1]

Another prophet, whose name is unknown, fired the imagination of the natives by advocating the construction of a New Jerusalem, saying that in a vision he had been shown a stone lying near a river, which was to be used as the cornerstone of the new city. In 1927 he founded the Church of New Salem, which rejected the Eucharist as a fabrication of the whites.[2] It is interesting to note that nearly all the visions in which the prophets receive their orders occur during thunderstorms or when lightning streaks the sky. Lightning is a favorite theme in native folklore, as is the Lightning Bird,[3] who, in the new cults, becomes the voice of Jehovah thundering above the clouds. The dead body of the prophet,[4] often seen in the visions, is said to signify the old native culture now destined to die and rise again in different form. Standing halfway between archaic paganism and Christianity, the Nazarenes reject both in their quest for something totally new. Shembe's attacks on Paul are attacks on all of Christian teach-

[9] Ibid., pp. 282–4.
[1] Ibid., pp. 111, 286; Eberhardt: op. cit., p. 37.
[2] Sundkler: op. cit., pp. 112–13.
[3] Ibid., p. 293. The sky, with its thunder and lightning *(shaka),* was believed by the Zulus to be the traditional center and the incarnation of their entire tribe, and had a position of prominence in their myths (Sundkler: op. cit., p. 287).
[4] Ibid., p. 214.

41

ing. He accuses the Apostle of having invented monogamy and promulgated it as a divine revelation to serve his own purpose, despite the fact that God had shown in countless ways his acceptance of polygamy. "The whites," says Shembe, "distort the Scriptures," to which the Ethiopian Church adds that the "old Bible was written only to cheat the black man. The Ethiopian Bible is the true Scripture given to the children of the House of Ethiopia."[5]

Racial segregation experienced by the natives in the very arms of the Christian church explains their turning away to found churches of their own. A Negro leader named Shabala, a pagan converted to Christianity and an active member of an independent church, once spoke of Jesus in these terms to a European: "Do you not understand that Jesus is not the God of the black man? I found that out when I came to this big city of the white people. . . . Here in the city are many white men, and Jesus is their God only. Here there are great houses built for him . . . but I cannot go into the houses of the white man's God."[6]

A tenet common to Zionist churches expresses the need for revolt from within against the present status of native society in order to make way for the New Jerusalem. This too, like many other ideas expressed by the messianic cults, stems from the Bible (Revelation 21:2–12), where the prophet of the Apocalypse sees the "holy city, new Jerusalem, coming down from God out of heaven . . . had twelve gates, and at the gates twelve angels. . . ." In the African's experience of Biblical interpretation by the white Christians, it seemed certain that the twelve gates would have become thirteen, the last one set aside for the use of the natives; the native church

[5] Ibid., pp. 277–8.
[6] Sundkler: op. cit., p. 280.

points to the promise of a New Jerusalem in which none of this will exist. Thus the name of Holy City, or New Zion, was given by Shembe to his center of worship on the mountain top.[7] The Zion Christian Church, founded by Ignatius Lekganyame in 1912 in the Transvaal and now a leading South African body, also has its Holy City, called Zion City Moriah, to express the fact that the natives are seeking not a kingdom in the hereafter but an immediate refuge on earth and a place of rest. This place shall be luminous, raised on high, a center of worship and of healing, where the faithful, gathering in large numbers, can sense their unity and freely give voice to their spirit of independence.[8]

At all times and in all places the church as an institution, by its very nature and purpose, is in conflict with the society from which it stems. By definition, the *ekklesia*, or church (*ekklesia, ekkaleo:* to call out), is a community detached or "called out" from its environment, for every church is born of a crisis in society. The native churches in South Africa, as in other colonial areas, merely represent one phase in the religious development of their society and are undergoing experiences similar to those of the early Christian communities of the West when the new faith was beginning to grow in the midst of a hostile society. In the West then, as in Africa now, the people were seeking a way out of their dilemmas in terms of religious regeneration. Now as then, a new church carries within itself contradictions and conflicts which come into full view only when the initial prophetic or messianic phase has been left behind. Such problems as ownership of land and of building sites, or the bitter conflicts over choosing a successor to the first chief, and many other

[7] Ibid., pp. 289, 291.
[8] Eberhardt: op. cit., pp. 36-7, 45-8.

43

difficulties of a secular nature, gradually bring about changes in the early structure of the movement.

The history of these native African churches shows that the first phase of their development is dominated by the prophetic figure of the founder. The second, usually starting after his death, produces an organized structure, governed by an organized priesthood.[9]

NYASALAND

Upon examining the religious movements among the native peoples of the Congo and South Africa, we find that all of them contain certain cultural elements common to the Negroes of those regions interspersed among the elements derived from local traditions and customs. Movements arising in areas at great distances from the Congo and South Africa bear the marks of experiences common to all peoples who live under foreign rule. This is an indication that the power of these movements to expand throughout a continent, shaking some of its people at the roots and threatening to engulf others as in a tidal wave, comes more from the universality of a racial reaction to similar circumstances than from a tradition rooted in local history. Among the movements which have expanded far and wide in Africa[1] is the Watch Tower, which had its start in Nyasaland in 1906 or 1907. It was introduced by Joseph Booth, a former Baptist missionary who abandoned his church to preach native religious autonomy throughout British Central Africa.

Also from Nyasaland came John Chilembwe, founder, in 1915, of the Providence Industrial Mission, a religious sect with an avowed anti-European purpose. A follower of Booth, Chilembwe was educated in the United States in the environ-

[9] Ibid., pp. 38, 55.
[1] Watson: op. cit., pp. 197–203.

44

ment that produced most of the movements for the protection and advancement of the Negroes, with which the later African groups established a close relationship. The Watch Tower movement[2] had a strong supporter in Elliott Kamwana, a Tonga from South Africa, whose deportation from Nyasaland in 1909 spurred the growth of this sect and of countless independent local churches derived from it, which took the common name of Church of Christ. The uprising against British rule at Shire Highlands in 1915 was a direct result of this religious ferment; the rebellion was put down by the authorities after much violence and bloodshed and many arrests.[3] To this day, the independent native churches of Nyasaland, although no longer engaged in revolutionary activities, are a safety valve[4] for the people's unceasing desire to achieve autonomy, at least religious, if not national and political.

WEST AFRICA

A number of dissident Christian sects have arisen in West Africa and many of them have flourished,[5] especially at Porto Novo, in Dahomey—all illustrating the merger of old traditions with Christian ideas, within a context of current social experiences. The Temple of the Fishmongers (Eledja), for example, displays a copper fish in front of the pulpit: the symbol of Christ as well as of the local trade. The Celestial

---

[2] G. Shepperson: "The Politics of African Church Separatist Movements in British Central Africa," *Africa*, XXIV, 3 (1954), pp. 234–8.

[3] Ibid., pp. 240–3.

[4] Ibid., p. 245.

[5] J. W. Dougall: "African Separatist Churches," *Int. Rev. Miss.*, XLV (1956), pp. 257–8; Balandier: "Messianismes et Nationalismes en Afrique Noire," *Cah. Int. Soc.*, XIV (1953), pp. 41–9; G. Bissainthe: "Catholicisme et indigénisme religieux," in *Des Prêtres Noirs s'interrogent* (Paris, 1957); G. Parrinder: "Les sociétés religieuses en Afrique Occidentale," *Prés. Afr.*, February-March 1958, p. 21.

Christians, which forbid the use of all medicines, both native and imported, practice healing with anointments, ablutions, and the sprinkling of ashes, thus combining old magic with the Christian sacraments of baptism and unction. The Church of the Oracles offers an especially curious example of pagan-Christian syncretism in its sanctuary, patterned after the mission chapels: the crucifix has been replaced by a mural depicting a large nut tree laden with fruit, nuts being traditionally used in the intercessory rituals of the local pagan sects. Church furnishings of pagan derivation are a piece of rope, a narrow wooden board, and a cup, as well as the images of birds and snakes.[6]

The cult of the Seraphim and Cherubim has a following of well over half a million in Nigeria and Dahomey, converts from Islam, paganism, or missionary Christianity. Prayer is their only form of worship, and they attribute to it the power to heal, to find work for the unemployed, and to make fertile the sterile. The cult was founded by Moses Orimolade Tunolase, a native Yoruba of Ikarre in Ondo province and a baptized Anglican. Stricken in childhood with paralysis of both legs, he sought recovery through prayers; and after ten years he had actually regained the full use of his limbs. He immediately set out to evangelize the natives around the country, teaching them how to pray. He frequently conducted prayer meetings in Lagos, Nigeria, but the attendance was always small until an extraordinary event changed his life and the future of his movement.

In 1925, during a Corpus Christi procession in which she was marching, a Yoruba girl named Abiodun Akinsowon suddenly noticed a celestial creature of wondrous beauty walking at her side. The divine companion remained with her three months, during which the girl was stricken with

[6] Parrinder: op. cit., pp. 21–2.

an obscure disease which left her at death's door. One day, in a state of unconsciousness induced either by a trance or by her delirious fever, she began to plead that Moses Orimolade be brought to see her, for he alone had the power to restore her health. The preacher was summoned and the girl was healed. Orimolade's success quickly increased his following and led to the establishment of a religious society, which he named Seraphim after he emerged from a trance and a three-day fast. A few days later, the angels appeared to a group of women accompanied by Cherubim, and bade them change the name of the cult to Seraphim and Cherubim.[7] The sect acquired a huge following in Lagos at a time when thousands of village people were pouring into the city, seeking employment as well as refuge from the disastrous effects of new economic and social patterns too rapidly imposed on tribal society.

In Lagos, Orimolade was revered as Baba Aladura (Father of the Prayerful), and surrounded by dedicated disciples who prepared themselves to go into the interior to preach in his name. In 1929 the young Abiodun Akinsowon organized her own following into an independent group which remained affiliated with the original movement. But by 1932, upon the death of Orimolade, the splinter groups had become so numerous that they were never able to unite, although they all subscribed to a common cult, ideology, and hierarchical structure. Throughout these smaller bodies there still prevails the classification of deacons, evangelists, prophets, and apostles, according to the spiritual development and degree of initiation of the faithful, each rank wearing a special dress to distinguish it from the others. Prayer is the core of the cult, which also practices baptism by immersion, confirmation into the faith,

[7] *Cherubim and Seraphim*, pp. 119–23; Parrinder: *Religion in an African City* (London, 1953), pp. 119–22, 141–2.

47

and communion made after a public confession. Images are forbidden, and hymns are sung in the Yoruba tongue, although some of them have now been translated into English. Every year thousands of members participate in a pilgrimage to the sacred mount of Olorunkole, where, in 1918, an angel appeared to warn the worshippers of impending disaster—the prophecy came true soon thereafter in the form of a great epidemic that raged throughout West Africa. The rituals, which last all night amid songs and dances, are often orgiastic, and the faithful go into convulsions to the rhythmic beating of the drums.[8]

In Nigeria new cults and dissident churches have multiplied rapidly in recent times. The Spiritualist movement, which appeared from Guinea around 1930, has a large following among the Anang people of the Calabar province in Southeast Nigeria. Here the Holy Ghost is cast in a magical role as coadjutor of God to heal wounds and cure sickness, to give wealth and longevity, to destroy the forces of evil in all their forms. The third person of the Christian trinity is identified with Ata Abassi, supreme being of the tribal pagan cult; the altar is regarded as his dwelling, and there all prayers and sacrifices are offered. The entire congregation usually falls prey to convulsive seizures during the services: many rise to make prophecies, others roll on the floor; still others run wildly through the streets, climb houses and trees, shouting incomprehensible words through the inspiration of the Holy Spirit. In these manifestations the Spiritualists may be likened to the followers of Kimbangu, to the Zionists, and to most of the other native religious movements.[9]

In vain, however, did the Spiritualists hope that their new

[8] *Cherubim and Seraphim*, pp. 123–34.

[9] J. C. Messenger: "Religious Acculturation among the Anang Ibibio," in *Continuity and Change in African Cultures*, ed. Bascom and Herskovits (Chicago, 1959), pp. 279–9.

religion would improve their lives. In 1936 and 1937 they were plagued by an invasion of locusts, many of their leaders died from various causes, and other disasters occurred, which they finally looked upon as the revenge of the ancient gods they had forsaken. A brief pagan revival followed, soon rejected by the young, who turned again to Christianity, partly because of their education in mission schools and partly because their contacts with the West had convinced them that salvation lay in that direction. The impact of the West on native Nigerian society appears to have produced a different reaction from that seen in other parts of Africa: here the younger generation became fanatical in its efforts to reject old traditions and adopt Western customs. The reckless speed with which they went about overthrowing the old to make place for the new produced a crisis as grave as that generated in other areas by the vehemence of the anti-European drives. The codes of the traditional society were broken down before other values, based on Christian concepts, had been understood and accepted, so that corruption, skepticism, and delinquency came to fill the vacuum where they had never existed before. This development adds further evidence that the natural laws which govern human life and society, as well as the basic values of any given culture, cannot be eliminated by fiat and mechanically replaced with extraneous patterns and values, without throwing society into chaos and turmoil.[1] No enduring change can come except from within—rising, as it must, from the experience and the need of society itself, which, even in a period of transition, cannot deny or reject its cultural history with impunity.

In his study of native churches, Geoffrey Parrinder classifies them into three groups: those founded on orthodox Christianity, those founded on prayer-healing, and the syncretic

[1] Ibid.

49

churches in which pagan customs are blended with Christian ritual.[2] This distinction, however, would appear to be somewhat unrealistic, since not a single native church, sect, or cult is free from a combination of the ancient and the modern, and since healing practices are found in all of them. From Parrinder's extensive listing of religious movements a few may be singled out for their special significance: the United Methodist Church founded in Lagos in 1917, in reaction to a campaign against polygamy launched by the Methodist missionaries, illustrates the conflict between Europeans and natives on the question of matrimony. Polygamy is prohibited by the missionary church on theological grounds,[3] whereas the indigenous people cling to it as a traditional aspect of their society. A good example of a syncretic church is the Orunmla movement, founded in 1943, also in Lagos, by a journalist turned prophet, A. E. Beyioku. This movement brings together, in the temple called Orunmla,[4] some elements of Christianity and the oracular Yoruba cult of the god Ifa. A strong critic of the independent native churches for their continued acquiescence in Christian doctrine, Beyioku—after being expelled from a native church—formed the Orunmla movement to implement his belief that the native people needed a cult of their own, completely apart from Western Christian forms, which instead revived the oldest religious traditions of the Yoruba. "I do not believe in political emancipation without spiritual emancipation as well," said Beyioku. Nevertheless, he professed faith in Jesus Christ, whom he regarded as an African, in fact as a priest of the god Ifa. "Let the image of God be African," he told his followers. "Let the angels be African as well and paint

[2] Parrinder: *Religion in an African City*, p. 109.

[3] Ibid., pp. 113–14; Parrinder: "Les sociétés . . . ," p. 21; T. Hodgkin: *Nationalism in Colonial Africa* (London, 1956), pp. 102–3.

[4] With regard to the oracular cult and the practices in use in the pagan rituals of the god Ifa, see Parrinder: *Religion in an African City*, pp. 31–6.

the devil any color you choose, but never the color of the
Negro race. Have faith in the cult of Orunmla and you shall be
saved!" The Bible is, in his eyes, African scripture written for
Africans, and his preaching emphasizes every reference to
magic and to divinations he can discover in the Testaments.
Christ himself, he asserts, was divining the future when he
wrote with his finger on the sand. This Yoruba movement
spread from Lagos to other areas and in 1946 was responsible
for the establishment at Ibadan of the Church of the Holy
Ethiopian Community. Its founder was a former teacher at an
Anglican school, who was also a Moslem for a short time before
beginning to preach the coming of an African incarnation of
God, who would bring Truth, Justice, and Love upon the
earth.[5]

In Nigeria, as elsewhere on the continent, there is a flourishing of Moslem movements, usually Mahdism, not without
some Asian influence. One sect which stands out from many
others is the Ahmadiyya: it was founded near Amritsar, in
India, by Ghulam Ahmad (1836-1908), a Moslem reformer
of the Koran, and brought to Lagos and Ibadan in 1923.
According to Ahmad, Christ did not rise from the dead and
therefore will not come again in the flesh, but his return occurs
through incarnation in other prophets, of whom Ahmad himself is the present one. The followers of Ahmadiyya regard
their leader as the Messiah, or Mahdi; they believe that Jesus
did not actually die when he was laid in the tomb and that
when he emerged from it, he set out for the East, ending his
journey in Kashmir, where a large Christian congregation
exists to this day. They believe that he eventually died at
Srinagar and was buried in the tomb which is still being
shown as that of Jesus Christ.[6]

[5] Ibid., pp. 126-9, 17-21. The religion of the Yoruba is typically
polytheistic.
[6] Ibid., pp. 79-80.

The Ahmadiyya movement is opposed to much of the
Islamic tradition, which it seeks to break down by demanding
equality for women[7] and the establishment of monogamy.
Although it does not openly engage in political action, it is
politically acceptable as a religious reform movement because
it combines native tradition with an effort to meet the natives'
need for secular progress and social change.

In Sierra Leone, the Church of the Master, which goes back
to 1930, assures its followers that their own missionaries will
eventually carry the African message into Europe, a prospect
which has caused this sect to make considerable headway in
the Gold Coast (Ghana) and Liberia. Their prophet, going
into trance, receives the "seal-words" which endow him with
magical powers.[8] The United Native Church, started in the
French Cameroons in 1922, is under the leadership of Lotin
Samé, who threw the city of Duala into a powerful ferment
when he sent his followers parading through the streets, wildly
singing anti-European songs.[9]

Religious movements in Liberia and the Ivory Coast have
revived, after a long period of inactivity, mainly because of
William Wade Harris, born at Garaway in Liberia and
educated at a local Wesleyan mission. A passionate student
of the Bible, Harris heeded the call of the Angel Gabriel in
1914, after a dream in which he was told to go out and
preach to the natives. He fought sorcery and fetishism without
quarter, condemning theft, falsehood, alcoholism, and adultery
as capital sins for which the unshriven would be punished
with eternal hell, while the just would gain an assured place in
heaven. He accepted polygamy but demanded that his followers be tolerant toward the Christian church which sought

[7] Ibid., pp. 77-8.
[8] M. Banton: "An Independent African Church in Sierra Leone,"
Hibbert Journal, LV, 216 (1956).
[9] Hodgkin: op. cit., p. 104.

to abolish it, and ordered the natives to respect the administrative authorities. Despite this conciliatory policy, however, the French viewed him as a threat to their security and sent him back to Liberia. The movement then began to decline until it was completely lifeless and apparently at an end; but World War II suddenly brought its old followers to their feet. Gathering in the abandoned chapels in great numbers, they planned and carried out a major construction program for new places of worship, and established new congregations beyond their own geographical boundaries. The magical aspects of the ritual present in Harris's cult[1] became more and more pronounced as new movements grew out of his original pattern, spurred by local prophets (Ake in the Lower Bassam, Boto Adai and John Avit at Divo and Lakota, and the prophetess Lalu in Deima).

Boto Adai has achieved renown as a healer who endows holy water with miraculous powers by his own exorcisms.[2] Maria Dahonon, later called the Prophetess Lalu, founded a cult at Deima, in 1942, using for her rites of healing and purification a special liquid; she had been given the formula in a trance, by a huge reptile with crocodile feet and buffalo horns,[3] called Ghobe Mele. This creature appeared to her in the forest and bade her mix the ashes from certain roots with water from the pool out of which he had emerged. Obeying the instructions, Lalu carried a large vessel filled with this

---

[1] With regard to Wade Harris, see J. H. Cooksey and A. McLeish: *An African Prophet: the Ivory Coast Movement, William Wade Harris* (London, 1934); B. Holas: "Bref aperçu sur les principaux cultes syncrétiques de la Basse Côte d'Ivoire," *Africa*, XXIV, 1 (1954), pp. 56-7; Schlosser: op. cit., pp. 241-66; Balandier: *Sociologie de l'Afrique Noire*, p. 418. With regard to neo-Harrisism, see Holas: op. cit., pp. 55-7; and "Le culte de Zié: éléments de la religion Kono (Haute Guinée Française)," *Mémoires IFAN*, XXXIX (Dakar, 1954), pp. 217-21.

[2] Holas: "Bref aperçu . . . ," p. 55.

[3] Ibid., pp. 58-9.

water into her temple, and every night the reptile renewed its magical powers by bathing in it.

OTHER AFRICAN MOVEMENTS

The native cults which have germinated all over Africa are far too numerous even to be listed here. But in addition to the major religious movements already described, it is important to note that in Kenya, for example, it was a messianic movement among the Kikuyu which sparked the Mau Mau uprisings and that many sects derived from the Kitawala and Ethiopian cults are still very active in that area (as Jomo Kenyatta's studies indicate). The Kiyoka cult in Angola goes back to 1920,[4] and the Bwiti rose among the Fang of Gabon in 1920.[5]

In Tanganyika, especially among the Nyakyusa tribes which live on the Nyasaland border, many independent churches that were started several decades ago have flourished. The African National Church moved in from Nyasaland in 1927 under Gordon Nsumba, who had worked with several South African cults; it is now headed by Paddy Nyasuru, who once taught at a Scottish mission. Another teacher from the same mission school, Silwani Ngemela, once a follower of the

---

[4] Balandier: *Sociologie de l'Afrique Noire*, p. 418.

[5] Ibid., pp. 419 ff. The Bwiti cult is widely diffused among the Ogooué of the coastal region and in Spanish Guinea. It is an esoteric cult founded on pagan-Christian syncretism, with a rich mythology of its origin greatly influenced by Christianity, with a Supreme Being (Mwanga), with holy objects or emblems, such as the Christian cross and the traditional harp (ngoma). During the ceremonies of initiation considerable use is made of the sacred *iboga* plant *(Tabernanthe Iboga)*, the consumption of which produces hallucinations and lethargy (it has an alkaloid content). The ceremonies include dances, songs, and recitation of myths according to traditional ritual, but with some Christian elements such as the worship of God and of Jesus Christ. A. V. Vilaldach: *La secta Bwiti en la Guinea Española* (Madrid, Instituto de estudios africanos, 1958).

54

Watch Tower movement, which he then abandoned,[6] established the Last Church of God and of His Christ. It proclaims his belief in Christian doctrine but, like so many other sects, is strongly anti-European in purpose, even though Ngemela himself is called by his followers "Our European." In this church too, paganism is evident among Christian rites and symbols, including open acceptance of polygamy as well as incantations and orgiastic dancing in honor of the dead which are often terrifying in their violence. Mission Christians abstain from these rituals,[7] thereby stressing the difference between native and white religious ideas, a fact further confirmed in the opening statement of the creed of the National African Church, which says: "We believe that religion is essential in the development of man, we believe that man must live according to his religious beliefs and that he is not allowed to belong to a church whose norms he does not accept." The creed further adds: "We believe that the task of the Christian church in Africa is to impart Christian teaching and education in conformity with the ways and customs of the native population, instead of imposing upon the Africans the unacceptable and unnecessary patterns adopted in European countries, such as monogamy, which finds no support in the Bible."[1]

Mahdi Mohammedanism must be included in any general survey of messianic movements in Africa, since its followers are scattered over many parts of the continent. According to this belief, the Day of Judgment will be preceded by a period of great confusion and oppression ending with the advent of a Mahdi (the enlightened, or the well-guided), who will be overcome in turn by Dajjāl, the Antichrist, until the Prophet Mohammed, returning to slay Dajjāl, brings justice in ac-

[6] M. Wilson, *Communal Rituals of the Nyakyusa* (London, 1959), pp. 171-2, 190-7.
[7] Ibid., pp. 174-90, 196-202.
[1] Ibid., p. 191.

55

cordance with the Koran. The belief in a redeeming Mahdi originated among the Shiites in Islam itself, causing dissensions and schisms in which political factors were closely intertwined with religious ones. Among the Shiites, the Zaidites believe that the Mahdi is not one particular person but rather the Supreme Being destined to come at the end of all time. Others, on the other hand, believe the Mahdi to be an Imam returning to save the world at some time after his own death.[2] Mahdism has often agitated the Moslem world: as in 1885, for example, when the preaching of Mohammed Ahmed in the Sudan was as political as it was spiritual. Inciting his followers to oust the foreigners from the land, he forced the Anglo-Egyptian forces to withdraw from Khartum.[3]

In the northern Cameroons a variant of Mahdism has sprung up in recent times; its leaders announced that, the Mahdi himself having already come and been dispossessed, the Dajjāl or Antichrist was now in power. They proclaimed the imminence of the end of the world, which, according to the Koran, was to take place 1,400 years after the death of the Prophet. Not without some justification, the Antichrist was identified with the effects of two world wars and with the growth of racial strife and segregation.[4] The ancient messianic tradition of Islam places Mahdism in the mainstream of current religious movements in Africa, where Mohammedanism has made inroads simultaneously with Christianity and in strong opposition to it. The growth of the Moslem faith is a significant aspect of Africa's religious ferment, and derives largely from

[2] Schlosser: op. cit., pp. 98-9; Hodgkin: op. cit., p. 112.

[3] Schlosser: op. cit., pp. 105-228; A. Le Grip: "Le Mahdisme en Afrique Noire," *L'Afrique et l'Asie*, XVIII (1952); M. Guidi: *Storia della religione dell'Islam*, cited in Tacchi-Venturi: *Storia delle Religioni* (Turin, 1939), Vol. II, pp. 335-8, 360-1; Banton: *West African City: a Study in Tribal Life in Freetown* (London, 1957), pp. 136-7; M. Cardaire: "L'Islam et le terroir africain," *Études Soudaniennes IFAN*, 1954.

[4] Hodgkin: op. cit., pp. 112-13.

its frankly anti-European attitude rather than from its efforts against paganism and other native religions. Moreover, Islam is less rigid than Christianity. Its doctrine is simple and elementary as compared to the complexities of the Gospels and the catechism; moreover, it does not clash with native culture or tribal society, this clash being one of the main causes of African antagonism toward the Christian missions.[5]

CONCLUSIONS

In all its varied forms, the striving for independence of the African people—as of many other emerging populations—has been encouraged by the disintegration of the native social patterns, by forced acculturation, by the efforts made to erase the traditional culture, by the centralization of political power, and by racial discrimination practiced as much by the missionaries as by the civil authorities.[6] The struggle has been shaped by native customs altered to suit new aspirations, the fundamental purpose of the new religious movements being the preservation of Africa's ethnic groups in the crisis which threatens to overwhelm them. Thus the religious cults have taken from the Bible such terms and messianic ideas as seemed to validate their own yearning for religious freedom and political independence. The cults actually transmute the hope for a spiritual Kingdom of God held out by the Scripture, into a hope that political, social, and cultural autonomy and progress may be enjoyed by the natives now, on this earth.

The history of Africa's messianic movements begins with a native interpretation of Christian teaching in pagan terms; it

[5] E. P. Skinner: "Christianity and Islam among the Mossi," *Am. Anthr.*, LX, 6 (1958) pp. 1102–19 (especially "Conclusions," pp. 1117–18).

[6] J. S. Coleman: "Current Political Movements in Africa," *Ann. Amer. Acad.*, CCXLVIII (1955); E. Ross: "The Impact of Christianity in Africa," *Ann. Amer. Acad.*, CCXLVIII (1955); H. Kuper: "The Swazi Reaction to Missions," *African Studies*, V, 3 (1946).

passes through apostolic and evangelical phases, in which large groups, exalted by their desire for renovation, blindly follow their prophets, on occasion stimulating them to take action of a political or even military character; and it culminates in a great blossoming of native Christian churches deeply imbued with secular significance and purpose. Outwardly, the established native churches represent a new phase in the relations between paganism and Christianity, both of which, having at first been rigidly entrenched in their antagonistic positions, now find a measure of balance and mutual understanding. These native Christian movements are never a "passive" imitation of their European models; on the contrary, they are an active force, which stimulates the indigenous people to seek emancipation and to build religious organizations of their own, as substantial as the Christian missions themselves. The label of "heretical"[7] or "dissident"[8] with which the missions tag the native churches is quite unrealistic. On occasion, the success of these churches has been described by the missionaries as "the failure of our mission to achieve its purpose,"[9] but the explanation offered more recently is that the native churches testify to the successful penetration of Christian teaching, their diversities being proof of the universal character of Christianity.[1] This change of attitude was forced upon the clergy by the growth of a strong and well-established nucleus of native religions, which they could not ignore; and it is important to examine the range of these movements in the perspective of history rather than merely in relation to the Christian church of the West.

[7] Balandier: *Afrique ambiguë*, p. 226.
[8] E. Bartolucci: "Problemi religiosi dell'Africa d'oggi," *La Scuola Cattolica*, II (1958); Parrinder: *Religion in an African City*, pp. 130-2.
[9] Dougall: op. cit.; Andersson: op. cit., pp. 264-8; R. T. Parsons: "Missionary-African Relations," *Civilizations*, III, 4 (1953); Ross: op. cit.
[1] Bissainthe: op. cit., pp. 134-5. See contributions to this in *Des Prêtres Noirs s'interrogent*.

As we have seen, one of the most influential factors in the growth of these churches and cults has been the nature of relations between the white man and the natives, and those personal experiences which gradually caused the indigenous peoples to look upon the missions as facets of European rule. The native church is thus to be regarded as the limit to which the independent movements will go in accepting the full doctrine of Christianity. It reveals a middle course between traditional beliefs and the new theology, a course discovered after much painful striving by the natives as they move toward political as well as religious regeneration. The burgeoning of new spiritual life among the Africans comes out of their struggle against an alien culture, from which, nonetheless, they have taken their new set of values. This process of transformation and growth, impelled by a force inherent in native society, is a reaction to, and a victory over, the crisis generated in the African continent by the clash between two very different cultural patterns.

The simultaneous attacks launched by the religious movements against the white man's presence and against witchcraft and black magic have a common origin. The Europeans brought into Africa a number of ills new to the indigenous populations, such as alcoholism, certain social diseases, some new and violent epidemics, moral corruption, prostitution, and theft, many of which were consequent upon greed for money and power. The tribal and other native codes could no longer act as bulwarks, weakened as they were by the white man's determination to root them out. Since the mass of the natives were unfamiliar with most of these evils and could not understand their origin, they imputed them to the influence of sorcerers against whose witchcraft they knew of no defense other than magic. The natives' fear of sorcery and their desperate quest for protection from its evils became all the more intense as the evils which had come in the wake of the white man increased. At first they multiplied their use of talismans and exorcisms; then, as the new religious movements began to preach against black magic and witchcraft, the natives turned to these cults for help and support, recognizing the traditional elements they contained and accepting the Christian ones now blended in with them. It was in the Gold Coast[2] that this trend first took shape; and it soon spread to other areas, where its growth coincided with the growing impact of colonial rule. In Zululand, for instance, Dr. Sundkler found that "the changes and upheavals have brought with them uncertainty and its corollary of the ever-increasing search for security against all threatening dangers, from ill omens to death." Some Zionist prophets appeared on the scene at this time, working powerfully against sorcery,[3] which the missions also opposed, and thus attracted followers because their doctrine combined elements from native tradition with Christian concepts.

A Rhodesian case history, studied by Audrey Richards, casts light upon the problem engendered by the destruction of native patterns of society, by the dispossession of tribal chiefs, who had always been the protectors of their tribes against witchcraft and the chastisers of those who practiced sorcery, by the intertribal rivalries developing in the mining areas, and by the sharp decline of moral values. A new craving for money set in among the natives, stimulated by the evidence that money could buy any kind of protection. The craving grew as the population became increasingly mystified and frightened by the actions of the whites, which they identified with the work of witches. Looking about desperately for help, they turned to their own tribal "witch-finders," whose prestige

[2] M. J. Field: *Akim-Kotoku, an Oman of the Gold Coast* (London, 1948), pp. 175–9.
[3] Sundkler: op. cit., p. 255.

and power thus began to rise again. From her study, Miss Richards concluded that, even though the power of sorcerers and witch-finders was only a figment of popular imagination, anyone who offered protection against the evil in the white man[4] established his hold on those who turned to him. It was natural, therefore, that any new religious movement which promised to expel the white man while also fighting the power of the sorcerers should quickly gain a large following.

In the final analysis, it may be said that all these religious movements have in common the following five salient traits:

1. A traditional pagan pattern, dominated by the mythical figure of a Supreme Being, which opens the way for the Judeo-Christian God. To this pattern belong such rituals as the worship of the dead and the belief in their resurrection; a magico-medical interpretation of baptism and of other Christian forms of ablution; the emergence of figures from animal mythology in the visions of their prophets and in the iconography of the various sects; all the incantations and collective phenomena of possession. In essence, the crisis arising from the clash between cultures has magnified the importance of such collective manifestations as are traditional in pagan societies, while it has also impelled them to seek their own historical and cultural background and to use it as the foundation for their new religious cults.

2. The battle against witchcraft and fetishism, in part traditional and in part instigated by the need to fight new evils arising in tribal society. Antisorcery in itself expresses the natives' obsession with security and their need for physical healing—the latter being met by the religious movements

---

[4] A. I. Richards: "A Modern Movement of Witch-finder," *Africa*, VIII, 4 (1935), pp. 458–60.

through the use of rituals, such as baptism, taken from Christianity.

3. The striving for autonomy and independence, now gradually expanding into the vaster concept of Pan-African unity.

4. The building up of an ecclesiastical organization, incorporating pagan features and headed by leaders who wield political as well as religious authority. These native organizations are usually at variance with the mission churches and often break out into open conflict with them.

5. The Judeo-Christian factor which the native religions have taken from the West and which, in most cases, orients them toward the Old Testament rather than the New. The Jewish God, the identification of Hebrews with Africans because of the persecutions suffered by both peoples, the defense of polygamy, and the acceptance of the Mosaic law are among the marks of an ideological as well as a political bond with the predecessors of Christianity.

CHAPTER

II

THE PEYOTE CULT

PREMISE

In the struggle of the American Indians against the white invaders, religion played a far more significant role than is commonly believed. In fact, to cite one authority in this field, religion became, for the Indians, a bulwark against the demoralizing effects of the European impact on their society. Frequently it was a religious drive which inspired and sustained their desperate efforts to rise up against the foreigners who had taken their land.[1] One of their most eminent chiefs, Sitting Bull, acquired fame and authority among his own people less as a military and political leader than as the apostle and prophet of the Ghost Dance, an "irredentist" religious movement which gave the Indians the courage and strength to carry on the struggle for independence.

In recent years, among many of the tribes on reservations religion has taken on a new form—the Peyote cult—which seeks adjustment in place of struggle. Peyotism, "the new

[1] Petrullo: *The Diabolic Root: a Study of Peyotism, the New Indian Religion, among the Delawares* (Philadelphia, 1934), p. 1.

religion of the Indians," does not convey the prophetic message found in earlier movements which promised the extermination of the white man and the restoration of all that existed before his coming. Within certain limits, Peyotism teaches acceptance of new conditions and provides its followers with the means of carrying out a new program of cultural emancipation.[2]

The Peyote cult did not spread without serious opposition from certain political forces which viewed it as an obstacle to the penetration of the white man's culture and religion among the Indians. Indeed, its opponents claimed that the peyote was a "narcotic" from which the Indians had to be protected—the missionaries and certain government officials entrenched themselves behind this argument to fight the spread of the cult.

The peyote is a plant which, when eaten, produces peculiar physiological effects. But it is not a narcotic and is not harmful. In view of the continuing controversy between those who oppose Peyotism and those who do not, the following statement, published in 1951 in *Science* by a group of American anthropologists who had made a study of the plant, deserves serious consideration:

> In connection with the current national campaign against narcotics, there has been some propaganda to declare illegal the peyote used by many Indian tribes. We have participated in the rites and partaken of the sacramental peyote. We therefore feel it is our duty to protest against a campaign which only reveals the ignorance of the propagandists concerned.
>
> Briefly put, the propagandists argue that Peyotists are simply addicted to a narcotic and intoxicant which they use orgiastically. . . . On the basis of our experience we

[2] I have turned to Petrullo for certain concepts; see pp. 1–3.

would say that peyote seems to have none of these effects. It does not excite, stupefy or produce muscular incoordination; there is no hangover; and the habitual user does not develop an increased tolerance or dependence. As for the immorality that is supposed to accompany its use, since no orgies are known among any Indian tribes of North America, the charge has as much validity as the ancient Roman accusations of a similar nature against the early Christians.[3]

An equally significant document appeared in the same publication the following year, penned by John Collier, one of the world's foremost authorities on Indians and U. S. Commissioner of Indian Affairs from 1933 to 1945. Collier, a remarkably intelligent and unbiased government official— and an exception in this field, as we shall see—wrote from personal knowledge not only of the Peyote cult but also of the problems of cultural and religious policy which were involved. Collier wrote:

I wish to express appreciation for, and to concur with, the communication dealing with peyote in your November 30th issue. The subject is of importance to American Indians, to civil liberties and to anthropology.

In late 1922, when Federal and State proscriptions against the Native American (Peyote) Church were being pressed, the peyote cult members at Taos Pueblo laid their cause before me. They offered (with an understanding of what was involved) to submit themselves individually and as a group to the fullest scientific investigation. They understood that such investigation would be pharmacological, biological, psychological and social and that it would involve experimentation using part of their number as a control group.

[3] W. La Barre, D. P. McAllester, J. S. Slotkin, O. C. Stewart, S. Tax: "Statement on Peyote," *Science*, CIV (1951), pp. 582-3.

In 1924, at a meeting of the Committee of 100 on Indian problems, I reported this offer; a resolution was enacted, calling upon the National Research Council to plan and execute an investigation into peyote. The Council never initiated this requested investigation.

Some years later, for the American Indian Defense Association, Donald Collier canvassed all the then existing literature on peyote, totaling some 400 published books and papers. His conclusion was identical with that set forth in the communication in *Science*. Subsequently, in 1933, I became U. S. Commissioner for Indian Affairs. I introduced the above-mentioned analysis into the Congressional Record . . . and I prohibited absolutely any interference by the Indian Bureau with the religious practices of the Native American Church. We were abused in a good many quarters for this action, but the administrative policy that we established has been adhered to . . . but there remain on the books of a number of States statutes that declare the ceremonies of the Native American Church to be misdemeanors; and there is an occasionally renewed drive in Washington to secure the classification of peyote as a habit-forming and injurious drug . . . it is hoped that the communication in *Science* will be given attention.[4]

The religious aspects of the problems created by the impact of the white man upon Indian culture are thus made clear. Moreover, the "irredentist" nature of the cult could not have been any more pleasing to those who formulate U. S. government policy than its pagan elements were to the Christian churches. In actual fact, however, Peyotism is based on moral elements—derived in part from Christian teachings—which have been embodied in well-organized and widely supported churches, whose rituals take place in a sacred enclosure, usually

[4] J. Collier: "The Peyote-Cult," *Science*, CV (1952), pp. 503–4.

a *tipi*, and culminate in the sacramental eating of the peyote button.

The peyote is a small-sized cactus (*Lophophora williamsii*), in the shape of a carrot, found in the Rio Grande Valley and farther south. The round top, or button, seen above ground, is eaten fresh or dried in the sun, and is sometimes made into an infusion and drunk as tea. Its most characteristic effects are a peculiar sensation of levitation, a vision of brilliant colored images, and an inordinately sharp perception of sounds and shapes. It produces visual and auditive hallucinations but no worse effects than occasional nausea, and is not habit-forming or deleterious. Its exceptional properties come from the alkaloids contained in the button, such as anhaline, mescaline, lophophorine, and others.[5]

The use of peyote originated south of the Rio Grande. As early as 1560, Sahagún described peyote as a cactus ritually used by the Chichimeca of Mexico.[6] Later, as it spread north, the peyote must have become known to the Indians of the

[5] The following nine alkaloids are found in peyote: anhaline, anhalamine, mescaline, anhalonidine, anhalonine, lophophorine, pellotine, anholinine, and anhalidine (La Barre: *The Peyote Cult*, Y.P.A., XIX [1938], p. 38). For their effects, jointly and separately, on an experimental basis, see pp. 139-50. For the experimental effects of mescaline on the human body, see L. Ceroni: "L'intossicazione mescalinica," *Rivista Sperimentale di Freniatria*, LVI (1932); R. C. Zaehner: *Mysticism, Sacred and Profane* (Oxford, 1957), pp. 1-29, 208-26. On the physiological effects of peyote in particular, see La Barre: op. cit., pp. 17-22. Quite recently, C. G. Barber, according to a more extensive definition of "narcotic" than the one in use up to now ("Narcotic is a substance capable of altering or distorting the subject's sense of self-perception and of perception of the world, and which is taken or administered chiefly for this purpose."), includes peyote among narcotics, at least in an anthropological and sociological sense. However, Barber states that the legal sense of the term "narcotic" may differ, and in this respect it is debatable whether peyote should be included among narcotics. (C. G. Barber: "Peyote and the Definition of Narcotic," *Am. Anthr.*, LI, 4 [1959]).

[6] B. de Sahagún: *Historia general de la cosas de Nueva España* (Mexico, 1830), Vol. III, p. 241.

United States, chiefly because of its therapeutic and hallucinatory effects.[7] By the seventeenth and eighteen centuries at least three ethnic groups were known to be using it: the Coahuiltec tribes of the Gulf, the Hopi, the Taos or Queres of the Southwest, and the marginal tribes of the southern Plains, especially the Caddoans. Between 1870 and 1885 the Comanche, Wichita, and Kiowa transformed the healing cult into an elaborate religious movement filled with social and political implications and with new religious elements derived from the Indians' contact with Christianity.

Peyotism, in its old form, was an individual cult in which the peyote was ritually used to heal sickness, to alleviate hunger and fatigue, to give protection against peril, and to produce supernatural visions. Modern Peyotism is a collective cult in which the therapeutic properties of the button still play a significant part but the problems engendered by the relationship between the Indians and the whites assume paramount importance.[8] The new Peyotism is widely accepted by the Indians of Oklahoma, Arizona (Navaho), Wisconsin (Winnebago), Utah (Ute), Colorado and Nevada (Washo and Paiute).[9] It was first made the object of a serious study in 1891,

[7] La Barre: op. cit., pp. 109-23; J. S. Slotkin: *The Peyote Religion: a Study in Indian-White Relations* (Glencoe, 1956), pp. 30-2. The name (*peyotl*) stems originally from the Nahuantl idiom of the Uto-Aztec tribes of Mexico and was in general use for an "object of smooth and flocculent consistency" (La Barre: op. cit., p. 16). The pre-Columbian people of Mexico knew the peyote and used it ceremonially. It is apparent, from ancient sources, that the term *peyotl-peyote* was promiscuously given to other botanical species which also possessed particular physiological virtues, such as *Sophora secundifolia*, commonly known as the mescal bean; the *Lophophora williamsii* (peyote) was variously called mescal, mescal bean, mescal button, etc. This served to create considerable confusion (La Barre: op. cit., p. 14-17).

[8] Slotkin: op. cit., pp. 30-4.

[9] See Dittman and Moore (Navaho); Merriam and D'Azevedo (Washo); La Barre, Slotkin (Kiowa and Oklahoma in general); Brant (Kiowa-Apache); Lasswell (Taos); Malouf (Gosiute); Petrullo, Newcomb (Dela-

by the distinguished anthropologist James Mooney. At the turn of the century Peyotism began to spread quite rapidly, just when the Ghost Dance was disappearing.

The Peyote cult assures the Indians of the fulfillment of the kingdom of God on this earth: "When all tribes have eaten it, then will come the end of the world." "When all the Indians eat this, the world will be made over, then all will be as He (God) wants it." The Indians ascribe these promises to Jesus Christ, thereby showing that Christianity had permeated their traditional beliefs.[1] However, in the Indian view, the triumph of "good" means attainment of it by the "road of Peyote," through all its rituals and practices—a "road" reserved to them alone and quite independent of Christianity. Peyotism demands religious independence for the Indians and opposes the methodical efforts of the whites to impose their own official canons upon the culture and religion of the aborigines. The history of Peyotism illustrates the social, cultural, and political forces which have influenced the religious life of the Plains Indians during the past seventy or eighty years and which have transformed an aboriginal cult into a new movement that merges elements of paganism with elements of Christianity.[2]

THE PROPHETS

The founder of the current Peyote cult, and its chief promoter, was a native of Anadarko named John Wilson, of mixed Delaware, Caddo, and French stock. Once an ardent pro-

---

ware); Opler (Mescalero; Peyotism lasted among them from 1870 to 1910); Opler (Ute); Stewart (southern Ute); Radin (Winnebago); Stewart (Washo, northern Paiute). [Complete references in Bibliography.]

[1] W. C. Mackern, cited by Slotkin: op. cit., p. 113.

[2] Barber: "A Socio-cultural Interpretation of the Peyote Cult," *Am. Anthr.*, XLIII, 4 (1942), pp. 673-5. For up-to-date material on peyote, see La Barre: "Twenty Years of Peyote Studies," *Current Anthropology*, I, 1 (1960).

tagonist of the Ghost Dance among the Caddoans, he changed his name to Big Moon, or Moonhead (Nishkuntu), because of a vision induced by peyote.[3]

Until the age of forty, John Wilson's life had been normal and uneventful: he traveled from tribe to tribe, as many Indians did, and came into contact with the white people, from whom he learned much which he later put to use in establishing the new cult of Peyotism.[4] In 1890 Wilson answered the call of Chief Sitting Bull to attend a great Ghost Dance meeting at Darlington, Oklahoma, on the banks of the South Canadian River, and in the course of the celebration was invited to eat peyote. Wilson had known all about peyote for a long time, of course,[5] but it was only after considerable reflection that he decided to try it, and went into seclusion with his wife in order to study its effects undisturbed.

Wilson's nephew, Anderson, later gave a detailed account of Wilson's retreat, of his eating of the peyote, and of the revelations he had as the result of it. "Peyote took pity on him," said Anderson, "and guided him into the heavenly kingdom, where, in a great vision, he saw signs and images representing events in the life of Christ, and was also shown the abode of the Moon, the Sun, the Fire and the Spirit Forces traditionally regarded as the ancestors and elders of the Delawares. He also saw the 'road' which Jesus had taken in His ascent from the grave to the Moon in the sky and was told to remain on this road for the rest of his life, so that he might be taken into the presence of Christ and of Peyote. He received precise instructions for setting up a sacred area in

[3] Petrullo: op. cit., p. 44.

[4] La Barre: *The Peyote-Cult*, p. 153; F. G. Speck: "Notes on the Life of John Wilson, the Revealer of Peyote, as Recalled by His Nephew, George Anderson," *G. M. H. Cb.*, XXXV (1933), p. 542.

[5] J. Mooney: "The Ghost Dance and the Sioux Outbreak of 1890," *Rep. B.A.E.*, XIV (1892-93), 1896, pp. 895-60.

the peyote tent, was taught chants to be sung during the rituals and shown all the particulars of the ceremonial to be followed in the new cult."[6]

The pagan foundations of Wilson's new Peyote cult, which he called the Big Moon, are quite apparent from the account of his visions, as are the Christian elements which he embodied in the rite—even though he loudly demanded the emancipation of the Indians from the influence of Western Christianity and rejected the Bible as a necessary means of communication with God. The Bible, said Wilson, was given to the white man because he had been guilty of crucifying Jesus. The Indians had no responsibility in this act and therefore the Bible was not intended for them. The Indians knew God's truth from the Peyote Spirit, but the white man needed Christ's word in order to learn it.[7] Thus, to some extent the role of Jesus was transferred to the Peyote Spirit, but the universal character of Christianity was ignored, since the new religion was intended to benefit only the Indians and became a force in opposing the people of the West.

The vivid memory of his first vision heightened Wilson's mystical tendencies and caused him to have hallucinations with increasing frequency. He composed songs, was a healer and a clairvoyant, and attained the prestige of a devoutly followed

[6] La Barre: *The Peyote-Cult*, p. 156; Speck: op. cit., pp. 540–2. The structure of the sacred enclosure of the Peyote ritual of the Big Moon cult founded by John Wilson minutely reflects the mythical model presented in the "revelation" received by the prophet. The mound of earth in the shape of a crescent, upon which the peyote is placed, rises at the back of the *tipi* and represents the ideal center, the focal point on which the participants fix their gaze. There the straight line ends that is traced on the ground from the entrance of the *tipi* to the Moon (the so-called "way of Peyote"). Two arms branch off from the line which form the cross of Christ. A "fire" is lighted in front of the "Moon"; a circle indicates the Sun; and one or two "hearts" represent the heart of Jesus and the heart of Peyote. Petrullo: op. cit., pp. 179–82, tables 3–6.

[7] La Barre: *The Peyote-Cult*, p. 159.

71

prophet,[8] to whom God spoke through an amulet he wore around his neck, consisting of a bull's horns surrounded by red feathers. The Moon played a major part in his visions, and in trance he ascended to it and was permitted to ravish its secrets.[9]

In order to salvage and restore the traditional Indian values, which were rapidly disappearing, Wilson imposed a strict discipline on his followers; he demanded perfect fidelity in marriage, forbade sexual indulgence, and banned the use of liquor. Although he never claimed to be a messenger of God, Wilson maintained that the Peyote Spirit had endowed him with the power to heal the sick, to remit sins, and to cleanse physical bodies of the effects of evil, thus guiding the Indians on the "road of Peyote" and eventually into the presence of the Creator.[1] Wilson died in a banal accident on his way home from a mission to the Quapaws, and his followers made his picture an object of ceremonial worship.[2]

The religion of the Big Moon, as the cult was called because of the crescent-shaped peyote altar, spread rapidly between 1890 and 1908 and attracted followers among the Seneca, Shawnee, Delaware, Quapaw, Potawatomi, and Osage. Several prophets followed in John Wilson's footsteps, among them his adopted son, Black Wolf,[3] and Victor Griffin, who preached largely among the Osage.[4] Gradually the original cult produced offshoots, which differed from it in ritual and interpretation, among them the Little Moon, the Western Moon, the Road of the Sioux, and others, all short-lived. The

[8] Mooney: op. cit., pp. 903-4; Petrullo: op. cit., pp. 78-86; La Barre: The Peyote-Cult, p. 159.
[9] Ibid., pp. 904-5.
[1] La Barre: The Peyote-Cult, p. 160.
[2] Ibid., p. 159-60.
[3] Ibid., p. 153.
[4] Ibid., pp. 112-13, 158-61, 167-72.

mainstream of the cult reached the Sioux, the Ute, the Washo, and other tribes in Nevada, Utah, and the Dakotas. Both the main cult and the offshoots revealed a combination of ancient tradition and Christian influence.

Among the major prophets who came after Wilson, we find Jonathan Koshiway, an Oto who promoted a highly Christianized version of Peyotism. Accepted by the Omaha and Winnebago in great numbers, this became the Church of the First-Born (later renamed Native American Church), which had a marked intertribal and Pan-Indian character.[5] Impressed by Jehovah's Witnesses and once a member of the Indian branch of the Church of the Latter-day Saints, Koshiway claimed to have discovered complete identity between Christianity and the native beliefs in which he had been raised. The bread and wine of the Eucharist were, to him, the equivalents of peyote. He identified the canonical virtues of Christianity with those held in high regard in the Indian religions and made great use of the Bible in teaching and in worship.[6]

As time passed, the Christian elements became more and more numerous in the Peyote cult, until Jesse Clay, a Winnebago prophet, gave strong missionary impetus to the movement in order to promote its Pan-Indian objectives and to seek legal recognition.[7] Between 1920 and 1926, John Jameson founded the Negro Church of the First-Born, which closely followed Koshiway's pattern, and such Winnebago prophets as Albert Hensley, Crashing Thunder,[8] and John Rave spread Peyotism among their own tribes.

John Rave appeared on the scene in the present century;

[5] Ibid., pp. 8, 167–9.
[6] Ibid., p. 167.
[7] Ibid., p. 171.
[8] For Crashing Thunder, see Radin: *Crashing Thunder* (New York, 1926), which I was not able to consult.

he traveled widely through Wisconsin, Nebraska,[9] South Dakota, and Minnesota, creating a deep impression wherever he went. A restless child,[1] Rave grew up with a feeling of uneasiness about the religious milieu in which he was raised. He participated in the rituals but never in the most important one, the Medicine Dance. As an adolescent, he had gone through the ceremonial intended to initiate those of his age into the secrets of their ancient religion by stimulating the first visions. At nighttime, as was the custom, he went with two companions his own age to an isolated spot to await revelation in fasting and prayer. But the fear of the dark soon overcame him, and instead of meditating in silence he yielded to the temptation of talking to the others and of inducing them to play. Having thus failed to live up to the traditions of his people, and more restless than ever,[2] he set out to seek communion with God in other places, traveling from tribe to tribe. Finally, in desperation, he joined a circus going overseas. But he was unable to stand the voyage; he returned sick and despondent and soon took to excessive drinking. This is a significant fact in relation to his later acceptance of peyote, because peyote is believed by some to have the power to cure alcoholism and prevent its recurrence.

In a way, John Rave's problem is symbolic of the problem of all the Indians, for it must not be forgotten that distilled liquors, a main cause of their moral and physical decline, were introduced by the white man and became disastrous for the aborigines. In the account of his experiences given to Paul Radin in 1910, John Rave said: "Before I ate peyote my heart was filled with murderous thoughts. I wanted to kill my

[9] In the middle of the nineteenth century half of the Winnebagos migrated into Nebraska. See Radin: "The Religious Experiences of an American Indian (John Rave)," *E. Jahrb.*, XVIII (1950), p. 252.

[1] Ibid.

[2] Ibid., pp. 254-9.

brother and sister." By his own admission, he was a gambler and a selfish, incontinent man.[3] His abuse of liquor finally upset his mental balance, and it was not out of mere curiosity that when he was traveling in Oklahoma and came to a peyote community, he quickly accepted the invitation to partake of the plant. This was the turning point in his life. In the visions brought on by peyote he suddenly found what he had sought all his life: he experienced the presence of God and came into contact with the supernatural and the divine.

John Rave described his "conversion" as follows: "During 1893-94 I was in Oklahoma with peyote eaters. In the middle of the night we were to eat peyote. We ate it and I also did. It was the middle of the night when I got frightened, for a live thing seemed to have entered me. 'Why did I do it?' I thought to myself. 'I should not have done it for right at the beginning I have harmed myself. Indeed, I should not have done it. I am sure it will injure me. The best thing will be for me to vomit it up.'" But his efforts failed and he lamented, " 'I am surely going to die.'" As the day broke he was able to laugh with the others. "The following night we were to eat peyote again. I thought to myself, 'Last night it almost harmed me! . . .' 'Well, let us do it again,' they said and I replied, 'Alright, let us do it.' So there we ate seven peyote apiece." On the third night he ate eight peyote, and his account relates the visions he had on each of three nights. On the first he was terrified by a big snake crawling toward him; on the second a hideous creature with legs and arms and a long tail ending in a spear jumped on him and, failing to strike him, jumped again. On the third night, says Rave, "I saw God. To God living up above, our Father, I prayed: Have mercy upon me! Give me knowledge that I may not say and do evil things! To you, O God, I am trying to pray. Do Thou, O Son of God,

[3] Ibid., pp. 284, 285-9.

75

help me too. This religion let me know. Help me, O Medicine! Grandfather, help me! Let me know this religion!"

The three visions are a mixture of paganism and Christianity, of ancient traditions and new concepts. The snake belongs to Winnebago mythology; it symbolizes the forces of destruction which had once engulfed a tribal hero called Hare. The second vision, of Christian influence, represents Satan and is related to Rave's fruitless boyhood efforts to complete his initiation. Finally, the nightmares give way to a vision of the Almighty, in which pagan and Christian elements become interlaced,[4] when Rave prays asking the Son of God to be his "medicine." His conversion to Peyote was completed after another revelation had placed him before the "true source of knowledge." "I seemed to see everything clearly," he said. "O Medicine, grandfather, most assuredly you are holy. Through all the years that I have lived on earth, I now realized that I had never known anything holy. Now for the first time, I knew it."[5]

Here we find the theme of mystical knowledge which recurs in all Peyote experiences. Because the peyote produces supernatural visions, its cult is accepted by its followers as the cult of "the one and absolute truth," and it is in fact a religion of revelation in which nearly all that has gone before and nearly all that is predicated on the ancient and outmoded customs must be condemned as error and sin. Public confession of faith and public confession of sin are required in Rave's cult[6] as an essential part of religious fulfillment. Thus, the Peyote movement comes to fill a void left by traditional beliefs which, under the changed conditions of Indian life, no longer have

[4] Ibid., pp. 267–8, 274.
[5] Radin: "The Winnebago Tribe," Rep. B. A. E., XXXVII (1915–16), 1923, pp. 389–92.
[6] Radin, in O. C. Stewart: "Washo-Northern Paiute Peyotism," U.C.P.A.E., XL, 3 (1944), p. 81.

reason to survive; in a historical sense, the cult becomes the solution to a dramatic crisis which shook all of Indian society even as it had shaken John Rave. The "past" to be renounced becomes a negative element identified with ignorance! "Now I know," says Rave, "that I had taken the wrong road and I shall never take it again. I was like blind and deaf . . . the Peyote is life, the only life, and only by eating peyote will you learn what is truly holy."[7]

However, it must not be assumed that rejection and condemnation of the past meant a complete break with tradition; on the contrary, cultural links are established between the old religions and the new Peyote beliefs. Among the Winnebago the new cult leans heavily upon the old Medicine Dance, an outstanding Winnebago ritual related to the myth of the creation of the world and of the voyage of Hare to the throne of the Creator.[8] The Medicine Dance traditionally provided the initiates with the personal experience of journeying to the realm of the Great Spirit and witnessing the regeneration of the world. The Peyote religion includes these experiences by placing them collectively on the plane of human redemption: the regeneration of mankind will occur when the Great Spirit becomes embodied again in the person of Jesus Christ.

John Rave's recovery as the result of eating peyote is a very important part of his experience. Said the prophet: "I was sick and it looked as if this illness were going to kill me. As soon as I ate the peyote, however, I was over my sickness. People who suffer from tuberculosis had no hope, but now they are beginning to recover." And he lists cases of persons cured of tuberculosis or of alcoholism by eating peyote.[9]

[7] Radin: "The Winnebago Tribe," p. 392.
[8] Radin: *Primitive Religion* (New York, 1957), 2nd ed., pp. 303–4; Radin: "The Religious Experiences . . . ," pp. 267 ff.
[9] Radin: "The Winnebago Tribe," p. 392.

However, it is also to be noted that Rave believed all physical ills to be visible manifestations of deeper troubles rooted in the soul and caused by the social[1] and historical crisis which brought alcoholism, tuberculosis, and other evils in its wake. He was convinced that peyote, used with persistence and faith, was the only remedy for these ills. When John Rave rejected the past, he was seeking to break away from the cultural pattern in the throes of crisis and to create a new one, unblemished by old stigmas. The emphasis on the healing power of the cult, taken in the spiritual sense intended by Rave, provided the basis for a doctrine of redemption and salvation.

Albert Hensley, a Winnebago prophet younger than John Rave, who was a Peyote follower in Oklahoma around the year 1910, had already introduced several Christian elements into Peyote doctrine and ritual which certainly influenced John Rave's thinking. It was to Albert Hensley that the Peyotists of Oklahoma owed their knowledge of the Bible and the use of its texts, for he translated them into the local tongue and taught his disciples to preach them. Until his coming, some Oklahoma Indians had used the Bible as an object of pagan worship, placing it alongside the peyote button during their rites, whereas the Winnebago laid the peyote on the Bible before consuming it. Hensley introduced the reading of the Scripture alternately with the singing of Peyote ritual chants. The texts, read by Indian boys trained for the purpose, were carefully selected to prove that Christianity had accepted and carried on usages and rituals of pagan origin. Thus, he identified the nighttime Peyote ceremonies with Jesus' choice of nighttime to pray in the Garden of Gethsemane.[2]

---

[1] Radin: "The Religious Experiences . . . ," p. 284.
[2] Radin: "The Winnebago Tribe," pp. 394–6, 421; La Barre: The Peyote-Cult, p. 73.

78

Hensley was unusually sensitive to the effects of peyote. He went almost instantly into trance and convulsions and attained extraordinary visions, which he recounted to his followers in great detail.[3] He differs from John Rave because he introduced Christian elements into his cult, but, like John Rave and others, he was explicit in formulating a Pan-Indian program. "You Indians," said Hensley, "are now fighting one another and it is for the purpose of stopping this that you must now shake hands and partake of food together." He then laid down the ritual in great detail, taught new songs, and exhorted those present to go forth and proselytize, saying: "Now go to your people to teach them all that I have told you. Go to your people in the North, and teach them."[4]

John Rave, who was illiterate, was captivated by Hensley's educated personality and, having understood the significance of the latter's innovations to the Peyote cult,[5] adopted them for his own. This gave rise to the religious Pan-Indianism which was later to have such an impact on the policy of the United States. Actually, the first indication of a Pan-Indian idea in Peyotism occurred when John Wilson, speaking to the Delawares at Anadarko and to the Wichitas at Dewey, demanded that all Indians, regardless of tribe, be invited to participate in the Peyote rite.[6] This idea was accepted by the Kiowa[7] and eventually by all Peyotists.

Another outstanding political and religious leader was a Delaware from Dewey, Oklahoma. His name was Elk Hair, and his conversion to Peyotism took a different course from the one which had led Wilson to the cult, although for both men the curing of their illnesses was of vital importance. Shortly after 1880, Elk Hair lost his wife and became gravely

[3] Ibid., pp. 404–8.
[4] Ibid., p. 399.
[5] Ibid., p. 421.
[6] Petrullo: op. cit., p. 33.
[7] La Barre: *The Peyote-Cult*, p. 60.

ill in body and mind. One day, in desperation, he allowed a friend, Johnson Rob, to give him peyote as medicine. Shortly after participating in the sacramental meal and without having prepared himself through fasting as John Wilson had done, he was cured. Elk Hair then established a new religious cult of his own called Little Moon, which differed greatly from Wilson's Big Moon.[8] Elk Hair's ritual, drawn from Cuyahoga and Comanche tradition, was totally devoid of Christian elements such as the belief in the grave of Christ, in the Cross, and in Jesus himself, all of which Wilson had implicitly adopted.[9] This is probably due to the fact that, in the Dewey reservation where Elk Hair was raised, aboriginal religious customs were strictly observed, despite many social and economic changes which the Indians had had to accept; at Anadarko, where John Wilson was raised, however, the Delawares had already lost faith in their traditional forms of worship.[1] In keeping with his attachment to tradition, Elk Hair stressed the healing aspects of the Peyote cult, whereas John Wilson emphasized new ideas gleaned through revelation. In the clash between the traditionalism of Elk Hair and the syncretism promoted by Wilson, the latter prevailed. The social and economic changes taking place in the Indian communities had paved the way for new religious forms, even as they had destroyed faith in many of the ancient beliefs. Wilson's rite gained following among the Plains Indians,[2] whereas the Little Moon cult never went beyond its own tribal circle until Elk Hair and his disciple James Webber recognized the need for

[8] Petrullo: op. cit., pp. 31-2, 41-3.

[9] Ibid., p. 45.

[1] Ibid., p. 136.

[2] The cult of the Big Moon branched out into myriad free individual forms at the hands of minor reformers (Petrullo: op. cit., pp. 137-8). For the many variations of the cult founded by Black Wolf, Jack Thomas, Enoch, John Quapaw, Jack Kushuwe, Quanna Parker, etc., see Petrullo: op. cit., pp. 105-30.

renovation, which they had once rejected. Soon Webber was making converts by saying: "Peyote will be the new religion of the Indians. It will be for all the Indians and only for the Indians."[3] The Little Moon merged with the Pan-Indian movements and eventually absorbed many Christian elements. Elk Hair himself said to his people that he now had pity for every man, for he "had learned this from Peyote." He suffered with anyone who sinned and prayed for rich and poor alike since all were equal and God provided for all. "When we die," he said, "we shall all have the same home . . . soon I shall have to prepare myself to enter the great brotherhood," and he prayed that God and Peyote might grant him clear vision to "practice goodness."

Much of what he was then preaching was Christian doctrine, especially the concept of life beyond death accessible to all believers. This found considerable favor with the Indians, who were becoming more and more despondent over the disintegration of their traditional society.[4] Their sorry state opened a door to Christian ideas, but it also fostered the new Pan-Indian feeling. This feeling, heightened by the bringing together of different tribes in a single reservation, overcame tribal enmities. The tendency toward tribal unification in turn offered fertile soil for the unification of various Peyote cults; and, in the end, the Christian concept of brotherhood[5] became the Peyote Brotherhood of All Indians. Thus the aborigines had reshaped Christianity to serve their own aspirations to independence and freedom.

Certain secular aspects of the Peyote cult must also be

[3] Ibid., pp. 76, 139.

[4] On the so-called theory of cultural disintegration, see R. H. Lowie: *Primitive Religion* (New York, 1924), pp. 188–201; Stewart: op. cit., p. 90.

[5] "Brother" is the term by which the Peyotists address each other. "Brothers and Sisters" is the form of address used by the minister when he turns to the followers during the rituals. Petrullo: op. cit., pp. 57–71.

pointed out in order to give a complete picture of the movement. For instance, the founder of the first cult, John Wilson, was accused by Elk Hair and others, not without justification, of setting a bad precedent in accepting compensation for his services as a minister of the sect.[6] This practice had become fairly widespread in other cults, for example, the Ghost Dance and the Shakers.[7] A council was held at Anadarko, at the request of the Kiowa,[8] during which Wovoka and Sitting Bull were publicly accused of accepting compensation in connection with the Ghost Dance. Sitting Bull defended Wovoka by quoting pronouncements made by the latter while in trance, and sought to exculpate himself by stating that his followers, of their own initiative, had brought him a gift of ponies, which he was quite ready to return to them. The role of public prosecutor at this meeting, which was very much like a trial, was taken by a Kiowa named Apiatan, or Wooden Lance, who had personally investigated the Ghost Dance among the Sioux of Pine Ridge, Nebraska, and had also questioned Wovoka in his own home at Mason Valley. Apiatan got the impression that Wovoka was not to be trusted or believed,[9] and the decision of the Anadarko council finally caused the Ghost Dance to decline among the Kiowa. Other tribes, however, rejected the charges brought against the prophets[1] and continued to follow the cult. The offerings of gifts or compensation to the prophet, who shared them with his disciples or assistants, gradually became an accepted cus-

[6] La Barre: *The Peyote-Cult*, pp. 158, 160–1; Petrullo: op. cit., p. 45.

[7] Stewart: op. cit., pp. 95, 97.

[8] Mooney: op. cit., pp. 911, 913–14.

[9] Ibid., pp. 908–14.

[1] It should be borne in mind that in calling on Wovoka, Apiatan had been motivated by a secret hope, namely, that of being able to communicate with his deceased son through the prophet. When he found no response to this request, he was disappointed. His impression of Wovoka was therefore subjectively based on emotional reactions.

tom and provided an incentive to spread the cult from village to village.[2] As time went on, the offerings helped to develop a priesthood, endowed with special social and economic privileges, which actively fought the old-line shamans and healers.[3]

Nonetheless, in a society as stratified and tribalized as that of the Indians and now subjected to the influence of a new money economy introduced by the white man, it was inevitable that a certain number of individuals should seek personal advantages by exploiting the ever-expanding field of religious renovation. Among those who allowed personal ambition and greed to govern their religious activities was Ben Lancaster, also known as Chief Gray Horse. Lancaster diffused the Peyote cult among the Washo and Paiute as late as 1936; such tribal prophets as Leo Okio, Raymond Lone Bear, and Johnny Wright had tried earlier, without lasting results. Leo Okio had turned out to be a fraudulent healer, and Lone Bear was an alcoholic later arrested for embezzlement of funds. Johnny Wright acquired notoriety by bringing charges against the other two and, eventually, by accusing Ben Lancaster of misleading the faithful[4] for motives which were neither religious nor honest.

Ben Lancaster was born in Nevada in 1880, and began at an early age to move from place to place, changing jobs when he felt that there was more money to be made elsewhere. Finally he became a traveling salesman for a Cincinnati company which packaged medicinal herbs, and it was in this connection that he made his first experiments with peyote. Almost at once he decided to introduce peyote among Indians who were not acquainted with it. He made his first converts among his family and friends, until the cult attracted a suf-

[2] Stewart: op. cit., p. 94.

[3] Concerning the antagonism between Peyotism and the shamans, see note 7, following.

[4] Stewart: op. cit., pp. 69–70, 96–7.

83

ficiently large following to justify his calling himself its priest as well as its promoter. By 1940, however, the cult had sharply declined,[5] and not until an obscure prophet began to preach the "Road of the Tipi" among the Washo was it revived; it is still actively growing among them.[6]

Ben Lancaster appears to have been an unprincipled opportunist who used religion for commercial purposes. His case is significant because it shows to what extent the Peyote cult allowed freedom of operation to its promoters.[7] Lancaster did not limit himself to emphasizing the medicinal and healing aspects of the cult, but devised a creed and rituals, which the Washo accepted. His success, at first not unlike that of Wilson and Elk Hair, who had been held in high regard, indicates how strong the need was for a new religious movement among the people he approached: they accepted whatever was offered and did not, perhaps because they were not willing to, investigate the motives and mores of anyone who claimed to be a religious prophet.

Certain students of the Peyote cult have minimized the broad social and religious issues involved in the acceptance of a cult that has had unworthy aspects, such as the personal dishonesty of a so-called prophet. Omer Stewart, whose evaluation of the functional aspects of Peyotism is very well

[5] Ibid., pp. 70-4, 94.
[6] A. P. Merriam and W. L. D'Azevedo: "Washo Peyote Songs," *Am. Anthr.*, LIX, 4 (1957), pp. 615-16.
[7] The individualistic factors include not only the forces which promoted and diffused the Peyote cult but also those which hindered and delayed its dissemination. The shamans were especially hostile to Peyotism, for the individualistic character of the religion meant that shamans were not needed as intermediaries between man and spirits. (Slotkin: op. cit., p. 47.) The obstinate opposition of the shamans may in certain cases account for the delay in the acceptance of a new religion, as among the southern Ute, studied by Stewart (*Am. Anth.*, XLIII [1941-42], pp. 303-8). The southern Ute rejected the cult in 1916, when it had been accepted by the neighboring tribes. They accepted it fifteen years later, in 1931.

founded, concludes, for example, that the introduction and growth of this cult were due entirely to fortuitous circumstances, such as unemployment among the Indians, or to the personal magnetism of its promoters.[8] There is an inescapable two-way relationship between society and the individual, between religion and the secular aspects of life, between the temporal and the spiritual. Personal magnetism, family ties, psychological and economic conditions are important in explaining the attitude of one individual who may accept or reject a cult, or perhaps yield to it passively while others in his group become ardent followers; but it is the social and cultural factors prevailing in society at a given moment which I believe are responsible for the rise, spread, and broad acceptance of a movement. I would find it impossible to evaluate the personal attitude of the Indians who accepted or rejected Peyotism unless I had studied the historical, cultural, and social conditions which prevailed when the swift and wide diffusion of this cult occurred among the Plains Indians after 1890, and had thus understood the collective needs which this religious movement expressed and fulfilled.[9]

We have viewed Peyotism through the individuals who promoted it—from Wilson to Rave, from Hensley to Elk

[8] Stewart: "Washo-Northern Paiute Peyotism," p. 98.

[9] The percentage of Peyotists in the various reservations and agencies differs from place to place, as is shown by data collected by R. E. L. Newberne (*Peyote* [Lawrence, Kansas, 1925], pp. 33–5) and cited by Stewart (op. cit., pp. 122–3). The percentages range from total refusal (as by the Sioux at Fort Speck) to 90 per cent support (as among the Omaha). Several factors influence acceptance or rejection, such as the attitude of the individual, his family and social environment, personal relationships with the promoter of the cult, and the character of the promoter, whose proselytism may have been motivated in some measure by hope of personal gain and self-interest, along with the religious feeling. Peyotism is still found among the Delaware (1952), especially among widely scattered groups which still also practice certain very ancient pagan rituals, such as the Great Race. W. W. Newcomb, Jr.: *The Culture and Acculturation of the Delaware Indians* (Ann Arbor, 1956), pp. 113–15.

Hair, and from Koshiway to Lancaster—but we cannot properly evaluate these personalities away from their background, since it is precisely the background which provided the conditions that made their messianic efforts successful. Despite the limited information available about these men, it is nonetheless possible to arrive at certain conclusions as to the connection between the personality of the prophets and the conditions in which they operated.

The rapidity with which Peyotism spread to all the Indian tribes in the United States and southern Canada is so extraordinary that it cannot be ascribed solely to the magnetism of the leaders. The membership grew largely through word of mouth, from group to group, tribe to tribe, even without the presence of a prophet such as those we have mentioned.[1] The absence of a powerful leader at the local level does not seem to have diminished the vigor of the movement or the enthusiasm of its followers, a fact which may be taken to indicate that the role of a guide or promoter is less important in the rapid diffusion of Peyotism than the conditions prevailing among the people who accepted it.

John Wilson's Peyote rite, and others stemming from it, were not, in a general sense, opposed to "coexistence" with the white man and his culture; whereas the Ghost Dance, which preceded Peyotism in different conditions and a different context, was openly hostile to the whites. This difference of objectives and attitudes does not, however, alter the fact that the Ghost Dance and Peyotism are linked, although it may explain the disappearance from the latter of many messianic elements which were paramount in the older dance cult. Whereas the Ghost Dance followers believed that the

[1] The spread of the cult is described and a list of names of local promoters provided in La Barre: *The Peyote-Cult*, pp. 112–23. More recent data has been gathered by Steward: op. cit.; and C. S. Brant: "Peyotism among the Kiowa-Apache and Neighboring Tribes," *South. J.*, VI (1950).

buffalo would return to expel the white man and bring about the millennium, the Peyotists accepted the idea of adjusting to the culture of the whites and the Christian belief in a Kingdom of Heaven.

The extraordinary spread of Peyotism and its departure from certain tenets basic in the Ghost Dance point up the importance of the social, political, and cultural conditions in which the Peyote cult developed. It gave voice to the special needs and demands of the Indians and signified the change in attitude from enmity and violence to conciliation. Peyotism too, like the Ghost Dance, contained a messianic message; but whereas the Ghost Dance promised restoration of the past, Peyotism announced a new dispensation and a renewal of Indian culture.[2]

MORPHOLOGY, DOCTRINE, RITUALS, AND MYTHS

Many Indians who call themselves Christian look upon the Peyote cult as a form of Christianity. The prophet Hensley said the following in establishing a link between Jesus and Peyote: "We read in the Bible that Christ spoke of a Comforter who was to come (John 14:16,26). Long ago this Comforter came to the white man, but it never came to the Indians, until it was sent by God in the form of this holy medicine. . . . It was given exclusively to the Indians and God never intended that white men should understand it."[3]

[2] Our interpretation of Peyotism as a basically social and cultural phenomenon is shared by B. Barber: "A Socio-Cultural Interpretation of the Peyote Cult," *Am. Anthr.*, XLIII, 4 (1941); and Slotkin: op. cit., p. 35. This interpretation, at any rate, is found in classic Peyote literature. See La Barre: *The Peyote-Cult*, p. 113; Petrullo: op. cit., p. 16, 25–6; La Barre: *Am. Anthr.*, XLVIII, 4 (1946), pp. 633–5.

[3] A. Hensley: *Letter to the Commissioner of Indian Affairs* (Bureau of Indian Affairs, Peyote Correspondence, 1908), cited in Slotkin: op. cit., p. 46, note 3.

The idea of Pan-Indian exclusivity is taken from the exclusive element in Christianity which the natives learned from the missionaries. The new Peyote followers accept Christian doctrine and respect the civilization of the white man, but they raise their claim to religious independence as a barrier against the white man's efforts to destroy their culture.

In the form Peyotism took at the end of the nineteenth century and still preserves, it is a nocturnal and collective cult which, through prayer, contemplation, and the ritual eating of the peyote button, enables its followers to achieve supernatural revelations believed to be the work of God. The theological and moral principles of Peyotism are laid down in the charter of the Native American Church, as follows: "The purpose for which this corporation is formed is to foster and promote religious believers in Almighty God and the customs of the several Tribes of Indians throughout the United States in the worship of a Heavenly Father and to promote morality, sobriety, industry, charity and right living and cultivate a spirit of self-respect, brotherly love and union among the members of the several Tribes of Indians throughout the United States and through the sacramental use of peyote."[4]

Peyotists believe that God has lodged a part of the Holy Spirit in the peyote, granting its use only to Indians; that by partaking sacramentally of the button the Indians are partaking of the Holy Spirit, in the same manner in which the white man partakes of the spirit of Christ through the consecrated bread and wine of the Eucharist; that the peyote, having both spiritual and medicinal powers,[5] is a panacea for all ills; and that its therapeutic efficacy is derived from purifi-

[4] La Barre, et al.: op. cit., pp. 582-3.
[5] Ibid.

88

cation of the spirit, which makes possible the visions that bring man closer to God.

God occupies an eminent and stable place in Peyote theology, whereas the roles assigned to Jesus Christ and the Holy Ghost are variable. Both are sometimes worshipped as Guardian Spirits, sometimes as national heroes, or as other spirit forces found in paganism.[6] The angels and demons of Christianity find their counterparts in similar mythical creatures of the pagan world and are identified from time to time as evil spirits, spirits of the four winds, or other forces of nature. Within the Peyote nomenclature we find such ancient mythical creatures as the Thunder Bird, the Mother of Mankind, the Moon, the Sun, the Fire; all of them have moved from mythology into Peyotism almost unchanged and have merged with the new Peyote Spirit, a more recent deity but also linked to pagan tradition.[7]

The role of the Heavenly Father was easily assignable within the Peyote cult because it could be identified with that of the Great Father Spirit, or Supreme Being of the Plains Indians, whereas Jesus and the Holy Spirit had no well-defined equivalents in pagan hierarchy. The healing power of the peyote also belongs to pagan tradition; it was used in old rituals long before the coming of the white man. The mystical nature of the ritual, centered on supernatural

[6] By "paganism" we mean native religious forms prior to the coming of the Christians. Paganism, in fact, has no significance other than, historically, that it is a form of religion which antecedes Christianity and to which Christianity is opposed. Naturally, every form of paganism is, in turn, the crowning phase of a religious-historical process determined by culture; it should not be evaluated in a negative sense, as is so often the case among those who use the word "paganism" to signify an inferior religious form. For the pagan religion of the spirit-forces, of the cultural heroes, etc., see Radin: "The Winnebago Tribe," pp. 284 ff.; Petrullo: op. cit., pp. 28–30; R. E. Benedict: "The Concept of the Guardian Spirit in North America," *Mem. Amer. Anthr. Ass.*, XXIX (1923).

[7] Slotkin: op. cit., pp. 69–70.

visions, stems from pagan initiations, when boys on the threshold of puberty went into retreat to await their first revelation in fasting and prayer; and the belief in healing is linked with the magical practices of the shamans.[8]

Ancient practices which had once had a strictly personal objective become collective and social in the new Peyote pattern. In place of a shaman healing a sick person, the Peyote rituals address themselves to a congregation which includes the sick: everyone partakes of the sacramental meal and remains together in contemplation and prayer to await the visions. Supernatural help was originally sought for the healing of a single person; Peyotism, instead, seeks salvation for the entire community. Visions attained during collective rites also serve to develop a socially conscious form of religion which draws strength from the unity and solidarity of all Indians. The Peyote cult thus becomes a religion of collective salvation and redemption after the encounter of the Indians with the white man has brought forth new social manifestations unknown in pagan times. Christian elements have been embodied in Peyotism (God the Father, the Holy Ghost, universal brotherhood, etc.), where they have found a link with the religion of the past (Great Spirit, spirit forces, etc.) or been able to meet certain new requirements of the people (need for unity, etc.); the rationale varies from case to case. With good reason, although with some oversimplification, Paul Radin said in regard to Peyotism among the Winnebago that the only new element in it was the peyote, along with a few Christian borrowings; all the rest had come straight from Indian tradition in keeping with Indian shamanism.[9] Likewise

[8] R. F. Benedict: *"The Vision in the Plains Culture," Am. Anthr.,* XXIV (1922), pp. 1–23; Ruth M. Underhill: "Ceremonial Patterns in the Great Southwest," *Amer. Ethnol. Soc. Monograph XIII* (Seattle, 1948), pp. 1–13.

[9] Radin: "A Sketch of the Peyote-Cult of the Winnebago," *J. Rel. Psy.,* VII (1914), p. 7.

Ruth Shonle asserts that at the root of the Peyote cult is the native belief in the supernatural origin of visions and that the Peyote cult took hold most deeply in regions in which this ancient belief had been most strongly entrenched.[1] Opler, writing of the Peyote cult among the Apaches, says that its popularity is due to elements which already existed in the local customs of the aborigines.[2]

Several other reasons which seem to explain the adoption of Christian elements into the Peyote cult are also worthy of attention. For instance, the Great Spirit of aboriginal religions, a disembodied benevolent spirit,[3] creator of the world and of its national heroes, is identified with the Judeo-Christian God because of similar attributes. Jesus, at times recognized as the Guardian Spirit and at others as the national hero of the tribe, is taken into Peyotism with an antiwhite implication reasoned out as follows: Jesus, rejected and killed by the white man, now protects the Indians, who are also being victimized by the white man; therefore He is one with the peyote. "The Peyote," says Hensley, "is a part of God's body,

[1] R. Shonle: "Peyote: the Giver of Visions," *Am. Anthr.*, XXVII (1925), p. 59.

[2] M. K. Opler: "The Influence of Aboriginal Pattern and White Contact on a Recently Introduced Ceremony," *J. A. F.*, XLIX (1936), p. 164. La Barre, too, insists on the connection between Peyotism and aboriginal culture; see *The Peyote-Cult*, pp. 7, 117. In this regard, the theory of "cultural compatibility" is not unfounded, as long as it is not generalized or isolated. According to this theory, "new institutions will be acceptable to people if the introduced complex is similar to some aspects of the indigenous culture." (Stewart: op. cit., pp. 89–90). In our view, this theory should be linked to another, whereby a new cultural complex is not acceptable unless its elements coincide with elements in the indigenous culture. Thus, rather than a "theory of compatibility," we should prefer to call it an active principle of dynamic continuity, in which the cultural transformation occurs not fitfully but through a continuing process of adjustment and adaptation. See Slotkin: op. cit., p. 53.

[3] Radin: "The Winnebago Tribe," p. 439; Petrullo: op. cit., pp. 28–30.

91

and God's Holy Ghost is enveloped in it."[4] Another significant example of the fusion of Christian ideas with Peyotism is the way native prophets use the Bible to promote their cults. Any Biblical mention of an herb is interpreted to mean peyote,[5] as in regard to the following passage from Paul's Epistle to the Romans (Romans 14:1-3): "Him that is weak in the faith receive ye, but not to doubtful disputations. For one believeth that he may eat all things; another, who is weak, eateth herbs. Let not him that eateth despise him that eateth not; and let not him which eateth not judge him that eateth; for God hath received him." These words are explained by the Peyote prophet to mean that the white man is "the one who believeth that he may eat all things"; "the one who is weak" is the Indian and the "herbs" are the peyote buttons. This particular passage is constantly cited by Peyote leaders in defending their cult against the white man's efforts to destroy it.

The survival of aboriginal beliefs within new Christian forms shows that one cannot erase by law a people's cultural and religious history nurtured by centuries of time and lying at the base of every phase of their life. The Winnebago Peyotists still pray to their pagan Creator, the Otos to the god Wakan, the Cheyennes to Mayan; and the Shawnees and Kickapoos worship the peyote because, as they point out, it was created with all things at the beginning of time, whereas Jesus came only a few centuries ago.[6]

Except for some tribal variants,[7] Peyote rituals take place

[4] Slotkin: op. cit., pp. 65, 70; 139, note 6; 116, note 37.

[5] The following quotations are used frequently by Peyote prophets: "God said, Let the earth bring forth grass" (Gen. 1:11); "And God said, Behold, I have given you every herb bearing seed" (Gen. 1:29); ". . . and every herb of the field before it grew" (Gen. 2:5); "And they shall eat the flesh . . . and with bitter herbs they shall eat it" (Exod. 12:8).

[6] La Barre: *The Peyote-Cult*, p. 166.

[7] The variations go back to the work of the founder-prophets.

at night,[8] in a special *tipi* reserved for this purpose. The faithful sit in a circle around a crescent-shaped mound of clayey earth, which is their altar. The peyote buttons are placed on the crescent, and a fire is lighted from logs laid to form a V inside the curve of the crescent. The followers of Wilson's Big Moon cult also draw a cross on the ground below the altar, but this is not done in the Little Moon. The faithful sing prayers to the accompaniment of drums, of rattles made from gourds, of flutes, and of whistles made from the bones of eagles, and finally they eat the peyote; the sacramental meal is shared with the sick who have come to be cured.[9] Before long, the worshippers go into trance and see visions, which often last through the night. In the morning they eat a ritual breakfast, which consists of parched corn, sweetened water, fruit, and other native foods.

Prayers and singing are led by one of the faithful who is regarded as the leader, assisted by four others; the ceremony is conducted with great dignity and solemnity in an atmosphere of ever-rising exaltation until hallucinations and visions are produced. The singing alternates with prayer, rising and falling with the mood of the participants; at times it reaches a high triumphant note, at others it falls to a soft crooning almost like a lullaby, or, again, it becomes a dolorous lament,[1] and the words seem to be comprehensible only to those who are in a state of ecstasy.[2]

[8] The ritual normally takes place each week and lasts from Saturday evening to Sunday morning. There are special gatherings for Christmas and July 1, which correspond to the two pagan New Year celebrations, as well as on special occasions, depending on individual decisions or on the illness of some person.

[9] In areas where the peyote does not grow, the followers made pilgrimages to areas where it could be gathered. Today peyote is purchased commercially and is dried and used as tea.

[1] Slotkin: op. cit., pp. 72–4.

[2] B. Nettl: "Observations on Meaningless Peyote Song Texts," *J. A. F.*, LXVI (1953), pp. 161–4.

The pagan elements found in Peyote theology are likewise present in the ritual: the place of worship is a *tipi* and not a church; the faithful remain seated rather than kneeling or standing as in Christian worship; the crescent-shaped altar is modeled after the moon, and the log fire is the sun; the musical instruments, the sacred objects used by the priest such as the feather fan and the rod, and even the days of the year chosen for the rituals are of traditional origin.[3] Baptism, adopted from Christianity, is performed by sprinkling the forehead of the postulant with peyote tea.[4]

The visions and hallucinations also reveal religious and secular experiences, drawn from aboriginal memory and combined with images and figures contributed by Christianity. The visions are populated by monstrous creatures, by the spirits of the dead appearing in heavenly beatitude, by kaleidoscopic colors, by indescribable forms, by hideous witches bound by their own evil doings, by magnificent landscapes, by nude women of superhuman beauty, by supernatural voices, by strains of music and song, and often even by the figure of Christ, regarded by the Indians as the Spirit of God made visible.[5] From their visions the faithful learn the "road of Peyote," which is their special Christian road. Such basic tenets of Christianity as universal brotherhood, taught by the missionaries, are accepted and used by the Indians to promote the idea of solidarity and union of all Indian tribes and therefore take on a social and political significance which is anti-Western in intent. The long-range goal of Peyotism is

[3] Radin: "The Winnebago Tribe," p. 388.

[4] Petrullo: op. cit., pp. 28–30; La Barre: *The Peyote-Cult*, pp. 57–92; Slotkin: op. cit., p. 72.

[5] Petrullo: op. cit., pp. 7–13; J. H. Steward: "Acculturation Studies in Latin America," *Am. Anthr.*, XLV, 2 (1943), p. 86; La Barre: *The Peyote-Cult*, pp. 140 ff.; Radin: "The Religious Experiences . . . ," and "The Winnebago Tribe," pp. 404 ff.

94

collective salvation as well as collective protection from the ever-present danger of tribal disintegration, which has threatened Indian society since the arrival of the white man.

The mythical origin of the peyote is told in a variety of ways. The Kiowa legend, for instance, tells of two youths, called south to engage in war, who left their only sister at home to await their return. After waiting and hoping for a very long time, the girl finally became convinced that they were both dead and gave way to despair and loud lamentations. Exhausted by grief and lack of food, she fell into a deep sleep, during which she heard a voice saying: "The brothers whose death you mourn are not dead, but living. . . . When you awaken, you will find at your side something that will enable you to bring them home." When the girl opened her eyes and sat up, she saw something protruding from the very place where she had lain and, digging with her fingers, brought forth a peyote plant. Obeying instructions received in the dream, she called a religious leader of her tribe, performed the first peyote ceremony, and built the first special *tipi* to serve as the place of worship. When the Indians who had come to participate in the ritual had eaten peyote, they went into a trance; some among them had a vision of the two young men wandering in a state of starvation amid the mountains of the Sierra Madre in Mexico. A party of rescuers was sent out, and the youths were found and brought safely home.[6] Their sister became known as the "Peyote woman," founder of the Peyote cult.

Among the Delaware, the legend is told in similar terms, although in a different setting: in the year 1860 a band of Comanche were pursued by a powerful enemy force. With the Indians was a woman who was gravely ill. The men hid her in a *tipi*, leaving with her a child who was old enough

[6] Mooney: "The Kiowa Peyote Rite," *Der Urquell*, I (1897), p. 330.

to care for her until they returned from battle. During the night, however, the child stole away to follow the men. The sick woman, fearing for his life, set out after him through the prairie, praying to the Great Spirit for help and protection. Soon, no longer able to stand on her feet, she fell on the grass, where she waited for death; suddenly, the figure of a tall Indian chief rose before her, saying that the child was safe and that she would recover her strength if she obeyed his command. Forthwith he instructed her to seek a certain plant which had great medicinal properties and to eat its buttons, after which she would be told how to establish a new religious cult. The woman crawled along the ground until she found the plant and after eating it was cured. In a second vision she saw the personification of Peyote and realized that the man she had first taken for an Indian chief had been the Peyote Spirit, who was now teaching her the prayers, songs, and rituals of the new cult to be established among her people.[7]

The legend told by Elk Hair was as follows: a little boy who had joined a band of Indian hunters slipped away from his elders to demonstrate his prowess in hunting alone. By nightfall the child had not returned and the party set out in every direction to find him. In vain the Indians wandered over the plains for many days, until the boy's sister, in desperation, set out to look for him in another direction. Without food or water she roamed the countryside for many miles, and finally collapsed from exhaustion and began to pray for death. As she lay in the muddy earth, her head pointing east and her feet west, her hand touched something cool in the earth while the figure of a man appeared at her side, saying: "Why torment yourself like this? Look at me: all your men are safe and your little brother is alive and well, for I have

[7] Petrullo: op. cit., pp. 34–7.

96

taken care of them all." The vision vanished, but the plant
she had been fingering in the mud began to talk to her through
the Spirit of Peyote. She was told to found a new religion
and, after eating the peyote, she saw her brother safe and
sound. "Take the peyote," said the voice, "it will restore your
health and you need never again worry about the world."[8]

The Winnebago believe that the cult originated with an
Apache hunter who lost his way in the forest and, after
wandering for several days without food, fell to the ground
at the point of death, his outstretched arms pointing east and
west. Suddenly his fingers touched something soft and cool,
half lodged in the ground. Making a supreme final effort, the
hunter raised a strange root from the soil, put it in his mouth,
ate it, and was quickly strengthened, as if a spirit had entered
his dying body, while he heard a voice saying: "I have caused
you to go through all this suffering, for had I not done it,
you would never have heard of the proper religion. I placed
holiness in what you have eaten. My Father gave it to me
and I was permitted to place it in the earth and I was also
permitted to give it to some other Indians."[9] Joe Washington, another Delaware prophet, gave a different version: the
peyote was first revealed to a warrior, the sole survivor of a
battle in which all his companions had been killed. Wounded
and alone, and on the verge of death, he too miraculously
found peyote and was saved.[1]

All the versions of the legend agree as to the manner of the
finding of peyote. In many of them the chief protagonist is a
woman who finds the plant in the spot where she had fallen
asleep or lost consciousness. This symbolizes a period of incubation during which she receives her first "vision." The

[8] Ibid., pp. 38–40. An identical version is cited by Petrullo, who learned
it from the Delawares at Anadarko; see pp. 40–1.
[9] Radin: "The Winnebago Tribe," pp. 398–9.
[1] Petrullo: op. cit., pp. 37–8.

97

woman's nearness to death and quick recovery also appear in every version, as does the healing theme. All these myths derive from religious beliefs common to primitive civilizations which drew sustenance from the soil.[2] At first glance it may appear contradictory that such legends should arise among hunters rather than farmers; but the explanation lies further back in their history. It has been ascertained that the Delawares, for example, originally had a mixed economy, in which the men hunted and the women cultivated the land.[3] Several other tribes abandoned farming only after the seventeenth century, when they acquired the horse from the white man and became hunters.[4]

It is also interesting to note that the agrarian elements in these legends have a parallel in the agrarian elements of the Peyote rituals: the center of the ceremonial area is a crescent, which represents the moon, and the legendary woman lying east to west has the same mythological significance as the moon. In the ritual, the peyote is placed near the tip of the crescent, even as in the legend the peyote was found by the fingers of a person dying with arms outstretched on the earth. A concept of redemption prevails in the rituals as it does in the legend: the moon, the woman, the plant growing out of the earth, and the earth itself are all endowed with life-giving power. Crescent, earth, and plant are also the three objects on which the worshippers fix their gaze as they sit in a circle in the *tipi;* from them they derive the power to achieve their regenerative visions. In the myth, the regenerative and redemptive force is constituted by the same triad: the woman, the earth, the plant. All the variations upon the legendary theme center consistently on the idea of salvation, beginning

[2] Jensen: *Das Weltbild einer frühen Kultur* (Stuttgart, 1948). M. Eliade: *Traité d'histoire des religions* (Paris, 1949), pp. 232–64.

[3] Newcomb: op. cit.

[4] V. L. Grottanelli: *Principii di Etnologia* (Roma, 1960), p. 147.

with the salvation of the individual hero or heroine and becoming gradually the salvation of society through popular
acceptance of the new religious cult.

The concept of moon and earth is also of agrarian origin,
whereas that of salvation from the mortal danger which faces
the founder of the cult has a broader social significance and
reflects the conditions of the Indians at the time. The wandering off in quest of a lost person, the warrior dying alone at
the end of a losing battle, hunger, thirst, and loneliness are
all symbolic of conditions which befell the tribes after the
coming of the white man. Hence, the promises and implications of the Peyote religion were such that the Indians could
not fail to reach out and cling to them as the drowning man
reaches for anything that floats his way. "The Great Spirit
has sent us peyote to help us," say the Indians. "I pray to the
Great Spirit and to Peyote."[5] And, by a mysterious power
known only to the Indians, the peyote transports them beyond
their problems into a realm of visions and of divine revelations.

PEYOTISM AS REACTION TO THE IMPACT
OF THE WHITE MAN

No segment of human society ever fails to react in some
tangible form when its traditional equilibrium is upset or a
crisis erupts in its natural environment. Following a sudden
change or an internal or external conflict which brings about
these conditions, human society will quickly strive to restore
its own balance by whatever means are within its reach. If
crisis comes from a clash so violent that human survival itself
is imperiled, there is a sudden rising to the surface of deep-
seated forces offering protection and salvation. These are the
forces of religious belief rooted in the people's own historic

[5] Petrullo: op. cit., p. 46.

past. They emerge to oppose the new perils and are revealed to society by the word of the prophets.

Toward the middle of the nineteenth century, the end of the Civil War precipitated an expansionist drive in the United States and the Plains Indians were suddenly confronted with major territorial upheavals and with a violent shake-up of their social, biological, and cultural environment. The white men moved in force into Indian land, compelled the tribes to retreat westward into areas very dissimilar to their native milieu,[6] and shattered the aboriginal economy by the ruthless destruction of the buffalo herds—as was the case between 1870 and 1880.[7] Nowhere did the policy of extermination and annihilation of native personality perpetrated by the colonial governments on both American continents reach such tragic dimensions as among the Indians of the North American plains.[8] To the survivors, virtually imprisoned in the so-called reservations, their economic resources all but destroyed, the experience was such a cruel blow as to seem unbelievable. James Mooney dramatically describes the situation as follows: It seemed to them like a dream of sorrow, a supernatural cloud of darkness to punish their derelictions, but which could be lifted from them by prayer and sacrifice. The old men told of years when the buffalo was scarce or had gone a long way off, but never, since the beginning of the world, of a time when there was no buffalo. The buffalo still lived beyond their horizon or in caves under the earth, and with its return would come prosperity and freedom.[9]

Tuberculosis and alcoholism were ravaging the tribes at

[6] Slotkin: op. cit., p. 12.
[7] Charles Hamilton: *Cry of the Thunderbird,* Ital. trans., *Sul sentiero di guerra* (Milan, 1956), p. 325; J. Collier: *The Indians of the Americas* (New York, 1947), p. 225.
[8] Collier: op. cit., p. 224.
[9] Mooney: op. cit., p. 906.

this time. Moreover, the disruption of their social and economic structure was further aggravated by forced acculturation following upon land seizure and tribal extermination, and was finally capped by religious persecution. John Collier himself admits that, "beginning about 1870, a leading aim of the United States was to destroy the Plains Indians societies through destroying their religions; and it may be that the world has never witnessed a religious persecution so implacable and so variously implemented. The successive and evolving reactions of the Indians to the irresistible proscription supplied a moving chapter to the religious history of mankind."[1]

The phase of the dramatic clash between whites and Indians (1865–70), which involved military attack and imperialist violence on one side and organized armed resistance on the other, was designed to expel all the aborigines from their land. It might, in effect, be called a "policy of genocide." The tenacious resistance of the Indians, however, forced the United States government to abandon this plan and to adopt a new policy, which in turn might be called a "policy of segregation." A number of tribes were concentrated in so-called Indian territory, and others were placed separately in various reserves created at that time (1870–85). This was actually the second act of the great drama, for, within the reservations, political interference soon began to undermine the native culture at the core of tribal life. Tribal ties were forcibly disrupted, chiefs were dispossessed, Western customs were imposed, children were taken from their families and sent to outside schools,[2] their vacations being spent as servants in white homes. The third act was the phase of acculturation, which began at this point and is still being carried on in an

[1] Collier: op. cit., p. 224.
[2] Slotkin: op. cit., pp. 8–12; La Barre: *The Peyote-Cult*, p. 113.

effort to produce total social and political conformity among the Indians.

This program was implemented in a variety of ways. One significant aspect of it was the passage by the United States Congress of the Allotment Act of 1887, probably the most insidious of all the attempts on the territorial integrity and security of the reservations. The Act abolished the accepted principles of tribal ownership and inalienability of Indian lands, which was still the binding force in tribal structure. Without the consent of the group, the land was parceled off into small lots and made available for purchase by outsiders. The inevitable and foreseeable consequence was the sale of land to the whites,[3] while the impoverishment of the Indians

[3] A dramatic illustration of the consequences of the Allotment Act may be seen in Omer Stewart's study of the Southern Ute in Colorado. His map of the reservation shows the fragmentation and wide scattering of the Indian-owned lots, as compared with the enormous majority of lots owned by the whites, which constitute a solid block. This is the result of an intricate policy by virtue of which the government bought back land originally assigned to the Indians, and allowed the whites to purchase or occupy it. The Indians, on their part, preferred to sell the land allotted to them; they were incapable of managing small farms, for which their lack of agricultural tradition and their habit of tribal ownership made them unsuited. By 1936, 40 per cent of land allotted to the Indians had been sold to whites.

As to the Indians' reaction to modern civilization, the survey shows the following: Tuberculosis is widespread, with high infant mortality; the Indians are not interested in, and refuse to accept, rules of hygiene. Lack of interest and apathy with regard to the land also characterizes the Utes, who work the land merely to produce enough for a bare living. Indian-held land yields much less than adjoining land owned by whites. The Indians prefer to remain idle or to gamble in the towns; they have very little interest in politics and almost never use their right to vote. The fact is that they have succumbed to the demoralizing effect of the attitude of their white neighbors, who treat them with disdain. The whites of Anglo-Saxon and Spanish descent in the area consider the Indians unworthy to vote since they do not pay taxes—exemption from taxation, free education, and social assistance are among the few advantages that obtain on the reservations. The apathy of the Indians in regard to civic

became increasingly tragic. The promoters of the Act asserted their aim to be to civilize and Christianize the natives, but neither of these goals was attained. What was achieved, instead, was the breaking up of the reservations.[4] The Indians reacted to the destruction of tribal unity with an unprecedented intertribal solidarity; indeed, they resorted to a vast Pan-Indian concept. Compulsory use of the English language, and the experience of being forced to adapt to Western ways while still striving to oppose them, provided the Indians with considerable common ground.

It was at this time, and in this setting, that the Peyote cult became established, as a native reaction to the white man's policies as well as to the Christianity of the missionaries. The missions were responsible for spreading tales of Peyote orgies[5] —both Protestants and Roman Catholics having come to regard the Peyote cult as a powerful enemy of their religious efforts. In the eyes of the missionaries, the peyote was a diabolical button, an evil influence, a gift of the devil to which

---

affairs, politics, and economic matters—even while they strive to preserve their own customs and traditions—is due to discouragement and depression produced in their society by the seizure of their land, the fraud perpetrated by the Allotment Act, racial discrimination, and the paternalistic attitude of the Bureau of Indian Affairs, which tends to discourage rather than encourage initiative. The racial discrimination practiced upon the Indians is evident from the answer given by a local politician when asked how he felt about the Indians; he replied that "any white man is better than any Indian." With regard to the scarce acceptance of the Peyote cult by the Ute at Ignacio, especially by comparison with the Ute of Towaoc—who are poorer and have fewer contacts with the whites— see Opler: "The Character and History of the Southern Ute Peyote Rite," *Am. Anthr.*, XLII, 3 (1940), pp. 468 ff.

[4] W. M. Daniels: *American Indians* (New York, 1957), pp. 43-4; Collier: op. cit., pp. 226-7.

[5] Anon., in Slotkin; op. cit., p. 126, note 14. That this statement is unfounded has already been proven.

the Indians had fallen prey.[6] Rarely, if ever, did these preachers even attempt to analyze the meaning of peyote from an Indian point of view.

The general attitude of the missionaries may be ascertained from the words with which Martin Gusinde, a distinguished ethnologist and a Roman Catholic missionary, concluded his study of Peyotism. Defining the cult as *Ersatzreligion,* or a synthetic substitute for Christianity, Dr. Gusinde wrote that a long time would have to pass before the followers of the Peyote cult would understand and experience the fact that their substitute religion actually left the mind and heart without comfort or support. His daily contacts with the Indians and his many long talks with some of them, he said, had taught him to have great regard for these "children of the plains who were once free," and as their true friend he would say to them, from the bottom of his heart: "Seek the truth and the truth shall make you free!"[7]

The author's inability to grasp the fact that Peyotism is an authentic form of freedom[8] for the Indians causes him to reduce the native religion, in his ecclesiastical evaluation, to mere aberration and vice, and thereby to deprive it of the cultural dignity to which it has a historical and human claim. In effect, Peyotism is a forward step taken by the Indians in their efforts to find a positive moral and religious role of their own within the setting of modern society. Naturally, the Christian churches could hardly fail to oppose the cult,[9] since their policy was backed by and in turn gave support to that of the government, whose main objective was to force

[6] Petrullo: op. cit., pp. 3–4, 14.
[7] M. Gusinde: *Der Peyote Kult* (1939).
[8] See Opler's review of the essay by Gusinde, in *Am. Anthr.,* XLII, 4 (1940), pp. 667–9. Opler assails the cultural presumption of Gusinde and his lack of understanding of Peyotism as a cultural phenomenon.
[9] B. F. Gassaway, in Slotkin: op. cit., p. 126, note 14.

the Indians to conform totally to the white man's ethnocentric pattern of life.[1]

The policy inaugurated by the Bureau of Indian Affairs at the outset of the twentieth century took a happy turn between 1933 and 1945 when John Collier, an exceptionally enlightened man, held the post of commissioner. His approach to the Indian problem was guided by his liberal beliefs in the principle of self-determination. He promoted the Indian Reorganization Act, which recognized the Indians' need for political and cultural autonomy; he halted the break-up of their territories and favored restoring ownership of the land to the tribes. Collier's program was designed to let the Indians live as Indians, and he sought to turn the destructive process of compulsory acculturation into a policy to foster natural assimilation.[2] But Collier's ideas did not endure beyond his tenure of office. By 1945 the United States government returned to its earlier views and again resorted to forced acculturation.[3]

In the meantime, however, intertribal and Pan-Indian solidarity had made such strides that by 1911 a group of highly educated Indians from the University of Ohio had founded the Society of the American Indians. By 1934 the Federation of the Indians of America had been established in Washing-

[1] Slotkin: op. cit., p. 8; Radin: *The Story of the American Indian* (New York, 1927), pp. 364-5; Collier: op. cit., pp. 242 ff.; Daniels: op. cit., pp. 47 ff., 167 ff.

[2] Daniels: "Indian Reorganization Act," pp. 47-53 (reprint from *Survey Graphic*, XXIX [1940], pp. 168-70). "The notion has obtained that the Indians were not capable of thinking for themselves, of having sentiments like other human beings, therefore they were not consulted or allowed a voice in the management of their personal affairs. Laws have been enacted and policies put into effect regardless of the Indians' wishes and not infrequently to their injury." F. La Flesche, letter to H. C. Phillips, cited in Slotkin: op. cit., p. 121.

[3] Slotkin: op. cit., p. 48.

ton, and ten years later, in 1944, the National Congress of the American Indians, a more powerful body, had taken shape in Denver. A Pan-Indian goal is evident in these groups, as it is in smaller ones formed in other parts of the country.[4] The persecution of the Peyotists was motivated by the nativistic and supertribal character of the cult, which ran counter to the religion of the white man as well as to his policies.[5] The following letter, read into the Congressional Record, makes clear what lay behind the false charge that peyote was a narcotic:

It is the missionaries that are continually writing about the peyote orgies, etc. From what I can learn, their fight is not based upon the actual physical harm done to the Indians by the use of peyote—that is an excuse to offer the public—but it is because the Peyote Church is gaining more converts than the missionaries. . . . Instead of going about quietly and really studying the drug or having it investigated by men qualified to do so, they jump in and begin telling the Indian it is no good, he is a fool to use it and Uncle Sam is going to stop it, etc. . . . and write letters about the peyote meetings that are as far from the truth (some of them) as we are from the sun. (Anonymous, 1923)[6]

[4] Ibid., p. 49.
[5] H. W. Vruwinck: *Peyote or Mescal* (U. S. Bureau of Indian Affairs, Peyote Correspondence, 1915), p. 1; *Peyote or Mescal as a Drug and Cult* (U. S. Congress, Senate Committee on Indian Affairs, 1937), col. 18310; J. D. Reichard: "Addiction," *Amer. Journ. of Psy.*, 103 (1946–47), pp. 721–30.
[6] *Letter to J. V. McClintic, Jan. 2, 1923*, U. S. Congress, Congressional Record 64, Pt. 2, pp. 1362–3; cited in Slotkin: op. cit., p. 126. It must be pointed out that recent observations on the effects of peyote in a ritual ceremony and of mescaline in laboratory conditions have given very disparate results. In effect, the environment and the social occasion surrounding the ceremonial partaking of peyote by the Indians are a determining

The zeal of the Bureau of Indian Affairs succeeded in influencing the passage of state laws against Peyotism, but a federal act could not be enacted in the face of the efforts of those who stood by the Constitution and the rights of the Indians. In 1923–24, however, the Bureau took it upon itself to place a ban on peyote, overstepping Congress, the Constitution, and judicial authority. It also forbade scientific research on peyote. James Mooney was removed from his observation post on the reservations and was never able to resume his studies.[7] When the Indians found that intertribal petitions, appeals to their constitutional rights, delegations to Washington, and other such steps would no longer protect them, they organized themselves to defend Peyotism as they had seen the whites organize to fight it.

One of their earliest organizations was the Association of Mescal-Bean Eaters, which spread from Oklahoma to Nebraska in 1906 and later became the Union Church.[8] The Indians were establishing "churches" to stop religious persecution; and soon several Peyote associations merged with the Union Church, which, in 1918, became the Native American Church.[9] By 1944 it had expanded on a national scale, and

---

factor even in regard to the symptoms of so-called "intoxication." In ritual circumstances one cannot really speak of "intoxicants." (Slotkin: op. cit., p. 151).

[7] Ibid., p. 153.

[8] A Peyote Society (perhaps another name for the Union Church) was established in 1911, with lodges and elected officers. That the "mescal bean" used by this society was peyote is attested to by the prophet Hensley (Roddy, cited in Slotkin: op. cit., p. 58, note 11) and by Thomas Prescott. The peyote should not be confused with the plant *Sophora secundiflora*, which was the object of another medicine cult.

[9] Jonathan Koshiway, an Oto prophet, proposed to the intertribal meeting held at Cheyenne, at which Peyotism was represented by Kiowas, Arapahos, and Otos, that the new intertribal church assume the name of the local Oto church (which would merge with the larger body), Firstborn Church of Jesus Christ. The Protestant influence of Russell and the

became the Native American Church of the United States. Between 1946 and 1955, two separate branches grew out of the main stem, the Native American Church centered in Oklahoma and the Native American Church of North America, covering northern United States. Both continue to exist, in addition to a large number of smaller local bodies that have the same objectives.[1] The religious resistance of the Indians thus defeated the opposition by means of structures modeled on those of the whites, and the native churches are now providing an answer to the need of the Indians for religious and cultural independence.

SYNTHESIS

The true significance of the Peyote movement cannot be appreciated unless the growth of this cult is viewed against the backdrop of the Ghost Dance. And neither Peyotism nor the Ghost Dance can be properly evaluated except in relation to the events which, at two different moments of history, provided motivation for each of them.

If we look deeply into these cults, we find that a polemical attitude toward the white man's culture is common to both, although the active manifestations of animosity differ in form. The Ghost Dance sought to inspire reaction to injustice and to the policy of violent expulsion of the Indians. The Peyote cult, which developed later and aimed to achieve Indian emancipation from the white man without violence, was a reaction to America's new nonviolent policy of forced acculturation.

Latter-day Saints was strong in this church and the assembly rejected the proposal because the name implied acceptance of the white man's church (First-born Church). The name Native American Church, which is filled with irredentist implications, was adopted instead. La Barre: *The Peyote-Cult*, p. 169.

[1] Slotkin: op. cit., pp. 57–62.

The Ghost Dance promised redemption and liberation at a time when the Indians were ready for rebellion, and provided the motivating force for uprisings such as that of the Sioux; the Peyote cult emerged when the Ghost Dance was being snuffed out and the Indians were forced to admit defeat, but when, however, the white man had changed his attitude and substituted assimilation in place of destruction. The new dilemmas that confronted the Indians resulted from the impact of law upon custom, of new upon old, of progress upon tradition. It was no longer a question of opposing armed Indian resistance to armed American force, as in the past; but, rather, a matter of finding deep-rooted means of arresting the gradual and inexorable advance of new techniques devised by the white man to eliminate Indian culture by superimposing his own upon it. The Ghost Dance had fed the fires of rebellion; the Peyote cult now counseled introspection and meditation. The time was ripe for evolving from the roots of native religious tradition a new doctrine incorporating enough of the white man's ideas to make coexistence feasible while also making it possible for the Indians to free themselves from the religious yoke of their masters. The Peyote cult was the fruit of the Ghost Dance in the same sense that peace is the fruit of war and that reconstruction follows upon revolution or defeat. Peyotism contains elements of Western culture selected to meet certain new conditions.

In essence, the basic elements from which the Peyote religion derives strength, significance, and appeal fall into five categories:

1. The elements of Indian paganism, expressed in the worship of the Great Spirit, in the belief in supernatural assistance, in visions and hallucinations, in the preservation of ancient myths and rituals in which the moon, the sun, and the Peyote

Woman have leading roles. The religious significance of the peyote fits into a framework of agrarian derivation, even as agrarian origins (in some cases of very distant date) exist in Indian society.

2. The part-magical, part-healing practices which stem from the old cult of the peyote, although they are not quite as old as the pagan legends that explain its origin. The healing aspect of Peyotism developed after the arrival of the white man, who brought with him a number of diseases hitherto unknown to the Indians. The need for physical healing increased, as did the need to cure the psychological malaise produced by the repressive policies of the invaders. Thus, the physical healing powers originally attributed to the peyote now also offered assurance that salvation of the entire race and of its culture could be attained by practicing the new religion.

3. The belief in salvation, often combined with the belief in a mystical knowledge of good and evil. The Indian prophets constantly repeat that through the effects of peyote they are able to discern the "road to good," as against the obsolete pagan way, now defined as the "road to evil." The facts inherently recognized in this doctrine are the failure of the cult of the Ghost Dance and the necessity to reach some form of understanding with the white man. Armed hostility and intransigence are abandoned as the Indians begin to understand the weaknesses that enabled the whites to defeat them, and begin also to strive for the good which they recognize in the white man's ways.[2] From a comparison between Western culture and their own, which may have been partly conscious and partly subconscious, the Indians arrived at a new evaluation of good and evil. However, since they still found it impossible to accept the white man's culture as

[2] Radin, *The Story of the American Indian*, p. 366.

"totally good," they devised a pattern of their own which combined aboriginal traditions with desirable Western elements.

4. Social solidarity, most recently developed, came in reaction to the anguish of being uprooted from the native habitat and of seeing tribal customs systematically destroyed. To some extent, intertribalism had already existed in the aboriginal society among the followers of dance cults,[3] but in the face of grave outside danger, solidarity took on new meaning, new vigor, and a broader, well-defined purpose.

The awakening of Pan-Indian sentiment among the Indians of the United States is reflected in the establishment of native churches in Oklahoma and other places. A specific manifestation of it is the periodical powwow,[4] or intertribal meeting, which consists largely of religious ceremonies lasting several days, with dancing as the principal form of worship and expression. The music and the movements of current powwow dances are a synthesis of ancient Indian and modern American features as well as a departure from the accepted custom of the past, which required the powwow dances to be those of the most influential tribe present. The powwow provides the Indians with a sense of their own strength and with confidence in their own power to act as Indians beyond the reach of the white man. This desire for unity, strong enough to override tribal differences and enmities, is the direct result of the white man's attempt to relegate the Indians to the reservation, a newfangled type of "ghetto," and of his

[3] C. Wissler: "General Discussion of Shamanistic and Dancing Societies," *Anthr. Pap. Amer. Mus. Nat. Hist.*, XI (1912–16), pp. 853–76.
[4] On the powwow, see Newcomb: "A Note on Cherokee-Delaware Pan-Indianism," *Am. Anthr.*, LVII (1955); B. S. Mason: *Dances and Stories of the American Indian* (New York, 1944), pp. 61–9. Slotkin, on the other hand, in "The Menomini Powwow" (*Milw. Anthr.*, IV [1957]), refers to the Dream Dance; its local name was powwow.

habit of regarding all Indians as Indians, without recognizing the various distinct Indian nations. Moreover, the establishment of separate schools and hospitals for Indians fostered a sense of oneness which the Indians had never had before and which led the Cherokee and Delaware, for instance, to urge intermarriage with other tribes. Intermarriage[5] obviously will operate radical changes in the structure of Indian society and is already paving the way for broader patterns of cultural expression and religious practice. The Pan-Indian movement is a product of the Peyote cult's advocacy of peaceful unification of all Indians and of a form of nationalism that transcends tribal limitations.

These major objectives differentiate Peyotism from otherwise similar religious cults in Oceania, where pan-native aspirations do not exist; they link it instead with the messianic movements of Africa, where Pan-African goals have come strongly to the fore in direct consequence of the white man's rule.

5. The religious elements of Christianity, similar in Peyotism to those found in other messianic cults, are in all cases the fruit of missionary work and are accepted by the aborigines merely as counterparts to pagan elements which they are determined to preserve. Basic Christian tenets are translated into Indian terms: Jesus is identified with the Peyote Spirit and Christian brotherhood with Pan-Indianism, although in the ritual it is only on rare occasions that the Christian deity plays a prominent role in the visions, dreams, revelations, or hallucinations of peyote eaters.

In conclusion, the Peyote cult has taken monotheism from Judeo-Christian teaching by merging the concept of One God with the Supreme Being of the aboriginal tradition; other

[5] Newcomb: "A note on . . . ," pp. 1042–4; La Barre: *The Peyote-Cult*, p. 166.

Christian elements have been transformed to serve Indian needs or have been rejected. In Peyotism, as in most other modernized versions of primitive religion, the Almighty God of the Jews and Christians is far more acceptable than the divine person of Jesus Christ, who, in the native view, evokes the alliance between Christianity and the white man's rule.

CHAPTER

III

OTHER PROPHETIC
MOVEMENTS
IN NORTH AMERICA

IN GENERAL, the prophetic and messianic movements of North America reveal two principal trends, which correspond to two different phases of Indian history. In the first phase, which was revolutionary and openly hostile to the whites, the religious trend reflects the yearning of the Indians for the recovery of their own culture, which was rapidly declining. Such movements as the Ghost Dance, and several which preceded it—the Dreamers, the Earth Lodge cult, the Bole Maru, and others—sought to salvage and renovate a culture already in crisis by rejecting the white man and his civilization. This trend is retrospective: for in these movements it is the past that offers the way to salvation.

The second phase, which started when the whites had taken and begun to develop the Indians' land, produced a religious trend that called for adaptation to the white man's ways, without, of course, renouncing religious independence. The Shakers, Peyotism, the cults of Kolaskin and Handsome Lake, which developed during this phase, show no longing for the past; rather, they focus their prophetic sights on change and progress.

HANDSOME LAKE, PROPHET OF THE IROQUOIS

The clash between whites and Indians in the Great Lakes region gave rise to a major prophetic cult among the Iroquois, founded in 1799 by a Seneca named Handsome Lake, or Ganioda'yo. His cult, called New Religion of the Iroquois,[1] or Gai'wiio, meaning "Good Message," soon spread from the Senecas of Burnt House, on the New York border, to the Five Nations, Onondaga, Oneida, Mohawk, Cayuga, and Tuscarora.[2] The "Good Message" is a syncretistic movement and a movement of adaptation. It is still active,[3] probably because it combined the Indians' traditional belief in a Great Spirit with the tenets of the Quakers, among whom Handsome Lake had been raised.

The Gai'wiio came forth during the American Revolution and, at that time, conveyed a warning to the Americans who had seized Indian land, that the Indians, too, wanted independence and sought liberation from the burdens of white occupation and control. The cult was strongly opposed to witchcraft and to the use of liquor—as was Peyotism—and engaged in a forceful drive to arrest the spread of smallpox

[1] M. H. Deardorff: "The Religion of Handsome Lake," ed. W. N. Fenton, *B. B. Amer. Ethn.*, CXLIX (1950), p. 80; L. H. Morgan: *League of the Ho-de-No Sau-Nee or Iroquois* (New York, 1901; New Haven, 1954), Vol. I, pp. 217-48.

[2] Deardorff: op. cit., pp. 80, 90.

[3] F. G. Speck: *Midwinter Rites of the Cayuga Longhouse* (Philadelphia, 1949); Deardorff: op. cit.

and of venereal diseases, which had appeared with the arrival of the white foreigners. In this regard, Gai'wiio resembles the messianic cults of Africa. It is a religion of salvation and seeks to preserve the biological as well as the moral and cultural integrity of the Indians.

Born around 1735 into a Seneca family of the Wolf clan, in a village near Avon, New York, Handsome Lake fled to Tonawanda with the entire population in 1799, when American military forces advanced into Indian land, setting everything on fire as they marched. Handsome Lake, already a Seneca sachem, was a member of the Executive Council of the Iroquois League when six Iroquois nations, meeting at Oswego, New York, decided to ally themselves with the British in order to fight the Americans. This decision was reached despite the plea for Indian neutrality voiced by Handsome Lake and by his half-brother, Cornplanter, also a Seneca chief, and despite the defection of the Oneidas, who had become Christians and chose to stand by the missionaries. Cornplanter, Joseph Brant, and Sayenqueraghta became officers in the Indian army fighting for the British, but Handsome Lake remained a private.[4]

When the war was over, Cornplanter negotiated the treaty between Pennsylvania and the Indians; he received for his people a territory at Burnt House, on the border of New York State, which had already been settled by a Quaker community. The contact and fellowship with the Quakers had an enduring effect upon the Indians, who grew to admire and love them deeply. The Quakers called upon the Indian families, talked to them in easy and friendly ways, and showed a great understanding of native religion and of all their problems and aspirations. Cornplanter invited a distinguished Quaker

[4] Deardorff: op. cit., pp. 82-3; Morgan: op. cit., Vol. I, pp. 26, 218 ff.

named Simmons to tutor his children, and the Indians joined the Quakers in great numbers.[5]

The Moravians, who had also settled on the banks of the Allegheny, had an outstanding leader named David Zeisberger, who, in 1767, had carried his missionary work as far as West Hickory in the lower Allegheny Valley and whose memory was greatly revered in those parts. The almost legendary figure of Zeisberger plays an important role in the myth associated with the origin of the Good Message. The Senecas tell that Handsome Lake, who habitually sought solitude by canoeing on the river, was followed one day. People saw him land near West Hickory, go into a cabin by the water's edge, and take a seat at a table while an older man read to him from a large book. The book, says the legend, was the Bible, which the re-embodied spirit of Zeisberger was reading to Handsome Lake.[6]

Quaker influence is evident in Handsome Lake's particular use and evaluation of the Scriptures, in his renunciation of pagan rituals, in his struggle against witchcraft, and in his habit of silent prayer and introspection. "You must not do anything bad, you must not say anything bad, you must not think anything bad," was the prophet's injunction to his followers. Introspection stemmed from his conviction that if an Inner Light from the Great Spirit could shine into the soul of the believer, it would separate good from evil; he demanded loyalty and gratitude to the Divine Giver for all gifts received, compassion for those in need and solidarity with their suffering, confession and repentance of sins, and total dedication to the work of the Great Spirit. Evil deeds, said the prophet, bring punishment in the afterlife and if they accumulate sufficiently they may even bring about the end of the

[5] Deardorff: op. cit., pp. 81–6.
[6] Ibid., pp. 87–8, note 6.

117

world.[7] The white man's Bible, according to Handsome Lake, was a good guide for him to follow, and he deemed it important to learn to read and write in order to consult it, although only the wisdom of the individual could help him decide upon the rightful use of a Biblical text.[8] The doctrine of Handsome Lake was transmitted in a document written down by his followers around 1900, after it had been passed along by word of mouth for many years.[9]

Handsome Lake had received his first prophetic revelation on June 15, 1799, at the home of Chief Cornplanter, where he lay dying of a grave and seemingly incurable disease. All hope for his recovery had been abandoned, and he gradually slipped into a trance, in which he heard a voice bidding him rise and go outside.[1] Obeying with great effort, he met three spirits in human form, who handed him branches of trees laden with fruit, telling him to eat the fruit and be healed. These spirits also admonished him, in behalf of the Great Spirit, against the Indians' intemperate use of liquor, and especially whiskey, and bade him go forth and preach a new doctrine of salvation. They also showed him the heavenly abode destined for those who would follow the new cult as well as a place of damnation ruled by evil spirits engaged in loading barrels of liquor on their canoes. The prophet, who had become ill because of his dissolute life, was cured. In

[7] Morgan: op. cit., pp. 246–7.
[8] Deardorff: op. cit., pp. 89–90; Morgan: op. cit., pp. 244 ff.
[9] The translation of the "code" of Handsome Lake, cited by the Iroquois Parker, was made in 1900, by a Seneca, Cattaraugus, but the Senecas look upon this text as being considerably "Christianized," as compared to the prophet's original text, which has been handed down by word of mouth.
[1] The "longhouse," the traditional Iroquois dwelling, is usually taken to be the symbol of the Iroquois League and is set aside by the prophet as the place of worship for his sect. Even in this respect, therefore, the new cult differs from that of the so-called "ecclesiastical," or Christianized, Iroquois, who worship in a "church" or chapel.

another trance the spirits told him that he would later behold the Great Spirit who had sent them as his messengers.

After a subsequent vision had shown him a deceased son and niece bitterly deploring the intemperance of the Indians, he again beheld the Great Spirit. This time he was instructed forever to forgo the use of firewater (alcohol) and to found a new religion from which all traditional secular dances and rituals were omitted, save the Worship Dance of the Iroquois performed at certain given seasons of the year and connected with the yield of the soil. The ceremonies to be retained were the New Year Festival, also known as the Feast of the White Dog, in which a white dog was sacrificed to the Great Spirit; the Strawberry Festival; the Corn Festival, or Festival of the Feathers, in which a Thanksgiving Dance was dedicated to the Great Spirit, to Mother Earth, to a culture hero called Heno, to the Three Sisters, and to several other pagan deities;[2] and the Festival of the Green Corn. Certain healing rites were also to be retained. These festivals were part of a great ceremonial cycle that coincided with the cycle of the seasons and the harvest, and could vouchsafe healing in return for tobacco offerings made to the gods.[3]

As to the adoption of Christian elements in the ritual, it is important to note that the sacrifice of the White Dog during the Great Festival of the New Year, with the sacramental eating of its flesh, is regarded by the natives as their form of the Eucharist. Likewise interesting is the fact that the cult accepts the monotheism of the Quakers, which is easily grafted

[2] Morgan: op. cit., p. 233.

[3] Deardorff: op. cit., pp. 90–1 (visions of the prophets), 93, 103 (cult), 80 (Longhouse rite); Morgan: op. cit., pp. 218–20, 224–48 (prophecy and cult). For the traditional feasts, see Morgan: op. cit., pp. 175–216. The feasts of the New Religion are individually described, according to seasonal chronology, in W. N. Fenton: "An Outline of Seneca Ceremonies at Coldspring Longhouse," Y.P.A., IX (1936); Speck: *Midwinter Rites of the Cayuga Longhouse*. For healing rites, see idem, pp. 141–3.

onto the aboriginal belief in a Great Spirit, but it rejects the New Testament and gives no role to Jesus Christ. It is only among the Cayuga that Jesus is identified with a local legendary figure known as the Fatherless Boy.[4]

A norm to guide relations between Indians and whites was also given to the prophet in a vision: whites were to be welcomed by the Indians and Indian children sent to school with the whites (that is, the Quakers). On the other hand, however, the Indians were to keep faith with their traditions:[5] one of their main obligations was not to sell their land to a white man. This was a significant command because lust for money had already induced several tribes to sell their land and to accept confinement in a reservation.[6] Absolute fidelity in marriage, responsibility for the children, and the strengthening of family ties were highlighted in the prophet's teaching,[7] which also forbade intermarriage with the whites because the Iroquois lineage had been created by the Great Spirit and was to remain distinct from that of the "pale face."[8] Special emphasis was placed on the moral significance of work, and all Indians were required to develop harmonious relations with their fellow workers. Handsome Lake attempted to solve the economic problem by introducing the plow, which he had learned to use from the Quakers—the only tool known to the Indians up to that time was a shovel, which was handled

[4] Deardorff: op. cit., pp. 100–1; Speck: *Midwinter Rites* . . . , pp. 3, 31, 127–8, 141. The Fatherless Boy of Cayuga mythology represents a founding hero of the traditional ritual cycle, which was accepted by Handsome Lake. It consisted of four periodical rites: Thanksgiving or Harvest, the Feast of the Feathers, the Skin Festival, and the Bowl Game Dance. The Fatherless Boy founded the first three rites and then disappeared; after a long time he returned from the dead to found the fourth rite; then he vanished forever. Speck: *Midwinter Rites* . . . , pp. 127–8.

[5] Deardorff: op. cit., p. 91.
[6] Morgan: op. cit., p. 230.
[7] Ibid., pp. 227–32.
[8] Ibid., p. 241.

almost exclusively by the women. The plow now called for
the stronger arm of the male; and once the use of the plow
had been accepted, the economic pattern of Iroquois society
underwent a major and progressive change. Shortly thereafter,
the Iroquois began to raise cattle and to establish personal
contacts with other people who traded, as they now did, in
the market places.[9]

Handsome Lake emerged as a prophet at a time when the
Iroquois were beset by tribal strife, by armed warfare with
the French, by the ever-growing spread of alcoholism and
disease, by the American occupation of their land, and by a
mass migration instigated by the Jesuit missionaries, who induced entire villages to move northward to the St. Lawrence
River under the protection of the French. These migrants
subsequently became enemies of their fellow tribesmen. By
1750 the number of the Iroquois had been reduced by half;
they knew that they were threatened with extinction.[1]
Ganioda'yo's new religion provided answers, through spiritual
revival, for many of these problems, and before long, self-
confidence had been regained and a new sense of security
had stimulated a noticeable rise in the birth rate. The old
Iroquois civilization, now renovated and revivified, was moving toward a more hopeful future.[2] The statement made by
Thomas Jefferson while he was President, in which he defined Handsome Lake's mission to his own people as "positive
and effective," caused the Indians to regard their prophet as
all the more worthy of esteem and support.[3] In essence, the
major achievement of Handsome Lake was the revival and
renewal of the best social and ethical values of the Iroquois.[4]

[9] Deardorff: op. cit., p. 94, note 7; Morgan: op. cit., p. 219.
[1] Morgan: op. cit., pp. 24, 218.
[2] Ibid., p. 222.
[3] Deardorff: op. cit., p. 94, note 7; Morgan: op. cit., p. 219.
[4] Ibid., pp. 102-3.

At his death in 1815, Handsome Lake was succeeded by his nephew Soseha'wa (Johnson) of Tonawanda, who carried on his uncle's evangelism, repeating his messages at all great intertribal and international powwows.[5] Handsome Lake had moved his religious center first from Burnt House to Cold-spring, then to Cattaragus, and finally to Onondaga; after his passing it was moved to Tonawanda, capital of the Iroquois Federation. His ceremonial clothing was preserved in the Longhouse, which soon became a place of worship for all tribes of the area and a "mother house" for other longhouses of this cult. Every two years a pilgrimage was organized to the Tonawanda center, with an international powwow to which preachers (hata'ha) came from far and near and at which a special council selected the new evangelists (hawanota). The method of choosing the new leaders and the invitations to outside preachers both stem from the traditional system of the Iroquois, who had always gathered at Tonawanda to elect their sachems. Public recitation of the doctrinal principles of Handsome Lake was a salient feature of the ceremonies. There was, however, no canonically recognized text, each preacher using the variants prevailing among his own people. But all of them adhered to the basic tenets propounded by Handsome Lake,[6] even though the Good Message was interpreted in a variety of ways, with greater or lesser punitive, magical, healing, or spiritual import. Even the actual reading differed; sometimes it was public and aloud, sometimes silent, sometimes responsive.

Three kinds of elements went into the making of Handsome Lake's new religion: (a) aboriginal religious elements; (b) Quaker elements; (c) the program of renovation which selected and gave its own interpretation to Christian elements

[5] Morgan: op. cit., p. 220–2.
[6] Deardorff: op. cit., pp. 99–100.

while also singling out for restoration and improvement many elements from local aboriginal tradition. The introduction of many functional changes in the tribal economy, such as the plow and the raising of cattle, gave a national character to the Good Message cult which strengthened its frank and open opposition to Christian church organization imposed from outside.[7]

An important event occurred in 1820. As a result of pressures from the missionaries who came to proselytize among the Seneca tribes, the Good Message movement split into two groups: one which accepted the Christian dogma with its exclusivistic attitude, the other which clung to concepts adopted from the tolerant and undogmatic Quakers.[8]

FORERUNNERS OF THE GHOST DANCE

A considerable number of messianic movements which emerged among the Plains Indians when their brave but useless fight against the Americans was at a peak come under the general definition of Ghost Dance.[9] The use of this term is justified by their commonly held belief that the dead would return to announce the dawn of a new day.

According to Mooney, the outstanding forerunner of the Ghost Dance was a movement founded by a nameless Delaware prophet who appeared in Tuscarawas, Michigan, in 1762, to preach a doctrine revealed to him in a vision. This doctrine held that the liberation of the Indians was to be accomplished by open warfare waged with native weapons, meaning bows and arrows rather than Western guns. The anonymous prophet also promoted intertribal unity, the immediate cessation of tribal strife, and abolition of polygamy

[7] Ibid., p. 97.
[8] Ibid.
[9] C. Du Bois: *The 1870 Ghost Dance*, U.C.R., XXXI, 1 (1939), p. 1.

and the use of liquor. He demanded immediate rejection of all white customs and usages, including firearms; he replaced aboriginal medicine cults with new healing rituals. Only the sacrificial rites and prayers addressed to the Great Spirit were to be retained. There was to be war against the British invaders, but the French were to be treated as friends and allies; and a great victory would bring freedom and well-being to all Indians.[1] This doctrine contained the seeds of many ideas which in later years were to motivate other religious movements started by Kanakuk, Smohalla, Tenskwatawa, and Wovoka.

The ferment created by this Delaware leader spread from tribe to tribe until an Algonquin chief named Pontiac established an anti-English confederation among the northwestern tribes of the Great Lakes. Pontiac's attack on the English ended in total defeat for the Indians, the chief himself having been ambushed and slain.[2] Forty years were to pass before another movement was initiated among the Plains Indians—its founder, this time, was Tenskwatawa, a Shawnee whose name means "Open Door." In 1795 the treaty of Greenville had obliged the Delawares, Wyandottes, and Shawnees to withdraw west of the Ohio Valley, which was occupied by the white forces; and in 1805 Tenskwatawa had the vision which impelled him to found a new cult prophesying Indian liberation. His doctrine required the tribes to resume all traditional customs while also fighting witchcraft and magic; liquor was banned, collective ownership of the land was to be restored, intermarriage with whites was forbidden, and all garments, instruments, and tools of European origin were to be given up without delay.[3] Tribal emissaries soon came from

[1] Mooney: op. cit., pp. 662-9.
[2] Ibid.
[3] Ibid., pp. 670-80, esp. p. 672.

near and far to seek Tenskwatawa's guidance: he was looked upon as the incarnation of Manabozo, a legendary Algonquin hero.[4]

Just as in 1762 the prophecies of the nameless Delaware had spurred the armed expedition led by Pontiac, so did Tenskwatawa's cult spur political and military action led by his brother Tecumseh, who used the intertribal solidarity built up by the cult to help organize his revolution. In the hope of halting the advance of the invaders west of the Ohio Valley, Tecumseh set up the greatest political federation in Indian history. But in 1811 the Indians were defeated by General William Henry Harrison's troops. The following year Tecumseh rallied his forces once again, this time allying himself with the British in the war of 1812.[5] The second defeat disproved Tenskwatawa's prophetic ability and the cult was abandoned. The need for a messianic movement was still strongly felt, however, and the continuing Indian struggle for independence, vain though it was destined to be, was fostered by a religious faith as deep-seated as it was compelling. "The Great Spirit gave this great island to his red children," Tecumseh had said in 1810. "He placed the whites on the other side of the big water. They were not contented with their own but came to take ours from us. They have driven us from the sea to the lakes, we can go no further."[6] "My father, the Great Spirit, holds all the world in his hands," said the Kickapoo prophet Kanakuk some years later, "and I pray to Him that we may not be removed from our lands. Take pity on us and let us remain where we are!"[7] Clearly the Great Spirit, supreme being of all Indians, guardian of

[4] Ibid., p. 675.
[5] Ibid., pp. 681–91.
[6] Ibid., p. 681.
[7] Ibid., p. 692.

125

justice and protector of the people, is at the core of all messianic movements.

The Federation of Northwestern Tribes fell apart after Tecumseh's death, and the Kickapoos, ceding all Illinois in return for a small reserve in Missouri, on the Osage River, signed the treaty of Edwardsville in 1819. But the Osages, who dwelt on that land, were the traditional enemies of the Kickapoos. In the end the Kickapoos refused to go into the reservation; many of them lingered in their villages while others migrated to Texas, where they would be as far from the Osages as from the Americans. Those who remained in their villages despite the white man's warnings were persuaded to do so by the prophet Kanakuk, who assured them that if they renounced liquor, destroyed all magical healing devices, and obeyed such fundamental commandments as "never kill, never riot, never lie," they would be allowed to live on their land for many more years until they found greener pastures in which to settle in peace and security.

To each family of the faithful the prophet gave a wooden tablet upon which were painted pictures representing the prayers to be offered daily to the Great Spirit in witness to the unity of the worshippers. Every Saturday they gathered for worship. Listening first to the prophet's sermon, they then held their tablets and recited prayers as they marched in a circle, stopping to shake hands with those they knew, until the prayer came to an end with words that referred to the House of the Father and the Heavenly Abode. Confession took place every Friday, the penance being a varying number of blows administered to the body with the prayer tablets. But Kanakuk could not win out over the Americans: his people were forced to migrate to Kansas, where he contracted smallpox and died in 1852. His followers, believing

126

that on the third day he would rise again, insisted upon waking
his body, and most of them died of the same disease.[8]

SMOHALLA, PROPHET OF THE DREAMERS

The cult of the Dreamers came into being among the tribes
that dwelt on the banks of the Columbia River, in Washington
and Oregon. They had refused to move into the reservations
set aside for them at Yakima, Umatilla, and Warm Springs
because they feared that once they were safely confined to
restricted areas, the whites would break their promises and
treaties and force them to relinquish even reservation land to
please any farmer who expressed the desire for it.[9] Smohalla
reassured them in the name of the Great Spirit, promising expulsion of the whites, the return of the dead, and the restoration of all the land to the Indians and a final military victory
over the Americans.

Smohalla, or Shmoqula, meaning preacher,[1] was born between 1815 and 1820 in the small village of P'na near Priest
Rapids, where the Columbia and Snake rivers meet. He was
raised in a Wanapum community consisting of fishermen and
hunters akin to the Nez Percés and Yakima. Smohalla was
called "Shouting Mountain" because of a widely accepted
belief that a portion of his revelation had come to him from a
mountain which, becoming imbued with life, had spoken to his
soul while he lay dreaming on the summit. Educated by
Roman Catholic missionaries, Smohalla proclaimed a cult
strongly marked by their influence. He fought valiantly in
the Yakima war of 1855–56, and four years later became involved in an accident which greatly enhanced his prestige as
a prophet and as a worker of miracles. Already known as a

[8] Ibid., pp. 692–700.

[9] Concerning Smohalla and his prophecies, as related to local events,
see Mooney: op. cit., pp. 708–15.

[1] Ibid., pp. 716–31.

healing shaman, Smohalla was challenged to a duel by a rival shaman called Moses, who left him for dead on the banks of the river. The rising waters carried the bleeding body downstream, where it was sighted and rescued by a white farmer. Slowly, on alien ground, Smohalla recovered but, instead of returning immediately to his own people, he traveled through Arizona, California, and parts of Mexico, finally reaching home, where he told the Indians of how he had died. He told them further that in the spirit world he had learned what the Great Spirit thought of the behavior of men. The Supreme Being, said Smohalla, deplored the way in which the Indians had forsaken their native religion and customs to follow the dictates of the white man. The people accepted his injunction to return to their own ways, for they had thought him dead and now he was alive in their midst.

His frequent trances, often lasting several hours, caused him to be called "the Dreamer." When he returned to consciousness, the people would listen to his account of the things he had seen and done and been told to do. He had seen the stars and planets in their course, could predict the eclipses, and now he preached a new cosmic theory. In the beginning, according to his theory, there was the Great Spirit, creator of the earth, of mankind, of the animal kingdom, and of all things. The first men created by the Supreme Being were Indians; from them came the French, then the priests, much later the Americans. Finally came the English, whom he called the King George's men, and, last of all, the Negroes. Of all these human beings, according to Smohalla, only the Indians were of original God-created stock. Therefore, the undivided earth belonged to the Indian tribes. "You ask me to plow the ground?" Smohalla asked the people. "Shall I take a knife and tear my mother's bosom? Then when I die she will not take me into her bosom to rest. . . . You ask me to cut grass and make hay and sell it and be rich like white men! But how dare I cut my mother's hair?" And to the white men who came to urge that the Indians accept the new Homestead Law, he said: "It is a bad law and my people cannot obey it. I want my people to stay with me here. All the dead men will come to life again. Their spirits will come to their bodies again. We must wait here in the homes of our fathers and be ready to meet them in the bosom of our Mother."[2]

Smohalla's cosmic theory reflects the needs of the aborigines who are tied to their land by bonds far stronger than those of ownership or production—by religious and spiritual bonds. The religion of Mother Earth is peculiar to the Indians who had always lived by hunting, fishing, and harvesting but had never farmed their land; and Smohalla was adamant in opposing the introduction of the white man's agriculture into the Indian communities. The argument he used to combat farming was that it would be a sacrilege to touch the soil from which the dead were to rise again.[3] Although Smohalla's cult was unmistakably hostile to the white men and rejected all cultural and religious elements which came from them, it seems to have had sufficient latitude to accept ideas which contradicted the prophet's personal stand. For instance, one of Smohalla's disciples, Ktai'aquan, advocated small-scale farming, horticulture, and cattle raising, provided that the old religious forms were preserved and observed.[4] The movement, therefore, embodies two opposite attitudes to Western culture, one which rejects it and one which partially accepts it. The first prevailed mainly during the early messianic phase of the movement; the second developed some decades later, when

[2] Ibid., pp. 721, 724.
[3] Lanternari: *La grande festa* (Milan, 1959), pp. 389–93.
[4] Mooney: op. cit., pp. 722–3.

Western goods, ideas, and systems had been gradually understood and absorbed into native culture.

The rites of worship began with a long procession headed by a rectangular banner—yellow to symbolize the plains, edged with green for the hills, and banded at the top in sky blue, with a central star to represent heaven. A large circle in the middle of the yellow field was the House of Prayer. The procession started from the old "Salmon House," once used to store dried fish and now transformed into Smohalla's church, where the religious ceremony was held. The responsive recitation of the litany, choral singing to the accompaniment of tomtoms, and dancing with a great variety of rhythms—the tempo being underscored by appropriate mimicry—constituted the ritual, which took place on Sunday, according to Christian practice. On special occasions, such as a burial, a traditional Lament of the Living and the Dead was performed. The worshippers stood against the walls attired and grouped according to precise rules, with the prophet in the center. Two major seasonal festivals were celebrated, the Salmon Dance in the spring and the Dance of the Berries in the fall, marking respectively the start of the fishing and of the harvesting seasons. The Spring Festival, also known as the Fisherman's New Year, involved libations and a banquet at which the young salmon was ceremonially eaten. Ritual excitement was heightened by singing, dancing, and the rhythmic beating of the drums, which gradually hypnotized the participants and sent most of them into trance, or dreams, as they were called in this cult. Visions were publicly narrated according to traditional custom,[5] the Dream Dance being regarded as the cure for every ill introduced by the white man.[6]

Smohalla's zeal gained a very large following, and, inspired

[5] Ibid., pp. 726–31.
[6] Ibid., p. 724.

by him, Chief Joseph, of the Nez Percés, in 1877 led his tribes in a major uprising in Idaho. This is another example of a religious movement that led to military and political insurrection, such as had occurred when Chief Pontiac, inspired by the Delaware prophet, marshaled his people to rebel, or when Tecumseh caused the Indian nations to revolt at the spiritual prodding of the Prophet Tenskwatawa. Smohalla had not intended his movement to produce a rebellion, because an agreement had been reached whereby the Nez Percés were ready to withdraw to a reservation. But the Americans staged a surprise raid on an Indian camp, stealing the cattle. The immediate reaction to this was open warfare, in which Chief Joseph held his own against the American troops from June until October 1877, withdrawing more than one thousand miles from Montana toward Canada, until he was finally forced to surrender. This defeat, however, did not put an end to Smohalla's movement. In 1883 his messianism underwent a resurgence stimulated by the sudden appropriation of Indian land by American authorities for the construction of the Northern Pacific Railway.

THE EARLY GHOST DANCE (1870)

The Ghost Dance first appeared in 1870[7] among the Paviotsos who lived between Nevada and California. Their prophet Wodziwob started the cult after a revelation received in 1869, but the movement had no real growth until two years later, when, spreading in two different directions, it reached all the tribes in the Western United States.[8] Wodziwob's vision had shown him a railroad train carrying the Indians' ancestors—

[7] Du Bois: op. cit.; Nash: "The Place of Religious Revivalism in the Formation of the Intercultural Community on Klamath Reservation," in *Social Anthropology of North American Tribes* (Chicago, 1955), pp. 412-20.

[8] Ibid., p. 1.

the first transcontinental train having made its maiden run in 1869—and he had been warned that these travelers would announce their return to earth with a great explosion. The dance itself was performed around a totem pole, according to older Paviotso dance traditions: men and women, holding hands, danced round and round, singing songs taught them by the prophet, who had learned them in a trance.[9] Wodziwob had an assistant named Numataivo, meaning Indian White Man, who was the father of a John Wilson,[1] better known as Wovoka. It was through Numataivo's ministry that a direct link was established between the Ghost Dance founded in 1870 among the Paviotsos and the Ghost Dance founded by Wovoka among the Paiutes.[2]

According to Mooney, Wodziwob's revelation occurred at the top of a mountain: the Great Spirit announced that a major cataclysm would soon shake the entire world, in the course of which the white man would vanish from the Indian land. The earth would open up to swallow the whites, while all their buildings, goods, and tools would remain for the use of the Indians. Other revelations appear to have warned that the Indians would also be engulfed in this great chasm, but that the followers of the new cult would come back to life after a few days, to live happily ever after. The Great Spirit would dwell among them in company with the risen dead, having fully established the heavenly era.[3]

The Ghost Dance movement initiated by Wodziwob was taken up by various Indian leaders, who promoted it as a cult of liberation and religious salvation. Frank Spencer, known as Wenyuga, carried it first to the Washos and later, along with

[9] Ibid., pp. 5–6.
[1] Ibid., p. 3; Mooney: op. cit., p. 701.
[2] Ibid., p. 4.
[3] Mooney: op. cit., pp. 701–4. Mooney uses the name Tavibo systematically, but we use Wodziwob.

other prophets, diffused it among the Modoc, Klamath, and other central California tribes.[4]

One particularly interesting event connected with Wodziwob's Ghost Dance is the encounter of this cult's followers with the Mormons, which occurred during Wodziwob's lifetime. Joseph Smith, who, in 1831, had founded the United Order of the Mormons or Latter-day Saints of Jesus Christ in northern New York, had prophesied that the Mormons would find the twelve lost tribes of Israel[5] and that a New Jerusalem would rise in a place where all the faithful would gather in a single community. Eventually Joseph Smith's followers came to believe that the Indian adepts of Wodziwob's cult were the descendants of those tribes, and sent emissaries to Oregon inviting them to join their Mormon brethren and be baptized. The Indians were told that "by being baptized and going to church the old would all become young, the young men would never be sick, that the Lord had a work for them to do and that they were the people chosen of God to establish His Kingdom upon earth."[6]

After this encounter, many Mormons joined the Ghost Dance cult,[7] while others joined Smohalla's Dreamers.[8] In 1892, when the later Ghost Dance established by Wovoka was at the peak of its popularity, the Mormons published a tract declaring that, as Joseph Smith had foretold, the Messiah had come to his people at the time appointed of His Father. The tract pointed out that, in 1843, Joseph Smith had announced that when he attained his eighty-fifth year of age (in 1890)

[4] A. H. Gayton: *The Ghost Dance of 1870 in South-Central California,* U.C.P.A.E., XXVIII (1930); Nash: op. cit., pp. 414-20.

[5] H. Desroche: "Micromillénarismes et communautarisme utopique en Amérique du Nord du XVII au XIX siècle," *Arch. Soc. Rel.,* IV (1957), pp. 75-6.

[6] Mooney: op. cit., p. 704.

[7] Ibid., p. 818.

[8] Ibid., p. 719.

the Messiah would appear in human form. In 1892 the Mormons felt able to declare that two years earlier, in 1890, the advent of the Messiah had occurred among the Indians and thus, by implication, identified Wovoka with the Son of God.[9]

The encounter, in America, of the Mormons with the followers of Wodziwob's Ghost Dance parallels the meeting of Jehovah's Witnesses with the messianic movements of Africa, which produced the Kitawala cult. On both continents, western and native religious drives, stemming from vastly different cultural, ethnic, and historic roots, were brought together by a common spiritual quest for deliverance from the contradictions and injustices apparent in human society. The affinity between the Latter-day Saints and the Ghost Dance in America, and between Jehovah's Witnesses and Kitawala in Africa, is derived from the similar nature of the problems that had come to beset both the Africans under colonial rule and the aborigines of America at the start of the Modern Age. The existence of a common motivation behind messianic movements originating in the Western world and others developing among primitive peoples casts light on the specific conditions in which these religious drives tend to occur: when there is antagonism between two different cultures, one striving to dominate the other, or internal conflict between forces in the same society.

THE EARTH LODGE CULT AND ITS OFFSHOOTS

In reviewing the prophetic movements which developed in or around 1870, one cannot fail to notice two distinct trends, identified, respectively, with the Ghost Dance proper and with the Earth Lodge cult which was derived from it. The difference between them is that, whereas the Ghost Dance focuses on the collective rising of the dead, the Earth Lodge

[9] Ibid., p. 792.

cult emphasizes the imminent end of the world, marked by
floods, earthquakes, and other cataclysms. Both doctrines,
however, are accepted in some degree by the two.

For example, the Klamath and Modoc followers of the
Ghost Dance expected the coming of Old Man Coyote, a
legendary figure highly regarded in their own mythology,
who would bring back the dead as well as all animal life as
soon as the grass was high in the fields. Circular dancing and
ritual songs were designed to hasten this event and to protect
the faithful from possible evils among the spirits of the deceased. Those who went into a trance during the ceremony
encountered the dead who were on their way back to earth,
where they would have eternal life side by side with the
faithful of the cult. The unbelievers would be turned to stone,
and the white men would be reduced to ashes by the holy
fire.[1]

The Earth Lodge cultists, while also awaiting the resurrection of the dead and the end of the world, sought physical
protection from floods, earthquakes, and other catastrophic
events by making underground shelters, usually in the form
of circular chambers with long corridors of access along
which the dance rituals were performed. The Earth Lodge
cult is found mainly in central California, especially among
the Pomos, Wintus, and Achomawis, who later spread it in
Oregon.[2] In the Oregon reservations of Siletz and La Grande
Ronde, however, this cult took the name of Warm House
cult, because the underground shelter, which was square instead of round, had a hearth in the center.[3] The followers
of underground cults frequently left their place of worship at

[1] Nash: op. cit., pp. 415–17.
[2] Du Bois: op. cit., pp. 1, 44, 53, 79–116, 132; Nash: op. cit., pp. 420–6.
[3] Ibid., pp. 27–31.

135

the bidding of the spirits, to journey to some distant place to meet the returning dead.[4]

The Dream Dance was an offshoot of the Earth Lodge cult which emerged in the Klamath reservation around 1875, when the latter movement had begun to lose vigor.[5] A shaman known as Doctor George developed the Dream Dance from the Earth Lodge cult which he himself had introduced among the Klamaths at an earlier date. The spirits of the dead returned to dance and sing in a circle, their faces painted in brilliant colors; and since the cult was chiefly a healing cult, the ritual took place around the sick, the shaman being instructed in a revelation to give the signal for the dance to begin.[6]

The Bole Maru cult, which rose among the hill Patwins and Pomos of central California, and another derivation of the Earth Lodge cult, discarded the belief in an imminent world catastrophe, and made afterlife the goal of its faithful and a supreme being the core of its doctrine. Bole Maru shows greater evidence of Christian influence than the Ghost Dance, the Dream Dance, or the Earth Lodge cult. Bole Maru prophets prohibit the use of liquor, forbid any kind of dispute among Indians, and preach an ethical code founded on the hope of a kingdom in the afterlife where the elect will attain prosperity and peace. Bole Maru includes both God and the devil in its dogma and accepts the Roman Catholic belief in eternal heaven and hell.[7] The Ball Dance was part of the Bole

[4] Ibid., p. 13.
[5] The Dream Dance of the Klamaths should not be confused with the Dream Dance of the Menomini. "Dream Dance" and "Dreaming Prophet" are current expressions signifying a number of prophetic movements among the Indians of North America. Indeed, in all these prophetic forms and among the prophets themselves the trances and visions (dreams) are commonplace.
[6] Nash: op. cit., pp. 426–35.
[7] Du Bois: op. cit., p. 133.

136

Maru rituals. In it a team of men and women faced each other across a bonfire, and each player tossed a rag ball over the flames to a partner on the other team[8]—this was an old game, the revival of which was intended as a challenge to the whites who were striving to suppress all Indian customs and traditions.

Another game, revived for the same reason, was the Ghost Dance hand game,[9] played in religious ceremonies as late as 1919, when its symbolic meaning was lost and the game continued as a sport. Around 1880, when the Arapahos and Pawnees introduced the hand game into the Ghost Dance, its significance was obviously political, for it expressed the Indian determination to revitalize traditional ways of life in defiance of the white man. The two competing teams were made up of members of different Ghost Dance sects and faced each other in circular formation, one member of each team starting the play. The first challenger held a coin in his clenched fist. After much gesticulation designed to confuse the opponent, he thrust both clenched fists toward the opposing team, and they had to guess which hand held the coin. Points were given for correct guesses and a score was kept; the play was preceded by ritual dancing and smoking of the ceremonial pipe.[1] All the participants wore full regalia. In earlier times the game had been a sport without special meaning and with no prizes attached to high scores,[2] but when it was revived as a religious

[8] Ibid., pp. 133-4.
[9] A. Lesser: *The Pawnee Ghost Dance Hand Game* (New York, 1933), pp. 322-37.
[1] Ibid., pp. 160-308.
[2] For the hand game and other games (guessing games, games of chance, etc.), see S. Culin: *Games of North American Indians*, Rep. B.A.E. (1902-03), 1907, pp. 267-327. It is likely that the hand game, and other games, among primitive peoples were originally rituals with a propitiatory motive. (See M. Griaule: *Jeux Dogons* [Paris, 1938], pp. 1-5). In this sense, even if one considers it symbolically, as a combat which later lost its symbolism

137

ritual, winning was taken to reveal deeper religious attachment to the Ghost Dance[3] and therefore endowed it with special significance in the quest for the ultimate goal of Indian independence.[4]

KOLASKIN, SANPOIL PROPHET AND CHIEF

While Smohalla's Dreamers were spreading in western Washington as far as the Canadian side of the Columbia River, another religious cult was being started in that general area, among the Sanpoil, Spokane, and Okinagan tribes, by a prophet called Kolaskin.[5] Unlike other local rites, Kolaskin's movement did not include ritual dancing but merely reflected the personality of its leader, who was a man of great political ambition and powerfully authoritarian views. The known facts about Kolaskin are a mixture of legend and reality, as they are about most prophets among primitive peoples; but it appears that after some twenty years of colorless existence, Kolaskin contracted a serious illness which caused his body to swell and become covered with sores, while his legs were completely paralyzed. He spent two years in this condition and nothing was found to relieve it; finally he went into a coma and was pronounced dead. His relatives were preparing for his burial when he suddenly came to life singing a song no one had heard before. He announced that he had actually died: his spirit had had a vision of the healing process going on in his body. The Creator (*Quilan tsuten*) had then instructed him to go forth to preach a new doctrine and found a cult that enjoined its followers to reject liquor, renounce theft and adultery, pray

---

and became a sport, the Ghost Dance hand game indicates a return to the oldest phase of the game.

[3] Lesser: op. cit., p. 311.

[4] Ibid., pp. 309–21.

[5] V. Ray: "The Kolaskin Cult," *Am. Anthr.*, XXXVIII (1936), pp. 67–75.

to God every morning and evening, before each meal and before setting out to hunt, fish, or engage in any important undertaking. On the seventh day of the week the faithful were to offer prayers in special ritual form, accompanied by special songs. Immediately a large crowd assembled around the revived Kolaskin, ready to obey his orders and pray as he required, until his recovery became evident before their very eyes.[6] He was then elected chief of the Sanpoil. His prayers have been preserved, and they appear to have been similar to those used in pagan mythology;[7] the songs, however, were improvised by the faithful as they went into trance. The ritual did not include dancing or music; neither did it induce seizures or exaltation and excitement. The faithful squatted silently in their place of worship, which was patterned after a Christian church.

Kolaskin had a second revelation, which caused him to predict that a flood would occur ten years later and engulf all humanity and that only those who followed his cult would be saved if they built a replica of Noah's Ark. The prophet ordered them to begin at once to set up a sawmill and gather lumber for the ark. The followers obeyed until the federal government forcibly put a stop to their activity,[8] but the movement continued to grow and for a time underwent considerable expansion after the occurrence of several minor earthquakes, in 1873, which Kolaskin had prophesied. Kolaskin, however, had by now become a despot rather than a prophet; he ordered the construction of a prison, and proceeded to throw into it all who refused to obey his orders. His authoritarian rule brought about divisions and rifts among his followers which finally exploded into violent feuds and open

---

[6] Kolaskin never regained the full use of his legs. Ray: op. cit., p. 69.
[7] Ibid., p. 70.
[8] Ibid., p. 71.

battles; finally the government had to arrest him and send him to the federal penitentiary. Upon his release, he abandoned the cult and retrieved his position as a tribal chief, but the cult itself did not decline until as late as 1930.

The fight against the abuse of liquor and all forms of corruption had a religious motivation engendered by the impact of the white rulers on Indian society. Kolaskin's objective was to so regenerate the religious strength of his people that they could resist the process of disintegration by which their culture was so seriously imperiled. In the prophet's personal experience with illness and recovery we see once again a symbolic representation of the sickness afflicting Indian society and of the possibility of recovery through the revitalization of ancient religious values.

Religious movements of this type still emerge among the Indians, even as recently as the late nineteen-twenties—the tendency to reform and change bearing the visible marks of Christian influence. An outstanding example is a cult founded in 1927 among the Pomo of central California[9] by a Pit River shaman named Albert Thomas, whose work was continued by Maggie Johnson, a Nidwok healer, and by Henry Knight and Clifford Salvador, all from Middletown Ranch near Clear Lake, about a hundred miles north of San Francisco. Their cult is based on new healing practices taught by the leaders after divine revelation; it combines old shaman methods with Western elements put to peculiar use, such as smoking American cigarettes over the body of a sick person as a means of curing the ailment. This cult, like many others, forbids liquor and vehemently condemns theft, adultery, and every form of lawlessness.

[9] J. De Angelo and L. S. Freeland: "A New Religious Cult in North Central California," *Am. Anthr.*, XXXI, 2 (1929).

ISATAI, COMANCHE PROPHET

Although it was short-lived, the Comanche movement, begun in 1873, has a place of its own in the general picture of messianic movements among the Plains Indians. The Comanche, who lived in the extreme southwest edge of the Plains and south of the Kiowas, used the Sun Dance as a vehicle for a new cult of their own, at a time when the Dance of the Prophet was making headway among most of their neighbors. The Sun Dance had been practiced by other buffalo hunters in this area, but it was not known to the Comanche, who devised it on their own chiefly in order to have a cult unlike that of their neighbors. The founder of the movement was Isatai, a shaman and a warrior of extraordinary power and prestige. He claimed immunity to the white man's bullets and the power to raise the dead, as the result of his having been taken to heaven to communicate with the Great Spirit. Isatai's doctrine was founded on certain premises derived from his own observation of events in several neighboring tribes, such as the Caddoans and the Wichitas. The latter had agreed to live on reservations and were now close to ruin partly because of poverty and partly because of depopulation. The Comanche prophet knew that a similar fate would befall his own people if they accepted the dictates of the white man. He also believed that if they marched on the whites to destroy them, power and prosperity would be theirs once again. Isatai assured his people that he could render every Indian immune to bullets and therefore certain of victory. And as soon as the meeting was concluded at which he announced his plan of attack, Isatai took command of a group of Comanche and Kiowa forces and set out for southern Texas on a punitive expedition against the white buffalo hunters with headquarters at Adobe Walls. The result of the Indian attack was of course disastrous, the Americans being armed with long-range guns. But although the prophet lost face and prestige for all time, the flame he had lighted did not go out, and in the following year the Indians attacked the American forts in the Plains. By 1875 the Comanche had been all but annihilated and Isatai's messianic movement had ceased to exist.

THE DREAM DANCE OF THE MENOMINI
INDIANS

The Dream Dance cult arose in 1879 from the Menomini powwow[1] in Upper Wisconsin. Like other native religious movements, this one, too, resulted from the impact of the white man upon aboriginal life, but it remained strictly a religion. It did not, like the older powwow, for instance, become both political and religious in its efforts to promote Pan-Indian unity. The antiwhite motivation is implicit rather than openly manifested; the principle of peaceful coexistence with the white man is recognized and accepted by the Dreamers. Nonetheless, the basic antagonism is revealed in a ban upon anyone who belongs to the Roman Catholic church[2] and in the exclusion of the English language from the Indian rites, even though English is the common language of the Menomini in secular life.[3]

Between 1949 and 1951, J. S. Slotkin made a study of the Zoar group in the Menomini community and found that the Dream Dance was going into a decline after the vitality it had enjoyed two decades earlier. His survey confirms facts gathered in 1911 by S. A. Barrett[4] among the Chippewas and

[1] Newcomb: "A Note on Cherokee-Delaware Pan-Indianism"; B. S. Mason: op. cit., pp. 61–91.
[2] Slotkin: "The Menomini Powwow," *Milw. Anthr.*, IV (1957), p. 14.
[3] Ibid., p. 94.
[4] S. A. Barrett: "The Dream Dance of the Chippewa and Menominee Indians of Northern Wisconsin," *Bull. Milw.*, 1, 4 (1911).

Menomini as to the ideological and ethical content of the cult, its legends, and other religious implications.

The dance, performed seasonally in spring and fall, and sometimes also to celebrate such occasions as a birth or a recovery from illness, retains its full pagan form and content. The rites, with their songs, dances, and invocations, are intended to establish direct and immediate contact with the Great Spirit and to entreat the deity to shower prosperity, abundance, and health upon the people. The large drum around which the ceremony revolves embodies the Great Spirit, and the rhythmic beating, gradually speeded to a climactic pitch, produces a state of excitement and frenzy strongly imbued with the dancers' feeling of oneness.[5] The calumet, which is only second to the drum in ritual importance, carries the offering of tobacco to the Spirits,[6] this custom being derived from the older Medicine Dance of the Winnebago tribes.[7] The continuing pagan tradition is also revealed by the structure of the priesthood, which includes officials with special roles to perform, such as those representing the Warrior Spirits, the Spirit of the Thunderbird, the Spirits of the Cardinal Points, the Gate Keepers of the Dancing Ground, the Guardians of the Calumet, and others.[8]

In addition to its traditional features, the Dream Dance has a major characteristic of its own: the message of peace, brotherhood, and tribal solidarity that echoes throughout the ceremonies and is expressed in the giving of gifts to all guests,

[5] Slotkin: "The Menomini Powwow," pp. 14–15.

[6] For the pipe as a "sacrificial altar," see Barrett: op. cit., p. 265.

[7] Radin: "The Winnebago Tribe," pp. 388–426; A. Skinner: "Medicine Ceremony of the Menomini, Iowa and Wahpetan Dakota," *Indian Notes and Monograph*, IV (1921); Radin: *The Road of Life and Death* (New York, 1945, 1953), 2nd ed.

[8] The Dancing Hall, a wooden building, is a relatively recent development, influenced by the West. Dancing was formerly performed out of doors, within a dancing ground. Barrett: op. cit., pp. 257 ff.

gift-giving being especially significant to the Indians.[9] The legend from which the Dream Dance originates strengthens its intertribal approach, for it tells of a Sioux woman who founded the cult among the Chippewas, the enemies of her own tribe; the hand clasp of Chippewas and Sioux is a salient feature of the dance, accompanied by a song called "The hand clasp of the Chippewas and the Sioux."

The legend runs as follows: in the year 1878, a band of Sioux was attacked by a detachment of United States troops. A young girl escaped by swimming out into the lake and hiding among the water lilies, where she waited for the soldiers to leave; but the troops remained and occupied the camp of the defeated Indians very close to the water's edge. After an interval of ten days, during which the girl stayed in the water without food, she heard a voice in the sky, and presently in a heavy cloud the Great Spirit came to rescue her. Praising her for her courage, the Spirit told her to establish a new religion among the Indians; and she was taught the forms and rituals. A drum was to replace the earlier smaller instruments which had proven incapable of keeping the evil spirits at bay, and the ethical basis of the new religion was to be the peaceful unification of all Indians. The girl obeyed the command and set out to preach the new religion among the Chippewas in order to reconcile them with her own Sioux tribe.

This legend has points in common with the legends of the Peyote cult,[1] such as the female founder being saved from mortal danger by the Great Spirit who then commands her to found a new religion based on Indian unity and peace. Like the Peyote cult, the Dream Dance is exclusively for the Indians and expresses their right to self-determination and religious freedom. Among the differences is the contemplative

[9] Slotkin: "The Menomini Powwow," p. 112.
[1] See the chapter on Peyotism.

144

character of the Peyote cult as opposed to the highly emotional manifestations of the Dream Dance; also, there are many elements of Christianity in Peyotism, whereas the Dream Dance is completely pagan and ignores the religion of the white man. This latter fact may have been in part responsible for the decline of the Dream Dance, while the Peyote cult, modernized by its absorption of Christian influence, survives and continues to have widespread appeal.

However, beyond these differences and similarities is one important fact common to the Dream Dance and to Peyotism: both arise from situations that have produced a dilemma in Indian society and both react to the clash between the white man and the aboriginal culture. The cultural legends become particularly meaningful once their symbolism is adequately interpreted: the imperiled protagonists represent Indian society now in danger of destruction because of its inability to meet the challenge of conditions brought about by the white man; symbolic also is the survival of the girl, who develops into a grown woman and is filled with a new awareness through which she founds a religion that will rally all Indians to a common cause of unity. This new religion could not have been Christianity for obvious political and social reasons. It had to be—as indeed it was—the outcome of native experiences, a genuine product of the movement to halt the drive of the white man.

THE SHAKERS

Shakerism developed among the Squaxin tribes of Puget Sound around 1881, promoted by John Slocum (*Squsacht-un*), who was probably born in 1838. Little is known about him except that during a grave illness in 1881 he went into coma one day at dawn and was believed dead until a late hour in the evening, when he suddenly came to, announcing that he had died and traveled through the sky but that the angels had barred his way because of his dissolute life on earth. He had been sent back into life to carry out the commandment of the angels that he preach a new religion and a new way of life.[2] In the comatose vision he had seen his own body dead and decomposing because of his sins—an experience common to many messianic cults, symbolizing the death of an old religion no longer able to meet the demands of its followers, in whom the presence of the white man has awakened new desires and new aspirations. The name "Shakers" comes from the bodily shaking of the worshippers during rituals, a manifestation partly derived from the shamans and partly from an interpretation of King David's dance before the Lord.[3] An effective leader in this cult was Louis Yowulac, or Ai-yel, who worked closely with its founder, John Slocum. Slocum himself had served with the Protestant church in the Skokomish reservation, although he had been baptized in the Roman Catholic faith.[4] After the miraculous recovery following immediately upon his vision,[5] he called a meeting of many tribes to proclaim the new cult he had been commanded to found. A wooden church was built, and soon the rumor spread

[2] The name "Shakers" was first given to the followers of Slocum by James Wickersham, their legal counsel, who had probably known the "Shakers" of English origin in America. Thus, a single name was used for two movements which were different both in ritual and in origin, although they were similar in certain regards, such as the "shaking" that took place during rites. The English Shaker movement was founded in 1750 in Manchester and in Bolton by Ann Lee, under the name of United Society of Believers in Christ's Second Appearing. It is a messianic movement with belief in the millennium; and it migrated to America to escape persecution. It settled in Mt. Lebanon, near New York, and spread to other parts of the United States, where it still has some followers. Mooney: op. cit., p. 741; Desroche: op. cit., pp. 72–5; H. G. Barnett: *Indian Shakers* (Carbondale, 1957), p. 333.

[3] Barnett: op. cit., p. 335.

[4] Ibid., p. 348.

[5] Mooney: op. cit., p. 752.

that Slocum performed miracles and raised the dead. The prophet claimed to have received his revelation directly from Jesus; hence his new religion was Christian. But the Presbyterian missions, backed by the civil authorities, waged war against his cult and even threw the founder and his disciples into prison.[6]

One reason for the persecution of Slocum by the Protestants was that the Shakers leaned heavily toward Roman Catholicism. Jesus has a leading part in Shakerism, and his passion is fully accepted, along with a duly consecrated place of worship, the crucifix, and much Roman Catholic iconography. The faithful make the sign of the cross several times a day, and always before and after meals. The shaking of hands, as a form of greeting, was taken to signify the exchange of a blessing, and the followers of the cult recognized one another by raising their right hand. The wooden table or altar for the rites was also adopted from Christianity, as were several other ritual elements.[7] The millennium was not ignored by Slocum, who promised the coming of a day when happiness and well-being would prevail and mankind would be healed.[8]

The striving for religious autonomy is expressed in the Shakers' rejection of the Bible as True Scripture on the grounds that the prophet himself had received direct revelation from Jesus Christ, the Bible now being an obsolete text for the use of the whites. The shaking of head and arms during the worship lasted from a few minutes to several hours[9] and was typical of such shamanistic sects as the secret Tomahnaus society, whose members went into trance and became completely rigid.[1]

[6] Ibid., pp. 747, 753, 756–63.
[7] Barnett: op. cit., pp. 308–36.
[8] Ibid., p. 295.
[9] Mooney: op. cit., p. 748.
[1] Ibid.

147

Other cults of this nature had flourished earlier on Puget Sound, such as the Dance of the Prophet initiated by one Tolmie, who gathered a following around 1834, and the movement started by the prophet Smohalla around 1870.[2] Shortly before Slocum received his calling, other messianic movements had sprouted in the same area; these were led respectively by Billy Clams and Big Bill. The latter, about to succumb to tuberculosis, had wandered away into the woods to hang himself from a tree, but on the threshold of the afterlife he had seen his dead brother standing beside him and commanding him to live and go forth to preach a new faith in One God, in the remission of sins, and in other Christian dogmas. Having thus miraculously avoided death, Big Bill prophesied the imminent coming of the Messiah to save the Indians. This is why Slocum, who appeared on the scene shortly after Big Bill's evangelism, was accepted by many as the Messiah, especially since he, too, had experienced death and resurrection.[3]

Shaker doctrine, in denouncing the medicine men and the shamans, fell in with the policy of the government. Indeed, Slocum himself maintained that his sickness and death had been the evil doings of a shaman.[4] At first the medicine men fought Slocum's cult, but gradually most of them accepted Shakerism. The principal purpose of the cult was to heal the Indians of all diseases, which explains the disappearance of the shamans from areas in which Shakerism was accepted.[5] The Shaker priest performs the healing ritual by ringing a bell over the sick person while everyone in the congregation kneels holding a lighted candle in each hand. This is to expel the

[2] L. Spier: "The Prophet Dance of the Northwest and Its Derivatives," *Gen. Ser. Anthr.*, I (1935); Barnett: op. cit., pp. 301–17.

[3] Barnett: op. cit., pp. 36–7, 49, 344, 346–7.

[4] Ibid., p. 28.

[5] Ibid., pp. 309–11.

evil spirit from the ailing body; the bell and candles borrowed from Roman Catholic ritual are also a link with ancient forms of Indian magic and exorcism. In the traditional ritual of the Tomahnaus society, for instance, the shaman went into trance, taking the spirit of the sick person with him and returning it cleansed of evil influences.[6]

Through belief in the Supreme Being, which stemmed from Indian tradition and which was accepted by the Shakers, the whole cult was conveyed to the natives, including its many Christian elements. These included Sunday worship, prayer, belief in heaven and hell and in angels and demons, acceptance of Christ as the Redeemer, of the Trinity, of Baptism and Confession,[7] as well as the proscription of alcoholic beverages, tobacco, gambling, and any other forms of intemperance.

Shaker history has a present as well as a past, for the movement is still very active among the Indians of the Northwest. After considerable persecution, the Shakers succeeded in claiming the protection of a law passed in 1886, which gave full citizenship rights to anyone who owned land. Soon thereafter, persecution ceased and the Shakers organized an independent church.[8] Shakerism traveled as far as the state of Washington and attracted the Squaxins, Chehalis, Nisovallis, Cowlitz, and other Indians of the Columbia River basin; it spread out in many directions, and today there are well-established Indian Shaker churches in the Northwest, in Oregon, in California, and in British Columbia. Among recent Shakers of note are Jimmy Jack, who proselytized among the Yuroks near Klamath in California, Peter Hekek, bishop of the Shaker church for nearly thirty years, and Annie James, John Slocum's younger sister.[9]

[6] Mooney: op. cit., p. 749.
[7] Barnett: op. cit., pp. 285–307.
[8] Mooney: op. cit., p. 757.
[9] Barnett: op. cit., pp. 3–10, 196–203.

The growth of the Shaker church is due to particular conditions prevailing among the Indians of Puget Sound and elsewhere in the Northwest, where after 1850 Indian life was seriously affected by American policy. Traditional Indian economy based on fishing and farming as well as traditional religion and social structure had all been wrecked—partly because of the white man's use of force and partly because of the Indian's own reluctant acceptance of the white man's way of life. The segregation of tribes into respective reservations had made it almost impossible for them to continue to trade with one another; and the ban on native religious festivals, on traditional marriage customs, and on shaman leadership had reduced them to a low mental and physical condition. Furthermore, a cleavage had developed within Indian society: Indian children had been sent to white schools and indoctrinated with modern ideas which their parents were not able to understand or to accept. Soon more and more of the Indians were seeking comfort for their dejection in the abuse of liquor, in gambling, in idleness, and in the general corruption of their mores.[1]

The religion preached by John Slocum offered a remedy for these ills. In fact, Shakerism was a typical nativistic answer to conditions prevailing in the reservations, especially the epidemics which occurred in 1881.[2] In many respects, including the fight against witchcraft, Shakerism resembles the Peyote cult, as well as many messianic movements found among equally unhappy aboriginal populations in Africa and in some parts of Asia. Shakerism, like Peyotism, seeks religious independence for the Indians, but it does not have a definite political goal. Both have taken a great deal from Christianity, and the Christian promise of redemption has enabled them

[1] Ibid., pp. 337-9.
[2] Ibid., p. 342.

to survive the adversities of time and history. Like the followers of the Peyote cult, the Shakers accept the idea of adjustment so long as their rights to religious independence are not endangered.

THE GHOST DANCE OF 1890

There seems to be little doubt that the most prominent prophet among those who launched new religious movements linked with native traditions was John Wilson, better known as Wovoka,[3] meaning "the Cutter." To him was due the extraordinary diffusion of the Ghost Dance of 1890, which spread from his own Paiute people to the Bannock, Shoshoni,[4] Arapaho, Cheyenne, Kiowa, Sioux, and other tribes, who in turn carried it from east to west and from north to south.[5] With minor local variations, the main theme of Wovoka's Ghost Dance, which is the return of the dead, the catastrophic end of the world, and the regeneration of Indian life after the disappearance of the white man,[6] departed but little from the Ghost Dance invented by Wodziwob, which had spread so conspicuously in other areas after 1871.

Wovoka, the son of Numataivo,[7] or Tavibo,[8] was born at Mason Valley, Nevada, in 1856, and was adopted by a local farmer named David Wilson, who renamed him John or Jack Wilson. Long before experiencing direct revelation, John Wilson had been widely known as a healing shaman. But it was in 1886, under the influence of a high fever, that he had the vision in which he was ordered to establish among his people a new cult called the Ghost Dance. Wovoka's first

[3] Mooney: op. cit., pp. 764–76.
[4] Du Bois: op. cit., pp. 802–15.
[5] Ibid., pp. 816–914.
[6] Ibid., pp. 785–6.
[7] Du Bois: op. cit., p. 3.
[8] Mooney: op. cit., pp. 701, 771.

revelation was preceded by an eclipse of the sun, during which the prophet fell asleep and was carried into another world, where he saw God and all the Indians who had died, now happy and forever young.

God instructed Wovoka to command his people to work assiduously, not to steal, lie, or fight, to love one another and to live at peace with the white man, even though they might still hope and pray for his disappearance from their midst. He also ordered that the Ghost Dance be performed at certain given times in place of most of the archaic festivals then still in use. The prophet was endowed with the power to govern time, rain, and other elements; he was to request his followers to wear Western clothes, setting them an example by wearing them himself.[9] "You must not fight, you must not do harm to anyone, do right always," were the basic tenets which the prophet put forward[1] in a setting of legends and myths similar to those found in the messianic cults of Africa and Oceania, such as the dead returning with gifts, the whites being carried away by high winds and leaving all their possessions to the Indians, and the buffalo herds being restored so that poverty, disease, and even death might be eliminated.[2]

Despite Wovoka's mild and conciliatory attitude toward the white man, all the more remarkable if compared to the attitude of other prophets, there was no place for the white man in his cult. The promised land was only for the Indians. It is not surprising, therefore, that the Ghost Dance should have so openly paved the way for the uprising of the Sioux.[3]

An unusual feature of the Ghost Dance ritual is the wearing

[9] Ibid., pp. 771-2.
[1] Ibid., p. 782. For the doctrine of the Ghost Dance in general, see pp. 777-9.
[2] Lesser: "Cultural Significance of the Ghost Dance," *Am. Anthr.*, XXXV (1933), pp. 109-15.
[3] Mooney: op. cit., p. 777.

of a white garment called the Ghost Shirt, fancifully decorated
with feathers, bones, arrows, birds, suns, and stars. It is worn
outside for religious festivals and beneath other clothing by
warriors because of its supernatural powers.[4] According to
Mooney, the shirt was adopted from the Mormons; all other
furnishings used in the Ghost Dance—such as bows and arrows, spears, and tomahawks—are of native tradition. The
dance itself lasts four or five days[5] and differs somewhat from
tribe to tribe; it takes place on an outdoor quadrangle, limited,
according to Cheyenne tradition, by four bonfires designating
the cardinal points. A totem pole of Kiowa and Sioux origin
rises in the middle. The Sioux, who begin their dance at dawn,
wear long trailing shawls, and only those who have had
personal revelations wear the Ghost Shirt. One or two
feathers are worn on the headband, but all beads, to which the
Indians are very partial, are removed from garments worn for
this ceremony. Although the prophet exhorted his followers to
wear Western clothing, the dance was performed in perfect
observance of tradition, as if to emphasize its significance as
a link with ancient customs and beliefs.[6]

The Ghost dancers, women as well as men, paint their bodies
to indicate the revelations they have received, and arrange
themselves in concentric circles, the arms of each dancer
resting on the shoulders of both neighbors, so that the vibrant
rhythm of the dance sways the worshippers as if they were
a single body. The mood quickly created by the dance is
conducive to collective exaltation and trance, the dance being
usually performed at night. The healers and those who have
most recently received revelations are in the center near the
pole.

[4] For the Ghost Shirt, see Mooney: op. cit., pp. 789–91, 916.
[5] Ibid., pp. 915–27.
[6] Ibid., p. 916.

The prophet and priest intone the first song, which is an invocation to the dead; it is promptly taken up in words and rhythm by the worshippers dancing round and round and is followed by a lament for the dead consisting of loud cries, ejaculations, and mimicry typical of the very oldest Indian rituals. Finally, all arms are raised together as the people ask the Great Spirit to give them power to speak to their dead. Almost at once the circle breaks up and the faithful, now in a paroxysm of exaltation, stamp their feet, contort their bodies, and shout: "Father, I come! Mother, I come! Brother, I come! Father, give me my arrows." Exhaustion finally causes them to collapse, most of them in a trance and some merely numbed by fatigue; but soon they are all on their feet again, repeating the entire ritual. The participants must fast day after day, making their daily ablutions in the nearest stream.[7]

In a mystical sense, the dance portrays the end of the world and its regeneration, but it also symbolizes physical healing[8] and spiritual redemption—in common with messianic cults all over the primitive world. The importance of physical cures is the prime reason that the originators of these religious movements are also proven healers, and Wovoka is no exception to this rule.

Wovoka's Ghost Dance started a proliferation of almost identical cults, in which the variants were usually a reflection of local or tribal traditions, or of the particular experiences undergone by a tribe at the hands of the white man. The prime movers of the Ghost Dance offshoots include Albert Hopkins, who, in 1893, called himself the "Indian Messiah" and originated a movement at Pine Ridge, Nebraska, designed to bring "unity, culture, and peace"[9] to several Sioux tribes

[7] Ibid., pp. 916–17.
[8] They believed that by participating in the dance and going into trance the sick would recover. Mooney: op. cit., p. 917.
[9] Mooney: op. cit., p. 893.

in that region; Sitting Bull, one of the best-known prophets and warriors, and recognized as a leader by the Arapahos, Cheyennes, Kiowas, and Wichitas of Oklahoma;[1] Frank White, who taught the Ghost Dance to the Pawnees;[2] and Black Buffalo, who carried it to the Oto, these last two having been imprisoned by the American authorities.[3] The Kiowas produced several prophets of their own; the best known are Datekan (1881), Pa'ingya (1887), Poor Buffalo (1890), and Apiatan or Wooden Lance (1890). A fairly recent derivation of the Ghost Dance appeared among the Pawnees as the Bear Dance,[4] but in general the Ghost Dance gradually became transformed or merged with the Peyote cult. Although Ghost Dance prophets were, for the most part, imprisoned and their followers persecuted[5] in order to force them to abandon the ritual, repression was to little or no avail. The cult expanded to the most distant regions of the northwestern United States.

The only barrier to the spread of this cult developed in the Southwest, where the Navahos strenuously opposed it. Some students of this interesting phenomenon ascribe it to the fact that the Navahos had not experienced spiritual and social deprivation, which is regarded as a major factor in the growth of all these religious movements.[6] Others[7] believe that the Navahos were skeptical by nature and privileged among the Indian population because of their prosperous sheep-, horse-, and cattle-raising economy. W. Hill[8] points out, however,

[1] Ibid., p. 895.
[2] Ibid., p. 902.
[3] Ibid., p. 903.
[4] Lesser: "Cultural Significance of the Ghost Dance," pp. 113–14.
[5] Mooney: op. cit., p. 902.
[6] Barber: op. cit.
[7] Mooney: op. cit., pp. 809–10; W. D. Wallis: *Messiahs: Christian and Pagan* (Boston, 1918), p. 140.
[8] W. Hill: "The Navaho Indians and the Ghost Dance of 1890," *Am. Anthr.*, XLVI (1944).

that in his opinion the Navahos were not skeptical in regard to the return of the dead or to the regeneration of the world; these beliefs belonged in their own tradition.[9] But they were perplexed and frighted by the Ghost Dance prophecies because of what they might lose if such prophecies were to come true.

My own view is that neither skepticism nor fear nor, indeed, a better economic status would in itself suffice to explain Navaho opposition to this religious movement. I regard their attitude, instead, as proof that history is not a prearranged concatenation of causes and effects which can be brought about artificially; nor does history always move in accordance with an empirically established norm. Every prophetic or messianic movement involves certain sociological and cultural conditions as well as the emergence of one or more individuals endowed with uncommon insight and natural prestige and powers. These factors—the conditions and the personality of the individuals—may be in a dialectical relationship to one another so that the appearance of a prophet is fostered or even engendered by the social conditions; or these factors may come to the fore independently of one another, each having its own positive or negative influence on the mass. It is certainly possible that the sociocultural conditions existing among the Navahos were not favorable to the concepts expressed by the Ghost Dance, but it is also conceivable that the lack of a native prophet to preach this cult in their midst accounts for the opposition to what was, after all, a religious movement from the outside.

In conclusion, the Ghost Dance, like all other messianic cults, contains aboriginal elements and elements borrowed from other cultures, largely Christianity, merged into a religious synthesis

[9] L. Wyman, W. W. Hill, I. Osonai: "Navajo Eschatology," *Univ. of Mexico Bull.*, Anthr. Ser., IV, 1 (1942).

designed to meet the needs of a native society seeking a solution to an unprecedented dilemma and striving to find a new road to survival. Although the hope of liberation offered by the Ghost Dance was shattered by the victory of the white man, the revival of religious faith which the cult produced bears witness to a vitality inherent in native religious life. This vitality continued to manifest itself in the prophets of adjustment, sometimes also called "reformers," who rose in strength from the ruins of Indian resistance.

CHAPTER

IV

RELIGIOUS MOVEMENTS
IN CENTRAL
AND SOUTH AMERICA

CENTRAL AMERICA

In Central America, and especially in the Caribbean, where the Negro population of African descent has suffered century-old oppression at the hands of European and American slave traders, conditions of life have prepared the ground for any religious cult which promises freedom and independence to its followers. Some of these cults are derived from traditional African religions and, until recently, have emphasized Negro antagonism to the whites; others, however, express the resentment of the lower class against middle- and upper-class people in their own society and are really engaged in class struggle disguised as a religious revival. All of them, however, provide the natives with a hope of salvation to be attained either through trance, visions, and incantations, or through new religious forms in which the Christian belief in the afterlife plays a paramount role.

158

A. *Jamaica*

The revival of traditional African cults, a widespread phenomenon among Afro-Americans in this area, appears to have been started in Jamaica in 1783 by an ex-slave named George Lewis. The Native Baptist cult, which he established on an Afro-Christian pattern, was eventually to become an intrinsic part of local Negro culture and a redoubtable rival to Christianity. The Native Baptists showed their strength especially between 1840 and 1865, during the uprisings at Port Morant, when they fought strenuously against the missionaries who had banned all their traditional cults, customs, and celebrations.[1]

Another nativistic movement, called the Great Awakening, swept through the island in 1861. Even the missionaries viewed it with favor until they discovered that its manifestations were "inspired by the devil." The purpose of the Great Awakening was to restore spiritual links between the Jamaican Negroes and their African forebears,[2] and found its expression in the wildest forms of dancing, in collective trances, in sexual orgies, and in flagellations following upon public confession of sins.

In 1920 Alexander Bedward, an almost illiterate laborer from the Mona district who had joined the Methodist church and was extraordinarily eloquent and persuasive, caused an upheaval all over the island with a new cult which was called Bedwardism after his own name. His widespread following consisted of people who regarded him as a prophet and believed that he would soon be taken to Heaven like Elijah and would then return to select those who had earned their heavenly reward. He prophesied that after his second coming

[1] G. E. Simpson: "Jamaican Revivalist Cults," *Soc. Ec. St.*, V, 4 (1956), p. 334-5.
[2] Ibid., pp. 335-6.

159

the whole earth would be destroyed by fire. Bedward was also a healer. He used water from the streams and the imposition of hands to invoke the power of the Almighty in his curative practices and called himself Christ, the Son of God. When his ascent to heaven failed to occur on December 31, 1920, according to his prophecy, Bedward announced that the Almighty had decided to delay the event until more of his followers had become worthy of eternal reward. Not long after this, he was arrested and committed to an institution for the insane,[3] but most of his followers continued to believe in him and revere him as their prophet.

In Jamaica, as elsewhere in the Caribbean, the most interesting forms of religious revival are found among the poverty-stricken populations of the cities. In such depressed areas as West Kingston, for instance, the thousands of newly arrived Negroes provide fertile soil for any religious cult offering a hope of change. This new urban proletariat, which yesterday was fairly secure in the rural areas, is today struggling to find even a miserably underpaid job, and ekes out a bare living by resorting to petty larceny, prostitution, gambling, and other crimes. Any religious movement that raises its voice against the whites and the local upper class, or protests against the conditions to which the Negroes are subjected, is bound to gain a strong following among this pitiful segment of the population. Some of these cults, such as the Ras Tafari, have an anti-European objective; others, notably the Afro-Christian movements of older origin, are chiefly concerned with the social struggle.[4]

Tafarism, or the Ras Tafari movement, began to take shape in 1930. It stemmed from the evangelism of Marcus Garvey,

[3] Ibid., p. 337.
[4] Simpson: op. cit., pp. 343, 408; "Political Cultism in West Kingston, Jamaica," *Soc. Ec. St.*, IV, 2 (1955), p. 144.

the Jamaican Negro who, in 1918, had established the United Negro Improvement Association to better the lot of the Negroes in Africa, the Americas, and elsewhere.[5] Garvey advocated the mass migration of the American Negroes to Africa—a mass return to the homeland—which the Tafari movement also promotes through two of Garvey's most effective slogans: "Africa for Africans!" and "One God, One Goal, One Destiny!" "Marcus Garvey," said a Tafari preacher, "was an international figure. He brought a philosophy to the Black Man. Garvey laid the cornerstone and the foundation. ... He was sent by Ras Tafari to cut and clear. ..."[6]

West Kingston is the principal center of the Tafari cult, but the movement is widely diffused throughout the island. The cult promises the American Negroes freedom and salvation when they return to Africa. Because its followers, in general, are almost totally ignorant of geography, they regard Ethiopia as Africa and dream of returning to the kingdom of Haile Selassie. The identification of Africa with Ethiopia comes in part from the fact that Ethiopia avoided colonial rule and has always remained independent. Thus, for Jamaicans, as for many Africans, Ethiopia is the symbol of Negro freedom.

The following concepts constitute the fundamental teaching of the Ras Tafari movement: the Negroes are the reincarnation of the ancient tribes of Israel which were exiled to the West Indies in punishment for their transgression of the Law; the white man is inferior to the black man; Jamaica is the black man's hell on earth; Ethiopia is heaven; Haile Selassie is the living God; Haile Selassie will make it possible for all persons

[5] G. Myrdal: *An American Dilemma: the Negro Problem and Modern Democracy* (New York, 1944), pp. 766 ff. According to R. L. Buell (*The Native Problem in Africa* [New York, 1928], p. 730), Garvey founded the United Negro Association in 1914.

[6] Simpson: "Political Cultism in West Kingston, Jamaica," pp. 135–141.

of African descent to return to their homeland; in the very near future the black man will be avenged by compelling the white man to become his servant.

The religious services held Sunday evenings begin with singing and are usually followed by this dialogue between the preacher and the congregation:

Speaker: How did we get here?
People: Slavery.
Speaker: Who brought us from Ethiopia?
People: The white man.
Speaker: The white man tells us we are inferior, but we are not inferior. We are superior and he is inferior. The time has come for us to go home. In the near future we shall go back to Ethiopia and the white man shall be our servant. The white man says we are no good, yet David, Solomon, and the Queen of Sheba were black. The English are criminals and the black traitors [meaning the middle-class Jamaicans] are just as bad. There is no freedom in Jamaica. The black man who does not want to go back to Ethiopia doesn't want freedom. Ras Tafari started Mau Mau. Ras Tafari says: Death to the White Man!
People: And to the Black Traitor! We believe in one God, one aim, one destiny. We believe in Africa for the Africans, at home and abroad![7]

The Tafari cult is not messianic and does not believe in visions or divine revelations. Its followers claim to have learned from direct personal experience the truths upon which their doctrine rests. Their position in regard to the religion of the whites is ambivalent: they favor it because it accepts the Bible and believes in a single God; they oppose it because of the policies pursued by the white man. They say: "Heaven is

[7] Ibid., pp. 135-6.

a scheme of the English to make the black man think that white men and black men will be equal in the sky, but on earth the white man isn't going to give the black man anything. Fraud has kept us back, the fraud of religion and politics." Tafari followers feel that colonial administrators and missionaries are one and the same thing: they regard the "police and the missionaries" as despicable people who have betrayed them and despise the whites as much for their politics as for their religion.[8] In 1953 there were at least a dozen different Tafari sects, each with its own leader or president, each administered by a deputy chief, a committee, and a secretary.

Tafari rituals are often conducted in the street: a red, gold, and green banner is carried aloft, flanked by a giant-sized photograph of Haile Selassie. Readings from the Bible are chosen largely for the antiwhite interpretations to which they lend themselves, the end of Babylon being regarded as symoblic of the end which will soon befall the white man's power. Their hymns are a call to action: "Africa awaken, morning is at hand No more are thou forsaken Ethiopia now is free!"[9] The nativistic view of Judeo-Christian doctrine is revealed by the following prayer used at the conclusion of their worship: "Deliver us from the hands of our enemies, that we might prove fruitful for the last days. When our enemies are passed and decayed in the depths of the sea, in the depths of the earth or in the belly of a beast, oh, give us all a place in Thy kingdom forever and ever. Selah."[1]

Tafarism, unlike many other cults, does not advocate political or military struggle to achieve its goals,[2] but holds out the promise that freedom will be found upon returning to African soil. It is, therefore, a typically *escapist* movement, rather than

[8] Ibid., p. 137.
[9] Ibid., pp. 133, 137–40.
[1] Ibid., p. 140.
[2] Ibid., p. 144.

a revolutionary force. This is due in part to the historical fact that its followers are descendants of Africans brought to these islands by European slave traders, and in part to the nature of their current relationship to the white man, which makes the very idea of revolution unthinkable and unjustifiable.

Today, although the Jamaican Negroes are almost universally Christian, there is an intense revival of pagan-type religions, linked to old African traditions. Among those derived from Euro-American Christian inspiration are the Church of the Brethren, Christian Science, the Salvation Army, the Seventh-Day Adventists, the Society of Friends, Jehovah's Witnesses, the Pentacostal Church, the Mission Church of God, and the Bible Students. Their following proves that the natives are everywhere in quest of new religious ideas through which to demonstrate their independent choice of a church, in opposition to the strict orthodoxy required by the church of the whites.[3]

Other significant Afro-Christian cults include the Pocomania and the Zion Revival, different from each other only in ritual: the former emphasizes the reading and interpretation of Scripture, while the latter highlights ritual dancing, magical healing practices, and collective phenomena of possession.[4] Their deities are taken from ancient African polytheism and given Judeo-Christian names such as Michael, Gabriel, Samuel, Rachel, Jeremiah, Jesus Christ, Jehovah, Miriam, Satan, the Holy Ghost, Moses, Solomon, etc. This recalls a similar process characteristic of Negro-American polytheism in Haiti (Voodooism), in Cuba (the Santería), in Trinidad (the Shango), in Brazil (the Candomblé), at Porto Alegre (the Batuoue or Para) at Rio de Janeiro (the Macumba), at

[3] Ibid., pp. 337-41.
[4] Ibid., pp. 352-5, 417-18. For the interpretation of Christianity in the polytheistic setting, see pp. 430-3. See also my discussion of the Voodoo cult (Haiti).

164

Pernambuco (the Zango).[5] The pagan names of the original African deities are no longer used, but both Pocomania and the Zion Revival are full of traditional pagan rituals from Africa, exploited by the Jamaican religious leaders to arouse popular protest against cultural and religious domination by the white man.[6]

The rituals of both Pocomania and the Zion Revival are performed in the open air around a pole sustaining a box which contains the Bible (Christianity), two wooden swords, a small ladder, and two wheels—the ladder for Jacob and Moses, the swords and wheels, weapons against alien tyranny. Both sects practice baptism by immersion within a pagan setting, and both have a clerical organization which includes several "equerries," called upon to restrain the faithful when convulsions and frenzy become excessive.[7]

In conclusion, the religious revival in Jamaica ranges from movements with political objectives, such as the Tafari cult, to sects which clothe their strictly aboriginal values and beliefs in Christian garb. All of them, however, take a definite anti-Western position which reflects the people's bitterness over religious persecution suffered at the hands of Protestant missionaries.[8]

B. *Haiti*

In Haiti, a French colony until 1804, the drive for independence, which began at the end of the eighteenth century and culminated in the proclamation of the Republic in 1804, was accompanied throughout by the rise of nativistic religious movements of a prophetic nature. It has been said that Voodoo, probably the most powerful religious force in the life of the

[5] Ibid., pp. 342–5.
[6] Ibid., pp. 430–3.
[7] Simpson: "Jamaican Revivalist Cults," pp. 360, 403, 466 ff.
[8] Ibid., p. 408.

Haitian Negroes, is responsible for the independence of the island.[9] Voodoo, almost wholly pagan and African under a veneer of Christianity,[1] continues to be a unifying force today even as it once polarized the cultural, political, and religious movements of slaves struggling to be free. The religious life of the Haitian Negroes underwent an upheaval and a transformation—first with the coming of the Christians to the island and again later, when religion became a powerful instrument in the struggle for independence.

From the start of French colonial rule in the second half of the eighteenth century, the living conditions of the slaves were intolerable, even from a religious standpoint, and the adamant opposition of the Christian rulers to all native cults added considerably to the hardships of life. Slaves, treated like chattel and forced to accept baptism within eight days of their arrival on the island, were forbidden to practice any religious cult outside of Christianity.[2] But these mass conversions were only expedient and nominal, for the Negroes secretly clung to their own beliefs and forms of worship, largely animism and fetishism. Soon, however, a new religious movement began to spread which was stronger than any tradition. Its appeal lay in the fact that it was linked both to African polytheism and to the efforts then being made on the Black Continent to unify all the tribal religions. Voodoo, as the new cult was called, eventually became the channel into which flowed every religious movement in Haiti.[3]

[9] J. Comhaire: "Religious Trends in African and Afro-American Urban Societies," *Anthr. Q.*, XXVI (N. S. 1), 4 (1953), pp. 106-7.

[1] A. M. Rigaud: "Le rôle du Vaudou dans l'indépendance d'Haïti," *Prés. Afr.* (February-March 1958), p. 43.

[2] Ibid., p. 47.

[3] Ibid., p. 53. In the Voodoo of Haiti there are powerful influences from Dahomey. Even now the esoteric idiom of the Voodoo adepts comes from the ancient language of the Fon. There are three rites in current Voodooism: Rada (the *arada* group), Nago, and Congo (from groups by the same

166

The movement of the "maroons," fugitive slaves living in the inaccessible mountains, had begun to gain ground in the middle of the eighteenth century. Organizing themselves to escape, the maroons had spurred the great slave rebellions of 1758 and 1790, and these movements were later reinforced by echoes of the French Revolution. In their hiding places the maroons practiced Voodoo rituals faithfully, and the cult became an increasingly powerful expression of their demand for liberation. The following episode, which occurred in the second half of the eighteenth century, underscores this fact.

Shortly before 1758, a prophet named Makandal had come to the fore in Santo Domingo. He was an African Mohammedan of illustrious descent who had been sold into slavery and who prophesied that the destruction of the whites would occur by poisoning. He was arrested at Limbé, in northern Haiti, and burned at the stake in the public square. Popular reverence for Makandal increased with his death, and his name was added to the list of invocations in the Voodoo ritual. He became a Father Loa, a saint in the natives' Christian theology and a god in their African tradition. A legend about Makandal soon spread: according to it, as the flames were rising toward his body, he was possessed by a loa and, letting out an unearthly yell, he broke away from the stake and escaped from his executioners. The name of Makandal is heard in Voodoo temples with those of other heroes of Haitian liberation such as Biasson, Dessalines, and Toussaint L'Ouverture. Makandal, endowed with invincible powers, became the Messiah of the Voodooists, who swore to avenge his martyrdom and to bring

---

names). Where the African groups are mixed, the three rites are used together, but with certain distinctions between them. Where one group prevails, its rituals prevail. The various rites are performed in their separate sanctuaries. The differences are notable in the liturgy, the songs, the dances, and the rhythm of the drums. Rigaud: op. cit., p. 54 *n.*

about justice and freedom.[4] From then on, forsaking the Creole language in use at the time, they resorted to the native idiom of the Africans. The Voodoo cult, once clandestine and obscure in the colonial lands, now became more obscure and threatening, with its overtly anti-European practices and its ever more pressing demands upon the colonial authorities.[5]

In Voodoo, as in the Afro-Christian cults of Jamaica and of other parts of Central and South America, there is interesting evidence of the impact of Christian teaching on the polytheistic religions at the ethnological level.[6] The loa, or mysteries, are the deities of Voodoo and represent highly individualistic mythological personages, each having a specific function of its own and all integrated within a sophisticated form of polytheistic worship. Christian influence has added certain figures of saints to the ranks of the loa, which are only pagan idols renovated in name and attributes. The principal aspect of Voodoo ritual is possession; it reaches a high point of frenzy as the dancing becomes increasingly wilder to the rhythmic beating of the drums, the rising of songs and choral invocations, accompanied by extraordinary mimicry, until the "deity" possesses the worshippers, riding them to prostration. The process is communicated from one person to another until possession becomes collective, pitched to a point of seeming madness.[7] This is typically an escapist cult, in which the

[4] Ibid., p. 55.

[5] Ibid, p. 56. The first known account of Voodoo by Moreau Saint Méry dates back to this time.

[6] The only other documented evidence of a clash between Christianity and polytheism at the ethnological level is found in Polynesian culture—where there is nonetheless a supreme being later identified with the Judeo-Christian God (see chapter 6)—and in the pre-Columbian cultures of the Americas (Aztec, Mayan, Inca, etc.). For the Afro-Christian cults of the American Negroes in general, see M. Herskovits: "African Gods and Catholic Saints in the New World," *Am. Anthr.*, 1937, pp. 635-43.

[7] A. Métraux: *Haïti: la terre, les hommes et les Dieux* (Neuchâtel, 1957), pp. 58-90.

followers take flight from the world through possession; it also reflects the yearning of the Negroes for liberation from the yoke of their oppressors. The striving for freedom was expressed in religious form because the political power of the foreign rulers was far too great to allow even the thought of political rebellion to make headway among the Negroes; at a later time, however, Voodoo did play an active political role in Haiti's struggle for freedom.[8]

SOUTH AMERICA

A. *Brazil—the Tukunas*

Among the indigenous populations of Brazil, the impact of European civilization has given rise, even in recent times, to prophetic manifestations which have affected certain aborigines more than others. The Tukunas, for example, who dwell in the jungles along the banks of the Amazon, and on the islets and canals at the point where the river changes its name to Rio Salimões, fostered the growth of a messianic cult started by a girl. Tukuna elders tell of a young woman who, at the beginning of this century, prophesied so effectively that a new religious movement was destined to emerge that the Indians of Peru and Brazil called a meeting of their chiefs to listen to her. While they sat enthralled by her words, the *civilizados*, or neo-Brazilians, surrounded the encampment, killed or wounded many Indians, and captured the prophetess. Manifestations of this kind occurred in several places, always inspired by visionaries and prophets who claimed that God had commanded them to chase out the white men.[9]

One of the best-known took place in 1941, instigated by a full-blooded Indian boy named Nora'ne, son of José Nonato,

---

[8] Rigaud: op. cit., pp. 56–67. See also A. Hill: "Revolution in Haiti, 1791 to 1920," *Prés. Afr.*, XX (1958), pp. 5–24.

[9] C. Nimuendajú: *The Tukuna* (Berkeley, 1952), p. 138.

who dwelt with his wife and children on the left bank of the São Jeronimo canal. Nora'ne was a small child at the time of his first visions. He was fishing from a little canoe at a spot where the jungle is flooded by the river, when a white man appeared before him and asked him for his catch and promised to be back three days later. The boy kept the rendezvous and the man returned several times to see him; this visitor was the heavenly spirit of Dyei or Tanati (our Father), creator of mankind and founder of the indigenous civilization.[1] The spirit came from the dwelling place of the heroes where all riches and gifts are preserved. Dyei told the boy to rally the Indians, to make a clearing in the jungle, and to erect a temple where certain ritual dances were to be performed. The spirit also announced that as soon as this command had been fulfilled, a deluge would engulf the white men, sparing only the Tukunas gathered in the temple at that time. Many Tukunas were on the site they had cleared, ready to start building the temple, when the owner of the land, one Quirino Maffra, threatened them with extermination by aerial bombing if they did not immediately disband. Maffra's purpose was merely to protect the interests of the white man by forcing the Indians to go back to work, but Nora'ne was told by Dyei, in a subsequent vision, that God was no longer protecting the Tukunas because one among them had violated the marriage taboo. Threatened by the whites and abandoned by their god, the Tukunas retreated and the movement petered out. Nevertheless, the religious rites prescribed by the young prophet are still being practiced.

Most of the prophecies rising among the Tukunas are revivals of ancient themes, such as the Great Deluge[2] or the return of the cultural hero coming to announce the liberation

[1] Ibid., pp. 121–2.
[2] Ibid., p. 141.

of his people and the end of the world. Some are based on visions, which are common among the natives when they approach puberty, but their purpose is always to instigate a drive to expel the *civilizados*. The continuing taboo on mixed marriage and the emphasis on the inexorability of divine punishment of those who transgress are intended for those Tukunas who, in derogation of their ancestral traditions, have accepted Western ways.[3]

The demand for freedom inherent in the Tukuna prophecies comes in consequence of the exploitation to which the Amazon Indians were subjected by the white man, especially between 1880 and 1920, and of the servitude which still exists in certain sections of Brazil, where despotic masters, *patrões*, rule the natives with an iron fist in defiance of the new and better laws passed by the government.[4]

The Tupi-Guarani

The Tupi-Guarani are indigenous populations well known in South America because they are periodically stirred up by religious and messianic revivals. The Tupis dwell in the basin of the São Francisco River in the interior of eastern Brazil. They are of the same stock as the Tupinamba tribes (Caite, Potiguara, Tamoyo, Timimino, Tupinamba, and Tupinaqui), which at the time of the discovery of Brazil by the Europeans were already settled along the Atlantic coast, between the northern end of the province of São Paulo and the mouth of the Amazon River. These coastal tribes are directly descended from the inland Tupis who, in the course of several centuries, until the sixteenth century, had migrated in great waves toward the coast. These mass displacements, inspired by native messianic movements, constitute an interesting aspect of

[3] Ibid., pp. 137–40, for Tukuna prophetism in general.
[4] Ibid., p. 9.

171

the religious life of these Brazilian aborigines.[5] The Guaranis, who are part of the Tupi-Guarani ethnical group, live on the border between Brazil and Paraguay and have also developed many religious cults and messianic drives of their own.

The Tupi migrations toward the Atlantic coast are attested to by historical documents, particularly the migrations which led to Bahía, Pernambuco, and Pará. As these tribes pushed out from their original habitat in the interior and began to invade the coastal regions, they encountered the resistance of the Tapuyas, a people who only spoke and understood the *gé* tongue. Quickly outnumbered and overwhelmed by the invaders, the Tapuyas withdrew into the forest to plan a counter-attack.[6] These peoples were still engaged in warfare when the first white explorers set foot in the region—although, according to Curt Nimuendajú, the Tupi invasion occurred long before the arrival of the Portuguese.[7] Métraux speaks of successive waves of Tupi tribes moving to the Bahía coast during the fifteenth century,[8] all of them impelled by a messianic quest for the "Land without Evil."

A Jesuit missionary, writing in the sixteenth century, noticed great religious ferment among the Tupinamba in a zone between Rio de Janeiro and São Paulo, where certain shamans had persuaded the natives to stop working in the fields, assuring

[5] M. I. Pereira de Queiroz: "Classification des messianismes brésiliens," *Arch. Soc. Rel.*, V (1958), pp. 25, 28–9; E. Schaden: *Ensaio etno-sociologico sobre a mitologia heroica de algunas tribos indigenas do Brasil*, LXI (1946), p. 54. For the migration of the Tupinamba, see Métraux: "Les Messies de l'Amérique du sud," *Arch. Soc. Rel.*, IV (1957); "Migrations historiques des Tupi-Guarani," *J. S. Am.*, XIX (1931); "The Tupinamba," in *Handbook of South American Indians*, ed. J. H. Steward, Vol. III (Washington, 1948).

[6] Métraux: "The Tupinamba," pp. 97–8.

[7] Nimuendajú: *Leyenda de la creación y juicio final del mundo como fundamento de la religión de los Apapokuva-Guarani* (São Paulo, 1944), p. 58. Pereira de Queiroz: op. cit., p. 4.

[8] Métraux: *La religion des Tupinamba* (Paris, 1928), p. 5.

them that the harvest would come of its own accord, that abundance would reach every home, that their enemies would surrender, and that old age would be transformed into youth. Lured by these promises, the Indians gave themselves up to ritual dancing day and night.[9] The same dream and promise of abundance induced other tribes to leave the native soil and strike out into the unknown, seeking a promised land where youth and happiness would last forever. The paradise they dreamed of came out of their own mythology, which offered seductive descriptions of a "Land without Evil" to which the Divine Hero retires after creating the world and endowing it with divine laws. To this land shamans, warriors, and even the common people may go, if they have given proof of courage and endurance during their lifetime.[1]

The oldest migratory movement with a messianic motivation occurred around 1539, when thousands of Tupinambas abandoned their settlements on the Brazilian coast, impelled by a religious urge to find the "Land of Immortality and Perpetual Rest" they had not yet discovered. After traveling nine years, they had crossed the South American continent at its widest point, and arrived at Chachapoyas in Peru. Here they told the Spaniards of fabulous cities to be seen and extraordinary riches to be uncovered, and so stimulated the imagination of the Europeans that the Spaniards set forth under Pedro de Ursua to find El Dorado.[2] Thus, the Indians and the Spaniards were pursuing the same chimera, albeit for different reasons: the Spaniards were seeking gold and riches; the Indians, a place of rest and a refuge from the dangers they identified with the presence of foreigners on their land[3]—foreigners who, having

[9] Métraux: "Les Messies de l'Amérique . . . ," p. 108.
[1] Ibid., p. 109.
[2] Nimuendajú: *Leyenda de la creación* . . . ; Métraux: "The Tupinamba," p. 98.
[3] Métraux: "Les Messies de l'Amérique . . . ," p. 109.

173

established their rule, were already trying to abolish all native traditions, customs, and religious beliefs.

The migrations of the Tupinamba were motivated chiefly by fear of the death and destruction which the shamans had foretold, as they announced that the end of the world was now approaching. The story of these long and adventurous wanderings through the continent, told to Nimuendajú by today's Indians as handed down by oral tradition, reveals how their ancestors withstood adversity, hardships, perils, and famine, in order to find the land of rest and beauty. Their shamans encouraged them to persist by performing miracles which produced food and water and made them "invisible" to their enemies. But when they finally reached the Pacific coast and found that there was no dream city, many of them resumed the long trek back, although some remained to found villages on the West coast.

During the sixteenth and seventeenth centuries there emerged a particular type of prophet known as *pagé*, also described as a Man-God or Demi-god, who founded cults and made prophetic pronouncements. The Demi-gods were powerful local shamans who came to the natives as religious leaders and reincarnations of the great mythical heroes of native tradition, announcing an era of renewal.[4] Sporadically, they opposed the rule of the white man and became spokesmen for those who had suffered outrages and humiliations at the hands of the Portuguese and Spanish clergy and laity. A nucleus of antiwhite resistance quickly formed around the prophet, cementing together villages and tribes in a religious drive to shake off alien pressures. The Demi-gods were healers who could also confer eternal life upon the faithful. They fulfilled the same role in South America as the Negro prophets in Africa, or the Indian prophets in North America, and had

[4] Métraux: "Migrations historiques . . . ," pp. 62–4.

the same ability to convince the natives that the regeneration of the world was around the corner. They are also not unlike the prophets of Asia and Oceania who founded new cults designed to pave the way for liberation from the white man's rule.

Claude d'Abbéville[5] describes the activities of one of these sixteenth-century prophets, who rallied a following of some ten thousand Indians around Rio de Janeiro, and started out with them on a great migration. The faithful so ardently believed in him that they withstood every sort of suffering and hardship during the journey, and were always rewarded with the miraculous appearance of food and drink to satisfy their needs. This prophet, part Indian and part Portuguese, claimed to have been born, not of man and woman, but of the mouth of God, who had sent him on earth to found a new religion and to lead the faithful to the Promised Land. In every village his ranks swelled, until a giant mass of fanatical people reached the neighborhood of Pernambuco, where they were stopped by the powerful mountain dwellers of the Sierra Ibiapabá.[6] The prophet died and hunger and disease reduced his followers to a handful.[7]

This particular episode had scarcely come to an end when a similar movement developed at Pernambuco. It was led by another shaman who urged the natives to follow him in quest of the "Land without Evil."[8]

The Guarani gave a new messianic significance to their traditional cults as they came into closer and more oppressive

[5] Claude d'Abbéville: *Histoire de la mission des Pères Capucins en l'isle de Maraguan et terres circonvicines* (Paris, 1614), cited in Métraux: "Migrations historiques . . . ," pp. 67–70.

[6] Métraux: "Migrations historiques . . . ," pp. 67–70.

[7] Nimuendajú: "Die Sagen von der Erschaffung und Vernichtung der Welt als Grundlagen der Religion des Apapokuva-Guarani," *Z.f.E.*, XLVI (1914), pp. 354–64.

[8] Métraux: "Migrations historiques . . . ," p. 70.

contact with the white man who now ruled their land. The first mention of their migrations occurs in 1515,[9] but their mass movements were frequently repeated down the centuries, always inspired by fear of the end of the world and by hope of finding refuge in an earthly paradise. The routes they covered varied; some took them to the Brazilian coast, others to the interior, others to the West. In 1921 Nimuendajú observed that the life, the thinking, and the actions of the Guarani were still dominated by these same fears.

In 1820 several large groups of Guarani from the southern foothills of the Mato Grosso banded together to go east to find the promised land they now believed lay across the ocean. Those who reached the coast were forced to accept the fact that they would never see the promised land, and it is their descendants who now inhabit the coastal regions of the province of São Paulo.[1] When in 1912 Nimuendajú encountered the descendants of the tribes of Paraguay, then settled on the Brazilian coast, he found that they had not yet given up hope of crossing the ocean to find the wondrous place their ancestors had not been able to see. Nimuendajú was invited to accompany them to Praia Grande, where he saw them perform incantations and ritual dances designed to rid their bodies of weight and thus enable them to fly across the Atlantic.[2] In our time, then, people of the Apapocuva, Tanygua, and Oguiva tribes were still trying to reach the "Land without Evil," hoping to avoid the end of the world foretold by their shamans centuries earlier.[3]

Among the Guarani of southern Brazil, the belief still prevails that a world preceding the present one was destroyed

[9] Schaden: op. cit., p. 151.
[1] Ibid.
[2] Nimuendajú: "Leyenda de la creación . . . ,"; Métraux: "The Tupinamba," pp. 93–4; Schaden: op. cit., p. 151.
[3] Métraux: "The Tupinamba," pp. 93–4.

by a cosmic cataclysm, and that the same terrifying event will occur again in the near future. The idea of a universal catastrophe derived chiefly from the preaching of the Jesuit missionaries who spoke of the resurrection of the body on the Day of Judgment. This was especially true among the Nãndeva and the Apapocuva, whereas among the Mbua of Paraguay the fear had no connection with Christianity[4] but was merely a carryover from tradition.[5]

Those among the Guarani who were not influenced by the promise of a land of beatitude identified the idea of a universal catastrophe with the rising of the dead, who would return to earth filled with anger and desire for revenge. Here, too, it is not difficult to detect a link between old myths and current living conditions of the Indians. For instance, in the village of Araribà, inhabited by more than one hundred Nãndeva-Guarani, there has recently been found a widespread psychosis that expresses itself in the form of discouragement and tedium, so serious as to border on suicidal mania. These Indians devote themselves intensively to rituals which enable them to escape from life into a state of mystical beatitude and personal perfection (*aguydjé*). Some cannot resist the yearning for death, which, in effect, is the traditional desire to reach a land where death has been overcome.[6]

The Guarani, like the Tupi and other South American aborigines, also had their Demi-gods and prophets who commanded large followings. From the diary of a missionary, Father Manuel Mingo, one learns that a religious uprising of the Guarani occurred near the city of Tarija in the year 1795, led by a native prophet who had a great following in the Mazaví region. Accompanied by a large crowd of natives,

---

[4] Schaden: op. cit., p. 152.
[5] Ibid., p. 154.
[6] Ibid., pp. 160–1.

the prophet came into the area in 1797, claiming not merely a direct contact with God but, indeed, that he was God.[7] He announced the Day of Judgment, when fire would pour out of the sky, when men would be turned to stone, the herds would be destroyed, and all who failed to accept his faith would meet with death. The prophet had a wife, whom he identified with the Virgin Mary. Finally, the Spanish forces[8] crushed the movement, which was only one of many of its kind.[9] In 1892 a similar situation developed among the Indians of the Ivu region, where the natives led by a tribal chief tried, by force of arms, to regain their independence. More than six hundred natives were killed at Curuyuqui, near the Ivu mission, but the survivors continued to worship the rebel chief as their God.[1]

At the end of the nineteenth century a messiah appeared among the Indians of the Içana River in northwestern Brazil. Calling himself the Second Christ, he healed the sick and commanded the natives to stop tilling the land, for the era of wealth and happiness was about to dawn in which the soil would yield its fruits without the touch of human hands. This prophet was finally arrested.[2] The Chiriguano, a warlike tribe in the foothills of the Andes, who had been converted to Christianity by the Franciscans several decades before, suddenly rose up against the Spaniards at the call of a native messiah named Apiawaiki, but the guns of the Spanish rulers soon put an end to this uprising.[3]

The Guarani tribes of Paraguay, on the other hand, pro-

---

[7] Métraux: "Migrations historiques . . . ," pp. 62, 81.
[8] Ibid., pp. 81–5.
[9] Ibid., p. 62.
[1] Ibid., pp. 85–7.
[2] Métraux: "Les Messies de l'Amérique . . . ," p. 111.
[3] Métraux: "Migrations historiques . . . ," pp. 62–4; "Les Messies de l'Amérique . . . ," p. 111.

duced demi-gods who, unlike the shamans, were in constant communication with the disembodied spirits and were themselves sons of the spirit, without an earthly father, wise with a wisdom drawn from another world, miracle workers, oracles, and creatures rich in magical powers. They claimed to have created heaven and earth and to have the power to bring down the rain. Father Lozano in 1875 wrote that one of these messiahs, having reached the Brazilian coast at Loreto, proclaimed himself able to overcome women and death, to be lord of the harvest, and capable of annihilating all creation with a breath. These prophets merely take unto themselves the virtues and attributes of their mythical ancestors and heroes, claiming to be their reincarnations. Even Nanderuvuçu, a hero of the Apapocuva-Guarani tribes, could breathe destruction upon the world and, in fact, claimed to have done so once in the past, to have then recreated the world, and to be about to annihilate it again.[4] Juan Cuara, another such Messiah, born at Guáira, where he had also been baptized, set out from his native village to incite the Indians to rebel against the missionaries. "You shall henceforth live according to our ancient customs," he ordered, "cultivating your traditional dances and drinking only your traditional beverages. You shall worship the dead and not the Christian saints, and in me you shall find your God." Another prophet gained a large following by promising the prompt extermination of all Christians, black or white.[5]

A certain Guiravera, operating between the Incay and the Ubay rivers, fomented fierce opposition to all Christians by performing such miracles as causing the trunks of trees to take on human forms, or causing demons disguised as angels to fall from the sky and to prostrate themselves at his feet seeking

[4] Ibid., pp. 71–3.
[5] Ibid., pp. 73–4.

179

redemption. He claimed to be a god and to communicate with heaven through his special messengers. When leading a procession of the faithful, he was always preceded by a warrior carrying an unsheathed sword, and walked with the slow powerful step of a conqueror.[6] Another Guarani, a prophet named Obera, formed a cult in which the pagan elements were blended with elements of Christian teaching, but his leadership soon instigated a rebellion openly intended to destroy all Christians. Born in Paraná and baptized at the Christian mission, he soon renounced the Roman Catholic faith to preach the new cult of the millennium. The ritual of his sect consisted of dancing and singing, forsaking any form of work, and the glorification of his own person. Proclaiming himself the liberator of the Guarani tribes, son of God born of a Virgin, messenger of his Father and author of every prodigious deed, Obera claimed to have captured a comet which at that time appeared in the sky and to have sealed it in a jar ready to be used against the Spaniards as soon as the natives had exterminated the Christians. Obera's mass following became increasingly a menace to the Spaniards in Paraguay; finally, knowing that an insurrection was now at hand, the Spaniards resorted to arms and brought about a battle in 1579 which put an end to Obera and his cult.[7] Lastly, another among the many Guarani prophets was Rodrigo Yaguariguay, self-styled god, who claimed that his mother was the Virgin Mary and his daughter Saint Mary, thereby creating a new Trinity to serve his own cause.[8]

In modern times, as Christianity and Western civilization have made deeper inroads among the natives, they have discovered new reasons to explain their past failure to find the

[6] Ibid., pp. 74-6.
[7] Ibid., pp. 76-9.
[8] Ibid., p. 79.

promised land. There was a time, they now say, when men prayed with true faith, ate fruit and honey, mingled in gladness with the other tribes, let their sex life be governed by abstinence—and many of them reached the Paradise beyond the ocean where death is no longer to be feared.[9] Today, by contrast, society has disintegrated and unity is lost. The white man has broken down the traditional tribal structure by introducing individualism and undermining native social and cultural values.[1] The long-awaited fulfillment of the promise cannot take place because the natives have committed sacrilege by accepting food and customs brought by the Europeans. The original native concept of the world in a religious sense now bears the somewhat negative imprint of the Christian belief in individual sin.

The old myths still provide a course for new migratory movements and new religious cults, but the motivation behind them, as behind the constant resurgence of apocalyptic beliefs, is the growing tension between natives and whites and the many new problems which confront the aborigines under foreign rules. Belief in the end of the world and in its regeneration, as well as in a heavenly kingdom, are the religious expression of people who yearn to break away (*end of the world*) from what now holds them, and to find a new world (*regeneration*) where the forces now arrayed against them will have been wiped out.[2]

C. *Colombia, Argentina, and Peru*

Among messianic movements in Colombia dating back to the coming of the Spaniards are three religious cults of libera-

[9] Schaden: op. cit., p. 161.
[1] Ibid.
[2] Pereira de Queiroz: op. cit., pp. 16 ff., 24–9, 111–12, 117–20; "Messiasbewegungen in Brasilien," *S. Jahrb.*, pp. 133–44.

tion which arose at Quimbaya and Antioquia in 1546, 1576, and 1603, all based on belief in the collective rising of the dead.[3] Another movement which also stemmed from the impact of Spanish culture upon the natives in Colombia was founded at Cartagena in 1613 by Luis Andrea: it combined the cult of the pagan god Buciraco with the worship of Jesus Christ and of St. John the Baptist.[4]

In Argentina near Buenos Aires, a significant episode occurred in 1870; it centered around the prophet Solares, who came after a prolonged drought had caused widespread famine, and whose miracles immediately won him a fanatical following. Solares announced that the time had come for the natives to throw out the Europeans and rid themselves of foreign rule, after which he would disclose to their view a miraculous city to be theirs forever. Spurring them to revolt with the promise of immunity from the oppressors' bullets, the prophet led the natives into a tragic battle which ended with the mass slaughter of his followers and his own lynching.[5]

In Peru, Juan Santos Atahuallpa occupies a special place among native prophets, for he built his prestige upon political authority and upon the great tradition of the Incas. In 1742 the Campas, who dwelt in the forest on the slopes of the Andes in central Peru, were stirred to rebellion against the Spaniards by a poor Quechua Indian named Santos Atahuallpa from the province of Cuzco. His success among the natives of this area, although he was an alien among them, testifies to the enormous prestige of the Incas, from whom he claimed personal descent as well as the right to the throne of the Sun beyond the confines of the old empire. The conversion of the Campa tribes to Christianity had begun, at least outwardly,

[3] G. Eckert: "Prophetentum und Freiheitsbewegungen im Caucatal," Z.f.E., 76 (1951).
[4] Eckert: "Zum Kult des Buciraco in Cartagena," Z.f.E., LXXIX, 1 (1954).
[5] Métraux: "Les Messies de l'Amérique . . . ," p. 112.

in 1635 with the arrival of the first Franciscan missionaries; by the middle of the eighteenth century, they had reached the Ucayali River and had discovered a new and shorter route from the basin of the Amazon to the Pacific coast. Their ambitious dream of providing an easy outlet from Peru to the Atlantic seemed within reach when this obscure Indian from Cuzco, Santos Atahuallpa—once employed by the Jesuits, who had educated him and taken him to Spain—wrecked their plans.

A fugitive from Spanish justice in Peru, where he had been charged with murder, Atahuallpa reached the village of Qusopango and, coming before the Campa chief, convinced him that he was a descendant of the Inca rulers, adding the title of Apu Inca to his name. He told that his family had been seized by the Spaniards and that he knew where the treasure of the Incas had been hidden; he declared himself ready to reveal the secret as soon as he had been restored to the throne. He also claimed to be the son of God, come to put an end to the servitude of the people and to deliver them from the burden of laboring for the white man both on the land and in the estates. The unbelievers, he said, would be exterminated and the faithful would receive all the wealth of the Spaniards. The most attractive feature of his plan was the liberation of the Indians from white rule, and this also drew the support of Negroes and mestizos. As to his religious program, Santos forecast the rise of a native Christian church with Indian priests, an idea he had probably acquired during a visit to Angola, where he had seen native clergy. His cult stemmed partly from tradition in that, for example, he recognized the sacred nature of the coca plant, the use of which had been barred to the natives by the Spaniards. The Catholic missionaries soon recognized the danger of this movement, closed their missions, and departed, while Santos began to gather arms, bows, arrows, and staves, to form a Negro garrison. In the guerrilla warfare which ensued, the natives held their own against the Spanish forces, for they knew the terrain and could find their way in the thick forests which sloped down to the banks of the Amazon River. Although the general uprising of villages and cities awaited by Santos on the plateau never came off, the Spaniards in 1750, unable to capture the leader, were forced to give up the rich lands which had been opened up by the missionaries. Nothing more was heard of Santos, although he probably continued to hold sway over the Campas until he died as the result of a strange incident in which a stone slinger, testing the prophet's claim to immortality, pierced his skull with a stone. For a century and a half, and until recent times, the Campas worshipped the burial place and the memory of Santos, for he had at least restored the dignity of their native traditions and held up before them the dazzling hope of liberty and of the restoration of the great realm of the Incas.

Santos did not remain without successors. Thirty years after his death, another Inca prophet, Tupac Amaru, also descended from an Inca warrior, revived the dream of a native Peruvian empire, instigating a violent insurrection which, for a time, seemed likely to fulfill the purpose Santos had dreamed of in vain.[6] Here, too, the natives seek in religious revival the strength to attempt to gain political liberation, exploiting the impact of Western civilization upon their own society to implement new ideas better suited to their aims. The religious movements started by these prophets bear witness to the popular quest for economic and social redemption, which they seek through such varied means as belief in an impending catastrophe from which new life will emerge, or

[6] Métraux: "A Quechua Messiah in Eastern Peru," *Am. Anthr.*, XLIV, 1 (1942).

as the dream of restoring the glories of the long-dead empire of their ancestors.

D. *New Messianic Movements in Brazil*

While there has been a great, if intermittent, flourishing of messianic movements among the Indians of South America, including those of Brazil, there have been few indications of religious revival among the Negroes of Brazil, although from time to time one or two native prophets have merged. Among these should be mentioned Febronio, who was arrested before he could muster a following; Lourenço di Joazeiro, who for a while carried on the movement started by Father Cicero, but was also caught by the police and his movement disbanded; João de Camargo, a healer who founded a cult compounded of Catholic doctrine, African traditions, and spiritualism; and the "Umbanda spiritualist sect," now very strong in southern Brazil among the Negroes, mulattoes, and whites, whose rituals consist of evoking the spirits of the African ancestors, as compared with the Kardecist spiritualists, who evoke the spirit of the departed Euro-Americans. The Negro population supports the Indian movements in a passive way, without taking any initiative of its own.[7]

Some students of this problem have furnished religious and sociological reasons to explain the scarcity and ineffectiveness of prophetic movements among the Negroes of Brazil. Others have regarded the high degree of integration achieved by them in Brazilian society as a sufficient explanation for this lack. Nonetheless, the Brazilian Negroes tend to cluster around such traditional African cults as Candomblé, Batieu, Zango,

[7] For prophetic movements among Brazilian Negroes, and related problems, see R. Bastide: "Le messianisme chez les Noirs du Brésil," *Le Monde nonchrétien* (July-September 1950); "Le messianisme raté," *Arch. Soc. Rel.*, V (1958); Pereira de Queiroz: "Autour du messianisme," *Prés. Afr.* (June-July 1958).

and Voodoo, which provide a good vehicle for their own need for religious individualism and autonomy.[8] The preservation and intensification of Afro-American cults is a common phenomenon among the Negro populations of Jamaica, Cuba, and other Caribbean areas; although such escapist cults as the Candomblé, Zango, and a few others, which combine Catholicism with paganism, certainly are a form of native liberation from the white man's rule, even they are confined to religion and do not reveal any political objectives.[9]

Nonetheless, Brazil is a land of modern prophets, rising among rural populations in which Indian, Negro, and white stock have now become indissolubly merged in a racial mixture that is predominantly white. The official religious environment is Roman Catholic, yet these movements reveal a close historical continuity with ancient Indian movements, in which belief in an earthly paradise and in a messiah coming to bring salvation is clearly expressed.

These messianic movements, rising out of Roman Catholic soil, profess strict adherence to Catholic doctrine and to the papacy, as in the case of the cult led by Father Cicero. In practice, however, they oppose both official Christianity and the present structure of society, with its class oppression and its local political leaders, who are also powerful landholders and wield despotic and arbitrary authority. These movements have deep roots of secessionist, anticlerical, and anti-European sentiment, which eventually come to the surface in a "holy war" against certain government institutions—the very principle of a holy war obviously running counter to the official Christian position—or in the founding of "holy cities" by local prophets to be the center of worship for the adepts of their sect, whereas Christianity recognizes only Jerusalem

[8] Pereira de Queiroz: "Autour du messianisme," pp. 72–6.
[9] Bastide: "Le messianisme raté," pp. 36–7.

as the Holy City; or in cults established by founders held up as healers, miracle workers, and saviors, messengers of God, or messiahs, destined to rise again from the dead.

João Maria, the "saint" who founded the Contestado movement in southern Brazil, went from village to village preaching that his Catholicism and not that of the priests was true Christianity, that his scripture and not the Gospel of the Catholics or the Bible of the Protestants was the true Word of God.[1] To this day, a century after his death, the return of João Maria is being awaited in countless rural villages in southern Brazil; even as in northern Brazil, where a century and a half ago the movement of Joazeiro gained a following, the resurrection of Father Cicero is confidently expected to occur.[2] The main goal of these prophetic movements in Brazil is the tearing down of the absurd social order which now prevails, and the restoration of the old monarchical system of native tradition, once the current republic has been abolished.

A closer look at some of the recent neo-Brazilian movements and at the historical and social background from which they stem reveals interesting facts brought to light in the excellent studies made by Isaura Pereira de Queiroz. There are three major messianic movements about which a good deal is known, and each of these takes its name from a Holy City founded or selected by its originator. The Canudos movement was started by Antonio Conselheiro and the Joazeiro movement by Father Cicero, both in the northeast regions of Brazil—an arid and squalid area in which disastrous periods of drought are invariably followed by equally disastrous floods. The Contestado movement, on the other hand, originated at the extreme southern end of the country in a mountainous region rich in forests and fertile soil. Its founder

---

[1] Pereira de Queiroz: "Autour du messianisme," pp. 13–14.
[2] Ibid., pp. 13, 16.

was a "monk" named João Maria, and his work was continued first by José Maris and then by the "virgin" Theodora.

These three movements all arose around the year 1870, but their development followed very different courses. The Canudos movement reached a peak in 1890 and was crushed seven years later as the result of an unsuccessful uprising against the government. The Joazeiro movement survived a critical phase in 1914 and prevailed in spite of the federal government and the Roman Catholic church—both of which were powerless before the magnetism and prestige of Father Cicero. It lasted until the death of its founder in 1936. The Contestado movement had gained considerable power by 1914, when it staged an insurrection which was finally put down by government forces in 1916, after which the cult declined. However, more than a trace of their passing has remained among Brazil's country folk, who are still imbued with a messianic sense of expectation.

The three movements, though springing up in very different areas, have a common historical and sociological background, which explains their origins and gives them a special significance for our own time. "These movements," writes Isaura Pereira de Queiroz,[3] "emerge in farming and cattle-raising regions of modest output, rarely if ever in the richer areas where sugar cane and coffee grow in abundance. The economy of these populations is therefore primitive, dotted here and there by the presence of a few wealthy farmers who raise cattle. These landowners are the 'elite' of the region and constitute the local authority. Their power is sometimes due to their wealth, sometimes to their descent from ancient land-holders, sometimes to personal prestige. The enormous spread

[3] Pereira de Queiroz: "Die Fanatiker des 'Contestado,'" S. Jahrb., V (1957); La Guerre sainte au Brésil (São Paulo, 1957); "Messiasbewegungen in Brasilien"; "Classification des messianismes brésiliens," pp. 7–13, 23–9, 111–20; "Autour du messianisme."

of the territory makes it impossible for the government to enforce law and justice in the interior; therefore, the administration must rely upon the co-operation of these local landowners, whose promise to fulfill the law is blindly accepted. The landowner keeps power and prestige in his own hands by organizing private armed bands which recruit every able-bodied man in his jurisdiction whenever a dispute breaks out over land demarcation or a family feud flares into the open. Therefore, the landowner, and not the government, is the real authority, since no government official can hope to set foot in a village without the landowner's consent. The social consequences of this situation are extremely serious.[4] Neither justice nor public administration can prevail if they run counter to laws enforced by the landowner in his own interests. The population has no protection against injustice and the repressive measures of the landowners, who are usually economic plutocrats and political despots, and often finds itself dragged into bloody clashes that break out among the wealthy families. There are no doctors to take care of the ailing bodies, no priests to take care of ailing souls. The situation is further aggravated by frequent vendettas, by banditry, and by minor local revolutions, which explode against this or that local dictator, who, once deposed, is succeeded by another, who follows the same pattern as his predecessor. On the other hand, the population has not experienced cultural clashes of any account, since the great distances and the lack of communications prevent direct contact with the developed and more progressive sections of the country . . . local culture, shaped during the early stages of colonization and stabilized under the monarchy, has remained more or less unchanged."[5]

[4] Pereira de Queiroz: "Classification des messianismes brésiliens," p. 8.
[5] Ibid., pp. 8–9.

As to the religious situation, it consists of a "mongrel" form of Catholicism,[6] in which there is a constant shortage of priests. This Catholicism fosters mass religious practices, such as novenas, processions, magical healing, and prodigies of every kind deeply tinged with paganism, and the emergence of "saints (*beatos*)," "monks," "sacristans," and laymen "prayer leaders"—sometimes the landowners themselves become religious leaders and organizers—who soon become miracle workers, healers, baptizers, personal counselors, and arbitrators of all disputes. In short, the picture is dominated by persons endowed with great prestige who play a role very similar to that of shaman or prophet, despite the Catholic setting in which they operate.[7]

Indeed, it is around these *beatos* that the messianic trends found within popular Catholicism tend to concentrate and assume new forms. The *beatos* eventually come to be regarded as the incarnation of a saint or even of Jesus Christ himself. This is the environment in which the neo-Brazilian messianic movements have been developing, and their founders, the *beatos*, are very similar to the men-gods of the native Indians, especially where they claim to be the reincarnation of God, even as the man-god claims to be the reincarnation of a great hero of native tradition.[8] Both promise an era of renascence and of salvation and a "golden Kingdom" on earth.

Certain *beatos* become itinerant preachers, traveling from village to village; others tend to settle in a given place, which eventually becomes their "holy city," the goal of pilgrimages and the center of evangelism. The Canudos, Joazeiro, and Contestado movements are three conspicuous manifestations of a phenomenon which has reached deeply into the rural

[6] Ibid., p. 9.
[7] Ibid., pp. 9–10.
[8] Ibid., pp. 10, 116.

areas of Brazil. Often the police intervene to disperse groups forming around a *beato*, before he has been able to establish an official see.[9] But despite the police, these three movements have put down deep roots in their respective "holy cities" and attract thousands of followers.

Significantly, Antonio Conselheiro was called "Saint Anthony" or "Good Jesus" as he went around the country-side preaching against crime, delinquency, and the many aberrations by which these areas were beset in the wake of constant family feuds and political strife. He taught that re-mission of sins was to be attained through personal suffering and renunciation of worldly goods and secular pleasures; he announced the coming of a cosmic catastrophe to precede the Day of Judgment and promised his followers the delights of a "holy city" of everlasting peace, happiness, and concord. His ideal city finally took shape in an arid region almost totally inaccessible but to which more than five thousand faithful flocked and of which he became the supreme chief. Thus Conselheiro was transformed from a mere prophet and evangelist into a messiah, a savior of men, and the reincarna-tion of Christ.

The sermons of Conselheiro, in addition to advocating mor-tification of the flesh and renunciation of worldly goods, sounded a note of rebellion against society and especially against that "particular institution of the Antichrist, called the Republic of Brazil, established in 1889." The prophet identified the advent of the golden age with the restoration of the monarchy, and his activity became a threat to the po-litical authorities. Moreover, his followers, in order to sup-port the "holy city," were constantly raiding the farms and herds of the big landowners. The clash inevitably came, and the government intervened with armed force. The rebels re-

[9] Ibid., p. 10.

191

sisted longer than had been thought possible, but in the end the "holy city" of Canudos was razed to the ground. Defeat was total, and Conselheiro died in abject poverty shortly before the bitter end.[1]

Whereas Conselheiro was a self-styled *beato* and therefore a layman, Cicero Romão Baptista, known as Father Cicero, founder of the Joazeiro movement, was a Catholic priest who had a parish in the village of Joazeiro, in the interior of the state of Ceará. His purpose was to revive religious fervor among his people while also bringing about much-needed improvement in the social and economic conditions of the area. At first he performed minor miracles, healing the sick and foretelling the future, thereby attracting an enormous popular following from far and near. The village of Joazeiro was the center of his work, and it expanded as the population grew, until it became a real city, the Holy City, the New Jerusalem. Father Cicero became the leader of an enormous congregation; he also instituted an ecclesiastical hierarchy which governed in opposition to the secular power, so that a state within a state finally emerged.

By 1914 relations between Joazeiro and the government had become critical and Father Cicero declared a holy war against the authorities with the intention of restoring the monarchy, a symbol of the Golden Age, which the populace expected would soon arrive. The followers of the prophet triumphed over the civil authorities by besieging the capital of the state of Ceará and forcing the governor to flee. Father Cicero, victorious leader of his people, chose to remain in Joazeiro, and was officially named lieutenant governor of the state of Ceará. Neither church nor state could weaken the prestige and power of this priest and prophet who had full control of the rural population.

[1] Ibid., pp. 11–12, 115.

The Canudos and Joazeiro movements were developing in the northeast while another movement was growing in the south, at Contestado. Its founder, an almost wholly legendary figure, is reputed to have been a "monk" named João Maria who, from 1835 to 1908, was said to have traveled throughout southern Brazil preaching a new gospel. He is probably a composite of several individuals who carried on the same form of evangelism. João Maria was also a healer, a wise mentor, and a judge in all disputes. Unlike Father Cicero and Conselheiro, João Maria shunned all collective manifestations and finally disappeared from the scene in 1908, leaving no trace of himself. Nobody believed that he had died, however; the populace lent credence to his own statement, often repeated in his sermons, that he would retire to the summit of a magic mountain at the end of his mission and there bide his time until the hour had struck for his return among men.[2] Many Brazilians still believe that João Maria will rise again.

A few years later, another healer appeared and claimed to be a reincarnation of João Maria. He founded the "holy city" of Tacquarussú, and the people accepted him as their "monk," now embodied in his brother José Maria. He organized the faithful and restored his own monarchy in accordance with the visions of João Maria. Soon he had induced the people to proclaim a certain illiterate landholder the Emperor of

[2] The idea of the resurrection of an important personage and the expectation of his return as a savior marks the Sebastian movements, which arose in Brazil in the seventeenth century and which expanded considerably in the ensuing two centuries. They are based on the belief that Don Sebastião, king of Portugal, who was killed in 1578 in the battle of Alacer-Kibir, did not die, but had returned among his men. The existence of many Sebastianites—who did not, however, organize a movement as such—is noted in the provinces of Rio de Janeiro, Bahía, Minas Gerais, etc. In the province of Pernambuco, in the middle of the nineteenth century, they give rise to the movements of Santa de Pedra and of Pedra Bonita. Pereira de Queiroz: "Classification des messianismes brésiliens," pp. 111–12.

South Brazil; this mild-mannered man was promptly deposed by government forces, which killed the "monk" and crippled the movement. But the flame was not readily extinguished. A year later, the faithful reorganized under the leadership of a youthful prophetess, the Virgin Theodora, who claimed to be receiving direct orders from the spirit of the "monk." The excitement spread and an insurrection broke out against the government, whose forces put it down after a long struggle that lasted from 1912 to 1916.[3]

The neo-Brazilian prophets have much in common with one another, such as the claim of being the Messiah, the reincarnation of Christ, or that of a Roman Catholic saint now come to save the people, and their proclamation of the imminent end of the world and the regeneration of mankind. Regeneration is explained in a mythical setting linked with some particularly painful experience suffered by the people, as well as with the promised restoration of the prerepublican era, the Golden Age which cures society of all ills. These Brazilian movements emerge from a strictly Roman Catholic background, but in them Catholicism is interpreted in pagan terms, highlighting the prophet or healer, who is not unlike the man-god of the Indian tradition. The prophet is linked both by function and spiritual significance with the prophets of the African cults, who also call themselves Negro Christs, and to prophets in other primitive cultures who claim to be the embodiment of Moses or of some other Biblical personage. In essence, they all attach themselves to the Judeo-Christian tradition and come to fulfill a new mission, that of saving society from current evils and of achieving freedom both from foreign rule and from the oppression of domestic institutions—goals they could not hope to attain by armed revolt without the power of religious faith to support them.

[3] Ibid., pp. 13–15, 115–16; "Die Fanatiker des 'Contestado.'"

Religious Movements in Central and South America

The religious manifestations also show clearly that, like other messianic movements, these have their roots in fertile soil conditioned by social, political, and religious oppression. In Brazil, however, they arise not from a clash between different cultures but from internal conflict. The movements which, like these, stem from an internal crisis rather than from an intercultural struggle resemble such modern European and American messianic cults as the Mormons, Jehovah's Witnesses, and others, also produced by domestic conditions that have thrown society and religion into a turmoil.

The religious movements of South America reveal an extraordinary variety of manifestations both at the level of native Indian culture and in the advanced modern society in which, although there are many ethnic groups, the European strain is predominant. All of them—the prophetic cults which often conceal a revolutionary purpose, the mystical cults which promise spiritual redemption, and the movements advocating social emancipation and restoration of an old order —are equally an expression of the anguish of people seeking a way out of dangerous and oppressive situations in the hope of achieving liberty and freedom from all oppression.

CHAPTER

V

MESSIANIC MOVEMENTS
IN MELANESIA

PREMISE

THE RELIGIOUS MOVEMENTS emerging in modern times in Melanesia from aboriginal cultures still tightly bound to tradition provide a remarkable example of what may occur when Western civilization and a native society come together with a major impact. Bursting upon the scene with spontaneous vitality, these movements show to what extent the aborigines feel the urge to renovate their own civilization. To this end, the elements of local traditional origin embodied in new cults have been remolded to fulfill new functions in a changing world. At the same time, many old rituals and legends, typical of a people whose agriculture is still primitive, whose lives are simple, and for whom fishing is the main source of livelihood, have been carefully preserved.

Melanesian messianism aroused serious concern in the missionary churches and colonial governments concerned. They came to realize that they could no longer ignore the yearning

196

for change and freedom which these cults expressed. The cults revealed, not an incoherent or inert mixture of tradition and novelty, but an active and creative transformation of fundamentals of Western culture, at the hands of native leaders, designed to serve the natives cause.

Aroused by a number of prophets and messiahs, the Melanesians have even abandoned their work in order to stage religious festivities, to welcome the rising dead, to celebrate the exodus of the whites, and to prepare for the arrival of riches and cargoes due to be brought from Europe by the resurrected ancestors. In the past, native agitation of this kind has occasionally led to antiwhite violence, but with the passing of time and the steady growth of cultural and commercial exchanges, native society has gradually accepted a fruitful integration of Western and Eastern ways.

This great burgeoning of messianic cults, promising the millennium, results from the turbulent encounter between two civilizations at a time when each is at a high point of its development. Western civilization, moving out of the primitive agriculture of the Middle Ages with an extraordinary development of crafts and skills, had come to the age of industry and the machine, the output of which was now finding its way into Melanesian society. The aboriginal civilization, on the other hand, had only just reached a stage of agricultural development which employed tools with amazing proficiency. The gulf between these two high points shook Melanesia to the depths. But it revitalized rather than destroyed the ancient culture, which quickly put out new and lively shoots in the form of religious movements heralding progress and freedom.

It is important to study the terrain that was so profoundly shaken by this encounter, to seek within it the old foundations of beliefs which underpin the messianic cults and, taking them

197

apart, view the component elements in the light of their historical background. Such a procedure will indicate that every phase of Melanesian culture, secular and religious, from archaic times to its encounter with the West, is reflected in most of these messianic movements.

MORPHOLOGY OF THE MELANESIAN CULTS

The Orokaiva group, an agglomeration of peoples speaking the Papuan tongue and living in an area that extends from the coast to the plateau of the northeastern interior of New Guinea, between Oro Bay and Mambara Bay, still offer the first fruits of the soil to the dead, in their major annual religious celebration. On this occasion, called *kasamba*, a number of little platforms, with diminutive flights of steps leading up to them, are erected outdoors on top of a "Taro House," to enable the Spirit of the Dead to reach the morsels of taro, dried fish, and other foods placed there as offerings for their use.[1] The aborigines believe that the spirits are with them during the *kasamba*, thanking them and speaking in soft sounds through the chirping of the geckos which haunt all native houses.[2] Nowadays, the celebration of *kasamba* is not tied to a given season of the year or to a special phase of agriculture in the area, but is staged whenever the natives so decide; it always attracts enormous crowds, who dance, sing, and partake of abundant food at the traditional banquets.[3] The *kasamba* is probably the transformation of the much older New Year Festival to honor the dead, now adjusted to new cultural needs as a salient feature of the Taro cult.

[1] F. E. Williams: *Orokaiva Magic* (London, 1928), p. 26; *Orokaiva Society* (Oxford, 1930), p. 271, table 25a.

[2] Ibid., p. 41.

[3] Ibid., p. 98.

THE TARO CULT

The Taro cult emerged not very long ago, promoted by a Bunandele prophet named Buninia, who was still living in 1928 or 1930, when Francis E. Williams made a study of this movement. In 1914 this native of the village of Taututu was visited by the spirit of his father, who had been slain in a raid many years before and who came to him accompanied by other spirits, all in the act of eating taro. The spirit instructed his son in the establishment of a new cult intended to increase the taro crops.[4]

Buninia told Francis Williams that,[5] as he was emerging from a trance, he had seen several youths come toward him bearing bundles of taro on their shoulders. They were the Taro spirits. Presently, he said, they had begun to beat their drums and stage a dance, which they told him should be incorporated in his cult. In 1917, when E. W. P. Chinnery called on Buninia, he was given a slightly different version of the event by the prophet, who said that he had been possessed by a Taro spirit or a Food spirit and had gone into a trance while working on his vegetable patch.[6] Whichever version of Buninia's account one may wish to accept, it is the visitation of the spirits which is important as the motivating power behind the movement, as well as the fact that the prophet had been in a trance. Trance is an essential part of the ritual, during which those who are possessed by the Taro spirit finally go into violent convulsions. The excitement of the individual worshippers is highly communicable. Eventu-

[4] Williams: *Orokaiva Magic*, p. 12. This is the textual account given by the prophet Buninia to H. Holland, at the Anglican mission. Other versions of the vision were given by Buninia to Chinnery and Williams.

[5] Williams: *Orokaiva Magic*, p. 13.

[6] E. W. F. Chinnery and A. C. Haddon: "Five New Religious Cults in British New Guinea," *Hibbert Journal*, 1917, p. 339.

ally every participant becomes possessed, but the first who fall prey to this condition are regarded as Taro-men or Taro spirits and have special authority over the group.[7]

This form of possession with convulsions links the Taro cult with other messianic movements in which such manifestations occur: for example, the "Vailala Madness," a cult of the Orokolo tribes on the Gulf of Papua, which was strongly antitraditional and emerged soon after World War I;[8] the Cult of the Prophet Saibai, which arose in 1913 in the Straits of Torres;[9] the Cult of the Prophet of Milne Bay[1] and the older Cult of Baigona, the Snake,[2] practiced among the Orokaivas, from which the Taro cult originated.

According to Orokaiva belief, Baigona, embodying the spirit of a deceased leader, had taught a Tufi native the rites of a magic cult which healed every sickness through the use of certain herbs and ritual baths. The adepts of this cult went into trance with manifestations that later became typical of Taro rituals. The Baigona cult did not last long, for it was soon replaced by Taro, but both are intimately linked to the worship of the dead. A re-embodied spirit and a deceased person appearing in a trance or dream motivate both sects, which, therefore, belong in the category of movements inspired by, and identified with, one or more particular spirits. Both in the Baigona and the Taro cults certain very ancient

[7] Ibid., pp. 449–51. Williams: *Orokaiva Magic*, pp. 10–16 passim.

[8] G. H. Murray: *The Vailala Madness*, Papua Report, 1919–20, pp. 116–18; Williams: "The Vailala Madness . . . ," *Anthr. Report* 4, 1923, pp. 1–72; "The Vailala Madness in Retrospect," in *Essays Presented to C. G. Seligman* (London, 1934), pp. 369–79. His prophets preached the abolition of traditional usages and ceremonies, and the expectation of a ship bringing riches, piloted by the returning dead.

[9] Chinnery and Haddon: op. cit., pp. 460–3.

[1] Ibid., pp. 458–60.

[2] Ibid., pp. 456–8; Williams: *Orokaiva Magic*, pp. 7–11.

traditions underlie the ritual pattern now influenced by an individual force.

The acceptance of a particular spirit as the originator of the cult,[3] a fact not in the native tradition, seems to have brought about certain changes in the form of the Taro feast, although its purpose continues to be the improvement of the crop. "The more *kasamba*, the more taro,"[4] was the tenet upon which Taro rituals had always been based; such ritual elements as trance and possession were added by the promoters of the new movement. The paramount importance of a Taro-man or prophet in the current Taro cult is shown by the fact that the followers do not decide to hold a *kasamba* until their Taro-men have experienced an ecstasy, followed by a trance and convulsions, during which they make known when the feast is to take place. Dancing, singing, community eating, and collective seizures constitute the core of the celebration. Mr. Williams observes that certain specific aspects of the ritual, as well as the *kasamba*, are adaptations of an older agrarian cult known as *pona*.[5] It is evident from the nature of Buninia's dream and from his belief in Taro spirits that the cult is simply a different interpretation of the traditional belief that the periodic return to earth of the spirit of the deceased had to be greeted with conciliatory offerings.[6] From the standpoint of the ritual, Buninia merely substituted the Taro spirits for the Spirits of the Dead; but in the broader prophetic sense he shaped the cult to meet the new economic and social

[3] Williams: *Orokaiva Magic*, p. 11. Buninia preserved the magical character of the Baigona cult. He and his followers were healers, and their efficacy was commensurate with the scrupulous execution of the *kasamba* rituals.

[4] Williams: *Orokaiva Magic*, p. 98.

[5] Ibid., p. 39.

[6] The very essence of Orokaiva religion, says Williams, is to placate the spirits of the dead. Williams: *Orokaiva Society*, pp. 279, 285-6, 287. For the return of the dead in Melanesia, see Lanternari: op. cit., pp. 93-137, 411.

conditions which, in Melanesia, as in other areas, were responsible for the emergence of messianic movements. Regardless of the specific circumstances which gave rise to the Taro cult, it is certain that the traditional religions were no longer adequate to meet the challenge of the changing times. Therefore, no sooner had the Taro cult begun to spread than it supplanted its predecessors.

The Orokaiva people believe that the returning dead give rise to a new era of prosperity by bringing an abundance of native produce. The followers of other versions of the same cult believe that the dead will bring with them European goods, instead of native-grown gifts. They expect metal tools, garments, and textiles, canned meats and tobacco, bags of rice, guns and other weapons, instead of fruits, berries, and edible roots.[7]

The Taro cult has an important place among the many messianic movements appearing in Melanesia—especially since the end of World War II—which have opened a significant new chapter in the history of these populations. Some of these cults have arisen in reaction to the arrival of the whites; others, as an effort to cope with changing internal conditions.

THE CARGO CULT[8]

Popular belief in the return of the dead bringing liberation and riches is found at the roots of almost every religious move-

[7] P. Lawrence: "Cargo-cult and religious beliefs among the Garia," *Int. A.E.* (1954), p. 1.

[8] The literature on the Cargo cult is growing apace, owing to the great diffusion of these movements in recent years. The problems connected with the rise and spread of these cults are many and different. It is necessary to analyze the traditional pagan religious structures within the modern cults—which is our major interest here. There is also the problem of the cultural policy of the church in regard to the natives, as well as a problem of administrative policy, which is of special interest to British and American researchers. For a bibliography of the numerous aspects of this phenomenon,

ment, accompanied by the belief that the dead will arrive aboard a ship. The modernized version, according to which a Western ship, manned by whites, will come to bring riches to the natives, has become the springboard for a number of newer movements generically called Cargo cults. These assert that when the Western ship comes in, slavery will be abolished, the natives will become the equals of the whites, and a new era of prosperity will have dawned.

A great variety of ideas, trends, practices, and influences—both ancient and modern, pagan and Christian—can be found in the Cargo cult. The "cargo" is identified by the natives with their European masters, both as tangible evidence of their wealth and as symbol of their mastery. By making it the object of worship, the natives strive to make use of the cargo and to abolish the concept of their own slavery by conceiving of it as a gift they receive from the white man. The expectation of an era of prosperity and well-being combined with the arrival of the ship is of Christian influence and is taken from the Gospel, which promises redemption and a new kingdom where human evil and human ills will not exist. Another link between the traditional worship of the dead and the newer

---

see the collection by Ida Leeson. The general works on the subject which deserve special mention are: F. R. Lehmann, 1935, pp. 261 ff.; G. Eckert, 1937, pp. 135–40; Eckert, 1940, pp. 26–41; G. Höltker, 1941, pp. 181–219; C. S. Belshaw, 1950, pp. 116–25; T. Bodrogi, 1951, pp. 259–90; A. Lommel, 1953, pp. 17–63; J. Guiart, 1951, pp. 227–9; Lanternari, 1956; Inglis, 1957; Stanner, 1958 (see Bibliography for complete references). Documentation on more recent manifestations of the Cargo cult is found in: R. M. Berndt, *Oceania*, XXIII (1952), 1, pp. 40–65; (1952) 2, pp. 137–58; (1953) 3, pp. 202–34; R. M. Berndt, *Oceania*, XXIV (1954) 3, pp. 190–228; 4, pp. 255–74; C. S. Belshaw, *Oceania* (1951), 1, pp. 4 ff.; F. C. Kamma, 1952, pp. 148–60; A. P. Elkin, 1953, pp. 90, 99 ff., 101; P. Lawrence, 1954, pp. 1–20 (Madang district in New Guinea). The most complete and best-organized work on Melanesian Cargo cults is the beautiful volume by P. Worsley, *The Trumpet Shall Sound.*

worship of the white man's cargo lies in the fact that the strange new industrial products introduced by the Europeans were so surprisingly different from anything the natives had ever seen that they immediately ascribed the creation of them to a spiritual world with which the white man was in contact. Because ghosts are white and the white man brings the goods, the cargo was a gift from the dead.[9]

The myth of the ship is actually the keystone in the structure of messianic movements in this part of the world. Not only do we find it in the cults described or mentioned thus far, but it is basic also among the Marindanim of New Guinea, who, upon seeing Dutch ships come to shore, believed them to have been sent by the dead to collect coconuts for the natives.[1]

In the year 1893, at Milne Bay, a prophet named Tokerau had foretold the coming of a cosmic era which would start with an authentic New Year and a true Feast of the Departed. Tokerau's message spoke of a terrifying cataclysm, with volcanic eruptions, earthquakes, and floods, which would strike whoever refused to believe in his new creed; afterwards, he added, the winds would suddenly change, coming from the southeast to bring fair weather and causing the fields to fill with taro and other foods, the trees to become laden with fruit, and a ship to come into port carrying the deceased to visit their families. At this moment the new era would begin.[2] The faithful who wished to survive disaster were told to refuse to touch any object made in Europe, so that what was

[9] In Melanesia, the returning dead are whites—clay-white is the color with which widows paint themselves during mourning, and the whites are called "claymen" because of their similarity to the color of mourning. A. Dupeyrat: *Festive Papua* (London, 1955), p. 14.

[1] N. Nevermann, cited in G. Eckert: op. cit., p. 139.

[2] Chinnery and Haddon: op. cit., pp. 458–60; "Annual Report of British New Guinea."

really a boycott of foreign goods became a new creed, once again wrapping up tradition, religion, and current political conditions into a single package.

Three prophets, referred to as the "generals" from Saibai (Torres Strait) and named Wageba, Anu, and Sagaukus, launched their messages in 1914; they commanded their followers to decrease their hours of work on the land and to visit the cemeteries instead, there to beseech the dead to return quickly to provide for them. They assured the faithful that a large vessel would reach the shores of the island, bearing the spirits of the dead and a large cargo of money, clothing, flour, axes, and knives, all items which they maintained used to belong equally to the natives but which the Europeans had gradually taken away from them through an abuse of their own power. Equality and justice would then triumph.[3]

A great deluge, as well as the return of the dead, is an inherent part of the message brought by Ronovuro, a prophet heard at Espíritu Santo in the New Hebrides in 1923: the dead, he promised, would land on the island from a ship laden with rice and other foods. But Ronovuro went even further: he told the natives that the Europeans would prevent the ship from landing so that the natives could not receive the gifts. He urged them to stage an uprising, in the course of which one European was to be singled out as the victim; he would be symbolic of the others. At that time a plantation owner named Clapcott was done to death by the mob.[4] An uprising of the same kind had already occurred there in 1908; and although there was a period of quiescence after 1923, by 1937 the movement was regaining strength. It reached a peak in 1947, when a "nudist cult" spread far and

[3] Chinnery and Haddon: op. cit., pp. 460–3.
[4] E. Raff: Appendix, in Williams: *Orokaiva Magic*, p. 100.

wide.[5] The violence which these movements often generated was deplorable. Nonetheless, they were reflections of a state of mind prevalent among the aborigines, who demanded intelligent, rational, and humane treatment. After making a careful study of these movements and of their consequences, R. R. Marett defines them as "a healthy sign of vitality in a people only too ready to succumb altogether to *taedium vitae*, under the conditions of more work and less play which foreign rule inevitably imposes upon them."[6]

In the Solomon Islands, at Buka, a Cargo cult emerged in 1931–32—its prophet predicting an imminent deluge that would engulf the whites and would be followed by the arrival of a ship laden with goods of every sort. The Buka population was ordered immediately to construct a place in which to store the bounty, while getting ready to repulse the colonial police—resorting to arms if necessary. The ship would arrive only when the natives were reaching the end of their own supplies; hence, they ceased working in the fields, to use up their supplies, and the authorities arrested their leaders. But the movement continued, in spite of its temporary loss of leadership.[7] In 1934 the ferment was again evident, this time instigated by a new prophet, Sanop, who claimed to be speaking for his predecessor, the prophet Pako, who had come to him in a vision. According to Sanop, the arrival of the ship would coincide with the resurrection of the dead. The natives again abandoned the fields to worship and offer sacrifices on the tombs of their forebears in order to hasten their return.

---

[5] J. Guiart: "Cargo Cult and Political Evolution in Melanesia," *Mankind*, IV, 6 (1951), pp. 227–8; "Espiritu Santo," *Nouvelles Hébrides* (Paris, 1958), pp. 197–219.

[6] R. R. Marrett: Introduction to Williams: *Orokaiva Magic*, p. xi.

[7] Canberra: "Report to the Council of the League of Nations on the Administration of the Territory of New Guinea" (1933–34; 1934–35); Eckert: op. cit., p. 138–9.

Sanop, too, was arrested and jailed.[8] The return of the dead bringing food and wealth was awaited also by the prophet Upikno at Gitua (Finschhafen, New Guinea) in 1933; he added that, once this had come to pass, the natives would enjoy immortality[9] on this earth.

The same promise, that the return of the dead would signal the end of an era and the start of a new one, is found in the prophecies of a preacher named Marafi, who proselytized in 1933 in the Markham Valley, on the Gulf of Huon. He claimed a close alliance with Satan, from whom he had received all power and who had enabled him to visit the dead in their kingdom. He had been informed of their imminent return to earth, on the morrow of a cataclysm which would spare only the followers of his cult. Since the dead would bring rice, meat, and other foods, there was no longer any reason for the natives to cultivate the soil. The natives promptly followed his counsel, but the authorities arrested the prophet[1] and sent the people back to their jobs.

The Vailala Madness, a cult which greatly influenced the Orokolo tribes, was founded on the conviction that the dead would return, on a ship laden with European goods, having assumed the appearance of Europeans.[2] Several times the rumor spread that a ship had been sighted, and local agitation followed. But in 1936 the entire coastline in the Arihava region was suddenly filled with flags, pennants, and huge dancing crowds when the call went out for all to foregather: this time the long-awaited vessel was really in view. The re-

[8] Eckert: op. cit., p. 138.
[9] Eckert: "Prophetentum und Kulturwandel in Melanesien," *Baessler Arch.*, XXIII, 1 (1940), p. 31.
[1] Ibid., p. 29.
[2] Williams: "The Vailala Madness in Retrospect," pp. 370 ff.; L. P. Mair: *Australia in New Guinea* (London, 1949), p. 64.

current outbursts of great excitement when everything seemed quiet were like the sudden flaring of a flame from a fire that seemed extinguished. Time after time the same idea recurred and was joyously taken up by more tribes which did not seem to have heard of it before.[3]

Between 1937 and 1938 the natives of Bogia in New Guinea were persuaded by a prophet named Mambu that the coming of the dead would transform the life of all the inhabitants. The whites, he said, had exploited the natives, but the hour of retaliation was now at hand: it was the dead, dwelling inside the Manam volcano, who had made, crated, and shipped the goods to New Guinea for the use of the natives; and each time a shipment came in, the Europeans had seized it for their own use. But, said the prophet, this would not occur again, for the dead had made and stored the goods in the volcano and were about to bring them down themselves to the people. The whites would thus be unmasked and their rule ended. The attack against foreign rule implied in this prophecy is directed against the missions and the plantation owners,[4] as well as against the government. The responsibility for the exploitation of native produce to the detriment of the natives is jointly shared by all European groups.

In 1942 another version of the prophetic Cargo cult began to make inroads among the Mekeo tribes at Cape Possession, on the Gulf of Papua. There a prophetess named Philo forecast the coming of a great ship, sent by the dead, to return to the natives the food and other goods stolen by the Europeans. As the natives gathered upon the shore to await the fulfillment of the prophecy, they went into trance, had con-

[3] Williams: *Drama of Orokolo* (Oxford, 1940), pp. 123–4.
[4] G. Höltker: "Die Mambu Bewegung in Neu Guinea," *Ann. Lat.*, V (1941), pp. 186–91.

vulsions, and experienced all the typical forms of collective seizure.[5]

The penetration of the Cargo cult into the traditional cult of the dead was revealed as recently as 1952 at Tikopia, on the Solomon Islands, where the civilization is Polynesian rather than Melanesian. In that year Raymond Firth was told by the Tikopians that they were in a state of great excitement because one of their leaders, Pa-fenumera, long deceased, was due to ship a cargo of goods for their use which he had obtained through his own personal contacts with the Europeans. The Pa-fenumera cargo was eagerly awaited for a long time.[6] On another occasion, a radio report monitored by a native over the mission radio, which warned of a coming storm in the Solomon Seas, was immediately transformed into the assurance that the end of the world had been announced.[7] The natives rushed to the fields to gather all the available produce for the feast to celebrate the end of one era and the opening of another for their benefit.

The Melanesians have also established cults in which the role played collectively by the returning dead in many other religious movements is taken instead by a single supernatural being—as in the John Frum cult, named after a spirit by that name. In 1940 there appeared at Tanna, in the New Hebrides, a prophet named Manhevi, who claimed to represent John Frum. He made many converts by announcing the imminent transformation of the island into a paradise, with the immediate improvement of living conditions for the natives. This would occur as soon as the last white man had been chased out of the island, and as soon as every piece of money received from the white man had been either returned to him

[5] C. S. Belshaw: "Recent History of Mekeo Society," *Oceania*, XX, 1 (1951), pp. 5–8.
[6] R. Firth: "The Theory of Cargo Cult," *Man* (1955), p. 142.
[7] Ibid.

or destroyed. Eternal youth and perpetual abundance would then be the people's reward. The natives were to restore the rituals, the dances, the polygamy, and the use of kava which had been abolished by the missionaries. This cult had a succession of prophets, all of whom were either put in jail or committed to an insane asylum. The cult of John Frum rose and fell several times, notably in 1941, 1943, and 1947. But in 1952 it was still so strong on the islands of Ambrym, Paama, Epi, and Pentecost that the colonial government decided it would be wiser and safer to release the prisoners.[8] One effect of this movement was that thousands of natives deserted the Presbyterian church, returning to the pagan cults which had been stifled by the Christians before they had even laid foundations for the necessary cultural and religious changes. According to prophecy, John Frum would return to earth as a living being to bring the makings of a golden age in which, without having to work, the natives would have every resource at their disposal. Implicit in this cult is the natives' intention of taking revenge on the whites because they had exploited them through the sale of imported goods and through the mining and development of copra.[9] The cult opposes the Presbyterian church for its failure to understand the indigenous people and their aspirations.[1]

[8] Guiart: "John Frum Movement in Tanna," *Oceania*, XXII, 3 (1952), pp. 165–77; "Forerunners of Melanesian Nationalism," *Oceania*, XXII, 2 (1951), pp. 81–90; R. P. Patrick O'Reilly: "Prophétisme aux Nouvelles Hébrides: le mouvement Jonfrum à Tanna (1940–1947)," *Le Monde non-Chrétien*, n.s. 1949, pp. 192–208; J. Poirier: "Les mouvements de libération mythique aux Nouvelles Hébrides, *J. S. Oc.*, V, 5 (1949).

[9] Guiart: "John Frum . . . ," p. 174.

[1] The Presbyterian missionaries, starting from the conviction that there was an innate inferiority in the natives, disregarded their cultural needs; however, they reminded them systematically of their one obligation, which was to "pray, pray, pray; and to sing, sing, sing!" (Guiart: "John Frum . . . ," p. 172.) Guiart points out that the underlying motivation for the movement was a desire for education; the natives could learn

Another "personal" cult which drew followers away from an established Christian church was founded in 1942 at Kadavu-Levu, in the Fiji Islands, by Kelevi Nawai, a prophet who called himself the "Vessel of Christ." He promised immortality to his followers, engaged in magical healing practices, boasted of bringing the dead back to life, and succeeded in depriving the Methodist church of nearly all its native members. He lived with several young women selected for their pulchritude, whom he called "Roses of Life," and put together a code of laws of his own. Eventually the police intervened. Even though Nawai emphasized the Christian aspect of his cult by calling himself "Vessel of Christ" and preaching the Kingdom of God according to the Gospel, his major appeal to the natives lay in his power to communicate directly with the dead, according to pagan tradition.[2] In this case, as in others, the merging of the old with the new, of paganism with Christianity, was the most significant aspect of the cult.[3]

Melanesia has also produced cults which demand the immediate destruction of all goods produced by the whites and all money put in circulation by them. These also advocate the return to traditional customs and systems of work, and the restoration of all rituals abolished by the missionaries. In an elementary way, they actually seek to raise the hope of the people in an era of abundance by sending them back to work bound by the promise to accept the cult's discipline. The irredentist implications of these cults—sometimes inac-

---

nothing from the missions which would elevate the level of their economic life. See also Annette Rosenstiel: "Long-term Planning," *Human Organization*, II (1954), pp. 5–10.

[2] A. C. Cato: "A New Cult in Fiji," *Oceania*, XVII, 2 (1947), pp. 155–6.

[3] A. Lommel (1953) has made a long list of cults in which the return of the dead is either absent or not documented (pp. 21–5, 30, 31–46 *passim*).

curately described as nationalistic—are common to some extent to all recent religious movements rising among native peoples, regardless of the precise wording of the prophecies by which they are preceded or of the rituals which accompany them.

A. P. Elkin noted that a careful evaluation of these movements revealed an increasingly strong determination on the part of the natives to achieve autonomy and self-government, but that the British authorities preferred to adhere to their traditional policy of "letting sleeping dogs lie."[4]

Andreas Lommel, whose study of these messianic movements is among the most thorough and enlightened made thus far, points to the profound significance of these cults as manifestations of a ferment of life among the natives, and urges that they be taken seriously into account by Western civilization, which claims to be humanitarian and democratic. There was a time, says Lommel, when the principal desire of the native was to live as his forebears had lived, but this aspiration has been abandoned. The natives now wish to live as

---

[4] A. P. Elkin: *Social Anthropology in Melanesia* (London, 1953), pp. 154–5. With regard to this aspect of the problem, see also Guiart: "Forerunners of Melanesian Nationalism," pp. 81–90; Belshaw: "The Significance of Modern Cults in Melanesian Development," *Austr. Outl.*, IV (1950), pp. 116–25; Poirier: op. cit.; Rosenstiel: op. cit.; H. I. Hogbin: *Experiments in Civilization* (London, 1939), pp. 125–39; T. Bodrogi: "Colonization and Religious Movements in Melanesia," *A. E. A. Sc. Hung.*, II (1951), pp. 259–90. Bodrogi, in particular, takes up the whole matter of colonialism and the renewal of political awareness among the natives, without allowing prejudice or any other concern to influence his purely scientific study of the phenomenon in question. As an example of the reverse, note the essay by S. H. Roberts: *Population Problems of the Pacific* (London, 1927), in which the author starts out with the conviction that there is "inbred corruption in the Polynesian race," that "the primitive people are cruel," that they have "elemental tendencies and every sort of turpitude" (pp. 28–32, 58–62), and from this point of view strives to explain the native depopulation which has played such a significant part in the crises that have brought on the religious movements of liberation.

the white people live, but without their presence;[5] they look, not to the past, but to the present. We are seeing a small world striving to capture the ideas of a larger one.[6] I would disagree with Lommel's comments in only one respect: the natives are not only looking to the present, they are fastening their sights on greater things for the future.

SPREAD OF THE MESSIANIC CULTS

The way in which these cults became diffused makes it possible to recognize not only their place of origin but also the particular conditions in which they developed. As soon as the first cargo boats began to come in from Europe, the inhabitants of the coastal area of New Guinea and of the smaller islands began to experience difficult situations and conditions which had no precedent in their lives. Large numbers of white men landed from the ships to unload crates of what, to the natives, were extraordinary objects. The Cargo cult came as an immediate reaction to the arrival of the ships, in the places were they landed; in the interior and in the central highlands, however, the messianic cults began to develop only as late as 1930, when the "miraculous cargo" was sent inland by air, accompanied by the first Europeans to be seen by the native tribes.[7] The messianic cults in the interior are linked to the airplane rather than to seagoing ships.[8]

The reaction of the aborigines to the landing of the first aircraft in their midst is reconstructed by Ronald M. Berndt

[5] Lommel: op. cit., p. 57.

[6] Ibid., pp. 57–8.

[7] M. Leahay and M. Crain: *The Land That Time Forgot: Adventures and discoveries in New Guinea* (London, 1937).

[8] R. M. Berndt: "A Cargo Movement in the Eastern Central Highlands of New Guinea," *Oceania*, XXIII, 1 (1952), pp. 40–50; Mair: op. cit., pp. 29, 35, 37, 65. For Cargo cults in the central highlands, see also J. Nilles: "The Kuman of the Chimbu Region," *Oceania*, XXI, 1 (1950), pp. 64–5; M. Reay: *The Kuma* (London, 1959).

from conversations with individuals who witnessed it. Dr. Berndt reports that on a certain day in 1930 the natives of the central highlands of New Guinea heard, for the first time, the roar and rumble of an airplane: terrified, they threw themselves on the ground and did not raise their heads until the sound had vanished, lest they be suddenly killed. As soon as they got to their feet, sacrifices were offered to the Spirits of the Dead,[9] and the fat from a slain pig was spread over the ground for the dead to feed on.[1] They also covered their bodies and heads with foliage from the croton tree, to protect themselves from the nefarious influence of the object they had clearly heard and only vaguely seen. The dramatic quality of this experience, soon followed by others, convinced the natives that the new era had dawned, especially once the whites began to unload amazing objects from their planes. An interesting fact is that the religious ritual carried out by the population was the one traditionally used to celebrate the annual Feast of the Harvest and of the Dead, and, as Dr. Berndt observed, the whites were included in the pattern of the existing beliefs as benevolent spirits which could easily become evil unless the proper precautions were taken.[2] Dr. Berndt does not appear to have noticed, however, that, in addition to general ties between this reaction and old native traditions, there was also a very clear and precise connection with the belief in the return of the dead, celebrated during the traditional New Year Feast of the pagans. For the natives of the highlands, the whites who alight from planes to unload their cargo are the same Spirits of the Dead whom the natives

[9] Berndt: op. cit., p. 50.

[1] Regarding the use of croton leaves as magical protection during the annual harvesting rituals, see A. Riesenfeld: "Fruchtbarkeitsriten Melanesien," *Inter. Archiv f. Ethn.*, XXXVII, 1–2 (1939), pp. 1–30.

[2] Berndt: op. cit., p. 52.

of the coastal regions identified with the whites landing from ships. In both cases, the arrival of these men was regarded as the beginning of the new cosmic era, since the experience was so extraordinary and so dramatic that in the mind of the natives it could only herald the dawning of the New Age.

The memory of this first contact with the white man continued to be a living force, which gave rise to collective trances and convulsions such as the natives experienced when they were possessed by the dead.

This was the millennium they had been waiting for, and soon, they believed, the gifts would be turned over to them, or at least shared equally between the whites and themselves. The celebrations grew in number and intensity; platforms were built all over the highland areas upon which to place the food for the dead; and structures were erected in which to store the expected goods.[3] Some natives went so far as to cut a path from the cemetery to the storehouse, to facilitate the work of the spirits.[4] The movement reached a peak in 1947, in the region between Mount Hagen and the Markham River, and spread beyond,[5] producing everywhere periods of excited expectation followed by others of disappointment and depression.[6] In 1953, when Dr. Berndt made his last survey, the agitation still persisted, kept alive by a succession of prophets.[7] In several places the population was ordered by its prophets to stop working in the fields and to begin to clear areas for the planes to land.[8] This occurred in such widely

[3] Ibid., pp. 53 ff., 59–65.
[4] Ibid., p. 59.
[5] Berndt: *Oceania*, XXIII, 2 (1952), pp. 137–58; 3 (1953), pp. 202–34.
[6] Berndt: *Oceania*, XXIV, 3 (1954), p. 191.
[7] Berndt: *Oceania*, XXIV, 3 (1954), pp. 190–228; XXIV, 4 (1954), pp. 255–74.
[8] Mair: op. cit., p. 65.

scattered places as the Fiji Islands,[9] New Caledonia,[1] and Malaita in the Solomons.[2]

At Santa Ysabel and on other islands of the Solomons, around the year 1939 a missionary started a revolutionary religious movement urging the natives to petition the government for seats on local councils and for fairer rules. The movement took the name of Cult of the Seat and the Rule, and staged anti-European uprisings, with a wooden seat and a wooden ruler for its symbols.[3] Forcefully repressed by the colonial government, the movement started up again in 1945, with such force that the administration was compelled to accede to its demands. The Masinga cult, which originated at Malaita in 1944–45, bore the same political imprint: the aborigines awaited gifts from the Allied troops, built structures in which to house them, and actively organized themselves to fight the local administration as well as the Christian missions. They demanded better pay, education, independence, and the departure of the whites. In 1950 the movement was still very active.[4]

A Cargo cult was started on the island of Manus, in the Admiralties, by a native of Baluan called Paliau.[5] He had fought as a sergeant in New Britain and had been given considerable authority over the elders of the village of Rabaul, where he probably heard of the cult founded by Mambu, who had lived there for some time before 1937.[6] At the end

[9] R. Asmis: "Die Farbigenpolitik der Briten auf den Fidji Inseln," *Kol. Rundschau*, XXIV (1938), p. 84; Cato: op. cit., pp. 146–56. See Chapter 5.
[1] M. Leenhardt: *Notes d'Ethnologie Calédonienne* (Paris, 1930), p. 44; Lommel: op. cit., p. 36.
[2] A. B. Lewis: *The Melanesians* (Chicago, 1945), pp. 37.
[3] Belshaw: "The Significance of Modern Cults . . . ," p. 119.
[4] Ibid., pp. 120–1.
[5] Berndt: op. cit., p. 153.
[6] Lommel: op. cit., pp. 39–40; Höltker: op. cit., p. 184.

of the war Paliau moved to Manus and there promoted his messianic movement, which was based more on personal prestige than on other factors. Nonetheless, his message announcing the rising of the dead and the arrival of gifts and freedom struck a responsive chord and had enduring effects.

In Netherlands New Guinea, the only portion of Indonesia to remain for a time under European control after the republic was constituted in 1949, native society and its prophetic movements are closely related to the culture and religious movements of Melanesia. One of the cults in this area was organized in 1953 among the Muju tribes by a prophet named Karoem. He had moved to Merauke with other natives to work in the sawmills. Soon after his arrival, Karoem was visited by a spirit who showed him how to lead the Muju out of their backward condition to one of complete fulfillment, wealth, and well-being. His followers, said the prophet, would throw off the foreign yoke, and enjoy for their own use the riches and goods brought by the white man, which they would then be free to accumulate. All taxes and tributes imposed upon the natives would be abolished, as would any contribution to mission churches. A great new city would rise, including a large factory, a mint for the coining of European money, and all sorts of shops. A huge ship laden with goods would be awaiting the natives at the port. The dead would then come to life, and the coconut trees would walk. Many traditional beliefs which go back to the origins of native society in this part of the world are peculiar to the Muju people and reflect their special customs. For instance, the Muju are given to lavish spending on feasts and celebrations, such as a marriage, when the family of the bride exacts a high price before giving her to the groom. The Muju society, which is aristocratic and plutocratic, indulges its taste for riches by amassing such strangely divergent items of

217

wealth as hogs and sea shells, the latter being used as trading currency. The prophet's promise that the goods of the white men would become theirs, not merely to use but also to accumulate,[7] could not fail to be immensely attractive to this tribe. So deeply did they believe in the coming of the millennium that in 1955 those who were gainfully employed at Merauke organized a voluntary savings campaign, setting aside a portion of their earnings to facilitate the coming of the New Day.[8]

The American liberators play an important role in the prophecies of Karoem, who announced that the powers held by Queen Juliana would soon be transferred to a woman called Marianne, not further identified except as the spirit of a deceased American. After this transfer, New Guinea and America would be united. The concept of an American in the role of liberator was also accepted in Africa, where it took root after World War II. The followers of Karoem were bound to certain rigid taboos, one of which forbade them to have sexual relations with local or Indonesian women, pending the arrival of the "shapely women" from America and Australia. The presence of the Dutch was tolerated on the island, as was that of the Chinese, but bitter hostility prevailed against Indonesians and Eurasians, who were regarded as dangerous rivals in agriculture[9] and trade. Nonetheless, one cannot fail to note that the growth of Karoem's cult followed upon a spell of Muju warfare against the Dutch. (In 1942 the Muju murdered a Dutch policeman, and in 1945 and 1946 several

[7] For an exhaustive and synthetic account of the culture of the Muju and their prophetic movements, see J. M. van der Kroef: "Culture Contact and Culture Change in Western New Guinea," *Anthr. Q.*, XXXII, 3 (1959), pp. 134-46.
[8] Van der Kroef: op. cit., p. 145.
[9] Ibid., p. 143-4.

well-organized Muju bands attacked government posts.[1]) Thus, this cult was an attempt to seek adjustment in the relations between the Muju and the whites after a period of bloodshed and struggle, even though the cult's ultimate goal is the emancipation of the natives from foreign rule.

Karoem was arrested by order of the Dutch government in 1955, but his prophecies had already spread far and wide among the Muju tribes of the interior, which were already holding séances to establish direct contact with the spirit of the departed in order to plan for their return.[2] As to the cultural, social, and political factors which fostered this cult, they are easy to find in policies pursued by the Dutch government and by the Christian missions with the aim of destroying the patterns of native society. For instance, the Muju always build their huts in the forest, fairly close to their fields of sago, to places which provide good hunting and good fishing or where hogs can be raised in a natural state. The colonial powers forced them off the land into the villages, where it was easier for the police to control them and the missionaries to convert them. The raising of hogs, which from time immemorial had been the greatest source of revenue for the natives, was forbidden by law, ostensibly for reasons of hygiene, but more likely in order to eliminate an obvious impediment to the development of village life. Such Western elements as currency, and such goods as shoes, fishing hooks and rods, textiles, and so on, were introduced into Muju society, but no education was provided, so that the natives believed European goods came from the spirit world. They were forbidden by law to accumulate money or to visit the city of Merauke, lest they be adversely affected by Western attractions; and children who were being taught in the mission schools were kept there long

[1] Ibid., p. 142.
[2] Ibid., pp. 142, 145.

after the normal period, in order to prevent their returning to the traditional culture. These policies were so oppressive that they produced just the reverse results from those the missionaries hoped to achieve. In fact, Christianity was looked upon not as a new and valuable religious force but as a magical instrument of the whites, designed to increase and strengthen their rule. The natives who allowed their children to be schooled by the missionaries expected them to learn the secrets of this magic and eventually to oust the whites and reject Christianity, after having attained an equal level of culture and authority.[3]

Among the best-known and most disconcerting of the messianic movements in Oceania is the Koréri, which was responsible for a chain of revolutionary outbreaks from 1938 to 1943 in the Schouten Islands, particularly on Biak, Numfor, and Japen. The movement was born on the island of Supiori. Begun by the prophetess Angganitha Menufaoer and continued by the prophet Stefanus Simopjaref, it quickly spread to these three major islands, each of which produced a prophet of its own. Koréri, which means Utopia or the Golden Era, expressed the certainty that liberty and riches were on their way. When the Japanese gained control of the islands, the Muju rose against them with great violence, and it was only with still greater violence that the rebellion was smashed and the movement brought to an end. The origins of the Koréri cult go back to the legendary personage of Manseren Manggundi, a beneficent popular hero reputed to possess the secret of the Land of the Dead, in virtue of which he had access to the source of all riches and all foods. Manggundi also had power to lead man to the threshold of the Golden Era by bestowing the riches he controlled; but the people, it was claimed, had not known him when he first came among them,

[3] Ibid., p. 141.

disguised as an old man, or when he returned later as a youth, regenerated by baptismal fire. Hurt and discouraged, he had departed westward, promising nonetheless to return.[4]

By virtue of this traditional myth, the prophets of the Koréri cult call themselves Konoors, meaning Heralds of the Messiah. At first they merely kept alive the hope of a better future, but later they also supported the people's determination to oust the foreign rule. Messianic movements based on this legend had risen, fallen, and risen again long before the Europeans came to the islands—their purpose in the early days was to provide the natives with something to look forward to with hope, beyond their miserable living conditions and the poverty of their land. The hero Manggundi, said the early prophets, would reveal the secret storing place of riches and food, when the time was ripe for him to appear in their midst. The people, oppressed by hunger and misery, accepted the myth and followed the cult, which spiritually alleviated their needs. We know that such movements had gained ground by 1855 and that no less than thirty-seven of them endured for different periods of time in one part or another of the region. Obviously they were unrelated to foreign rule, as the natives of the interior had no knowledge of it at that time. There was, however, an instance, recorded in 1855 on the Schouten Islands, in which local inhabitants refused, for religious reasons, to pay taxes to Tidore, then ruling the district of northwestern New Guinea.

Several Koréri movements, which, for one reason or another, came to an end around 1943, have recently taken a new

[4] F. C. Kamma: *De messiaanse Koréri-Bewegingen* (The Hague), pp. 39–51. In another version the hero is called Manarmakeri; pp. 27–38, 52–61. For this movement, see also J. V. De Bruyn: "De Mansren cultus der Biakkers," *T. T. L. V. K.*, LXXXIV, 4 (1949).

lease on life in several parts of New Guinea, revived by underlying political motivation.[5]

AUSTRALIA AND ITS LACK OF LOCAL PROPHETS

The abundance of messianic and prophetic cults among agrarian populations and the almost total absence of them among tribes which live by ordinary hunting is an interesting and by no means accidental fact.[6] Australia, for example, is a sterile soil for prophets, even as it is devoid of traditional rites such as the worship of the dead or the offering to them of the first fruits of the land. The Melanesians, who are an agrarian people, have a vital religious history, whereas no such history exists among the Australian aborigines, who are hunters. Tradition has shallow roots among people who do not live on the land but are constantly moving in quest of prey. They also lack the rituals traditionally connected with the harvest season, which account for the continuing vitality of most of the messianic cults.

The clash between European and native culture occurred in Australia as it did elsewhere in the non-Western world, but its effects were different from those seen, for instance, in Melanesia. The establishment of Christian missions among the aborigines and the resultant mass conversions created a number of serious problems. These have been studied by Caroline Kelly in her survey of several communities in New South Wales and Queensland. The funeral dirge, which, from time immemorial, the natives had chanted over the bodies of the deceased, is at least one traditional element to which the local

[5] Kamma: *op. cit.*, pp. 236-9. See also G. J. Held: *The Papuas of Waropen* (The Hague, 1957). For very recent prophetic movements in Dutch New Guinea (Iriam), see Bureau for Native Affairs, 1958.

[6] For example, the Bushmen and the African Pygmies ignore the experience of prophetic cults. Schlosser: op. cit., p. 400.

222

religious communities have clung tenaciously, although the mission sought to eradicate it by forbidding it in unequivocal terms. As a result, all funerals were conducted either by or in the presence of a Christian missionary. However, as soon as the missionary had withdrawn after sundown, the natives carried on their own ceremonies until dawn, painting the body of the deceased and following all their ancient rites.[7] As Dr. Kelly points out, if by "converts" one means individuals who have changed their lives by repudiating ancient ways and adopting new ones, the Australian aborigines are not "converts" at all.[8]

Pagan tradition reacts strongly to protect itself from any element—be it technical or ideological—introduced by Christian or European cultures. Arnhem Land is one of several regions where the natives have remained "pure" and primitive and practically untouched by Western influence.[9] In the village of Oenpelli, for instance, the aborigines have preserved their first impression of the Europeans, which they had in 1925, and it is one of fear. Fear has remained the collective reaction of this village to the whites: fear of being touched by them, fear of their policemen, fear of their food, which the natives systematically reject, fear of Western weapons. This is actually an expression of their sense of inferiority, further borne out by this statement from a native: "In the world of the white man there is one 'very important man' and all the visitors who come here are his emissaries, merely sent to discover if everything is going well for them down under."[1] They take this attitude even in regard to scientists who have

[7] C. Kelly: "Some Aspects of Culture Contact in Eastern Australia," *Oceania*, XV, 2 (1944), p. 149.

[8] Ibid., p. 148.

[9] Elkin: *The Australian Aborigines* (Sydney-London, 1954), 3rd ed., p. 330.

[1] C. H. and R. M. Berndt: "Oenpelli Monologue: Culture Contact," *Oceania*, XXII, 1 (1951), pp. 26, 27-9.

223

tried to question them for purely scientific purposes. Today the Australian aborigines are striving to overcome their sense of inferiority by learning to read and write—not the language of the Europeans, however, but their own indigenous tongue.[2] In this respect, they are making a dual effort to defend and strengthen their own culture, while also imitating the whites, whose superiority they recognize. This effort has produced a new cultural awareness, which some observers have, not too appropriately, defined as "race consciousness."[3] Actually, it is a form of intelligent but passive syncretism, a policy of enlightened self-interest, which the natives have adopted even in regard to the labor demanded of them by the whites. The natives will work only in exchange for payment in kind, such as tobacco, sugar, tea, flour, and iron,[4] and by this means are trying to strengthen their biological as well as their cultural defenses against the damage already done to their stock by the practices of the Europeans and their appropriation of the best land.[5]

Poverty and a decline in population have had serious effects on the religious life of the natives, and have promoted the revival of ancient myths as well as the belief in the end of the world. If such a belief existed in their tradition,[6] it was not of major importance to the majority. Andreas Lommel, who has made a special study of the Kurrangara cult in Kimberly (northwestern Australia), finds that it was fairly widespread

[2] Ibid., pp. 32 ff.

[3] Lommel: "Modern Culture Influences on the Aborigines," *Oceania*, XXI, 1 (1950), p. 21.

[4] Elkin: *The Australian Aborigines*, p. 324.

[5] Ibid., pp. 321–2.

[6] The death of humanity and the end of the world furnished the content for myths from time immemorial. See K. Langloh Parker: *The Euahlayi Tribe* (London, 1905), pp. 75–6; R. Brough Smith: *The Aborigines of Victoria* (London, 1878), Vol. I, p. 466 ff.; R. Pettazzoni: *Miti e leggende* (Turin, 1948), Vol. I, p. 460.

among the Ungarinyin and Worora tribes,[7] but had only recently made headway among the Unambal. He was able to observe its growth among the Unambal and notice distinctly the gradual grafting of new ideas and new elements upon ancient cultural roots. The traditional myth of Kurrangara concerned an ancestor named Nguniai, regarded as the inventor of law and of all technical instruments, and the originator of circumcision. He was also the creator of all objects sacred to the cult, such as the tables of the law, which were endowed with such power that the initiates, whose bodies were rubbed with them, would have killed everyone within reach, had they not washed their bodies immediately after the ritual.[8] In 1938, at the time of Lommel's observations, the cult of this legendary hero had already been endowed with certain new features, some of them borrowed from Christianity. The hero of the new religious cult is no longer Nguniai but his son Tjanba, who can also make tables of the law endowed with superlative powers, but his strength consists chiefly in being able to spread such dread diseases as leprosy and syphilis. Tjanba can now distribute other Kurrangara objects all over the land by traveling by airplane, automobile, or ship. He carries a gun and many iron tools and only asks to be given tea, sugar, bread, and canned meat, which are consumed during ritual ceremonies.[9] As a benevolent hero, Tjanba, like his father, represents native tradition, but, being supplied with European goods, he also represents the Western elements now embodied in the cult. Syphilis is associated with Europeans; hence Tjanba can spread syphilis. Native society has been deeply hurt by the policy of the Europeans; hence Tjanba announces that the end of the world is at hand[1] and that, in fact,

[7] H. Petri: "Kurangara," *Z.f.E.*, LXXV (1950), pp. 43–51.
[8] Lommel: "Modern Culture Influences on the Aborigines," p. 22.
[9] Ibid., p. 23.
[1] Ibid.

it will occur as soon as the sacred instruments of Kurrangara have traveled from the south to the north, at which time no more tables of the law will be produced.

Although Ronald Berndt disagrees with some of the conclusions reached by Lommel in regard to the psychic collapse[2] of the Australian aborigines and their consequent inability to procreate, he agrees substantially with the significance attributed to the religious cult and to the myth behind it. Lommel also believes that the natives, owing to the clash with the whites, are now more interested in the future than in the past; but because their view of the future is dark and forbidding, their attitude toward life[3] is filled with sadness and marked by great apathy. The Unambal tribes are truly obsessed by the certainty that the world is about to come to an end, and are fatalistically awaiting what is to be the final dispensation from the north: the Maui cult, which will bring new venereal diseases and death to all living creatures.[4] The same pessimistic obsession prevails among the Ungarinyin and Worora tribes, whose lives have already been indelibly scarred by the certainty of the impending catastrophe.[5]

It is interesting to find that the missionaries deliberately ignore the Kurrangara cult, so long as its ceremonies are performed out of sight.[6] This attitude implies recognition, on the part of the church, of its inability to eliminate pagan beliefs until the economic, social, and political conditions of native life have been greatly improved. A. P. Elkin clearly sees the course to be followed if the Australian aborigines are ever

---

[2] Ibid., pp. 14–20; Berndt: "Influence of European Culture on Australian Aborigines," *Oceania*, XXI, 3 (1952), pp. 229–35.

[3] Lommel: op. cit., p. 24.

[4] Ibid.

[5] Petri: "Das Weltende im Glauben Australischer Eingeborenen," *Paideuma*, IV (1950), pp. 349–62.

[6] Lommel: op. cit., p. 25.

to assimilate Western culture. The process, he maintains, must occur in several phases: first, at the economic level; second, at the political level; and third, at the social level—the religious level remaining untouched until the third phase is over.[7] His view indicates that among aboriginal populations religion reflects the social, political, and economic conditions of life and that, therefore, religious patterns cannot be changed until the structure of secular society has been altered.

The subservient condition in which these natives must live under European rule has deprived their religious movements of such positive manifestations as are seen in the messianic cults of the Melanesians. The Australians have adopted a passive resistance, hoping to ensure the bare survival of their ethnic group, but also believing that the decline of their population is a clear warning of the imminent end of the world.

A historical explanation for this is also to be found in the seminomadic way of life of many Australian communities. The exploitation by the whites of arable land and pastures has deprived the natives of hunting grounds,[8] or compelled them to work on the white man's plantations; or, worse still, has caused them to be sent abroad to work. In these circumstances, it is hardly surprising that the hunting instinct of these primitive peoples has sought out its prey in the white man's herds, giving rise to problems and hostilities of every sort.[9] Only a few small groups can still make a living hunting the kangaroo. The aboriginal culture, wrenched from its economic, social, and even geographical moorings, is gradually

[7] Elkin: *The Australian Aborigines*, p. 332.

[8] From the early decades of the nineteenth century the sheep raisers invaded the country from New South Wales and moved into the center and the west. "Hungry for land, they flouted government regulations which protected the natives, and were themselves called 'squatters,' as had been the colonizers first sent into Australia as deportees." C. Luetkens: "L'Australie, pays de la laine," *Cahiers Ciba*, 22 (1949).

[9] Elkin: op. cit., pp. 322–3.

disintegrating. It must accept either servitude or assimilation, even though it is engaged in a last-ditch defense of its values and traditions. The character of these religious cults, passive and strongly conservationist, differs totally from that of cults in Melanesia, where the social and geographical foundations of native society resisted the West and continued to provide a basis upon which the people could build the hope of liberation and renewal.

THE MESSIANIC THEME AND THE CARGO THEME

Scholars have pointed out that certain of the Melanesian cults express the people's desire for adjustment[1] to the modern culture of the West, whereas others are a religious reaction to alien control[2] in a setting of poverty,[3] and still others are an attempt to stabilize native culture and status through self-determination and autonomy.[4] It must be added, however, that certain cults stem from a combination of these efforts and factors.[5] Whatever the combination, these movements must be evaluated for what they are, namely, the product of an

[1] Berndt: "Reaction to Contact in Eastern . . . ," p. 274.

[2] M. J. Herskovits: *Man and His Works* (New York, 1949), p. 531.

[3] Linton: op. cit., p. 238.

[4] F. M. Keesing: *The South Seas in the Modern World* (1942), p. 78.

[5] R. Firth, in *Elements of Social Organization* (London, 1951), p. 111: "The new native movements are essentially reactions by the native peoples themselves, without European prompting, to the new forces introduced through contact with the West. They express on the one hand native dissatisfaction with existing conditions. On the other hand, they are attempts to get an adjustment. This adjustment is sought through native means . . . the values of the organization are conceived as applying to corporate unity: it is the good of the community which is an ostensible object of the activity. They can see no immediate way of attaining their end save one—by relying on certain elements of the traditional beliefs—which through the help of the ancestors or the help of their magical performances, they can constrain ships and aeroplanes to come and land supplies to meet their wants" (pp. 112–13).

agrarian society's reaction to an alien culture, which appears among them in the form of religious evangelism and of hitherto unknown material goods. They are newly garbed manifestations of ancient traditional religious ways, such as the Feast of the New Year or the cult of the dead. Missionary evangelism, combined with the old native beliefs, has produced new prophets, who, in effect, are pagan imitations of the Christian Savior. The new theme of the Messiah is a re-elaboration of a theme found in pagan cults: the idea of a legendary hero becoming embodied in a prophet is traditional; the idea that he will disappear once his task is accomplished, promising to return bringing liberation and riches to his followers, is borrowed from the life of Christ.[6] Modern native cults do not invent new personages or new ideas: they only give new life and form to ancient pagan beliefs, and endow the old art of magic with new powers to meet new needs. The message of the missionaries, grafted on ancient patterns, has enriched the trances, visions, and convulsions of the shamans with new meaning. The traditional worship of the dead and belief in their return has been modernized by the addition of an assurance that the dawn of the new age will also bring to the natives the food and material riches of the white man.

The Cargo cult represents the reaction of people living in cultural and material poverty to the sudden appearance among them of new and unimagined riches from across the seas. It echoes Christianity with its promise of the hereafter and con-

---

[6] Concerning the mythical complex of the hero who vanishes and returns, or promises to return, see R. H. Codrington: *The Melanesians* (1891; New Haven, 1957), pp. 166–7 (New Hebrides); Andersson: op. cit., pp. 259–62; Kamma: op. cit., pp. 62–85, 229 (Dutch New Guinea); S. C. Handy: "Polynesian religion," *Bernice P. B. Mus. Bull.*, XXXIV (1927), p. 296 (Hawaii).

tains a variety of beliefs and rituals, some traditional and some new.

THE RETURN OF THE DEAD, THE GREAT FEAST, THE SHIP OF THE DEAD

The ritual theme of the return of the dead to their villages takes active shape during the festival of the New Year and is historically linked with the agricultural activities of the population. Just as an entire village will turn out in the fields to work, and works in order to feed itself, so the dead, during the yearly festival or at night when the living are asleep, will move collectively into the village, seeking food to sustain them. The villagers work together to produce the food; the dead return together to take their share of it. This, say the natives, is the price which mother earth, in which the dead are buried, exacts in retribution for the sacrilege committed by those who disturb the soil with their work. The burden of sin weighs upon the people until the dead have been satisfied, after which normal relations are resumed between the living and the earth, and man can again till the soil while nature obeys its own laws. At the end of a year, when the compounded cost of the oft-committed agricultural sacrilege becomes overwhelming, the collective conscience of the people can only be cleansed of sin by the celebration of the redeeming rites of the Great Feast. In this manner, the Melanesians link their belief in the return of the dead to the Annual Feast, which today is still held in the old traditional framework.[7]

The Cargo cult, which the Melanesians have added to their older cult of the rising dead, is also inherent in their experience as an agrarian people. The same general idea of the arrival of a cargo is found in many African, Indonesian, and American

[7] Regarding the relationship between the two theses, see Lanternari: op. cit.

religious movements in agrarian tribes or hunting tribes with an agrarian past.[8]

The Cult of the Ship of the Dead, peculiar to the Melanesians, represents the integration of a modern experience with a belief carried down almost unchanged from archaic times. Thus far, students of these movements do not appear to have realized[9] that the belief in a ship of the dead laden with miraculous bounty is simply the revival, or the reshaping, of the ancient belief in a vessel conveying the dead, which has always prevailed in Oceania.[1]

The belief that the final dwelling place of the dead is an island across the sea is common to the natives of Melanesia, Polynesia, Micronesia, and Indonesia, and is also the belief that

[8] Even Schlosser is in agreement in recognizing in the return of the dead one of the universally recurrent elements in the prophetic movements, like the return of the oxen in Africa, the buffalo in America. "Der Prophetismus in niederen Kulturen," *Z. f. E.*, LXXV (1950), p. 68.

[9] The only author who appears to perceive, or indeed to emphasize, the relationship between the traditional cult of the dead and the arrival of cargo from Europe is Andreas Lommel. "From the cult of the dead," he states, "there derives all the traditional religious life of the Melanesians. For them, it is not conceivable that the cargo should come from Europe, the existence of which they are not aware; for them the cargo comes from the world of the dead." (*Z. f. E.*, LXXVIII [1953], p. 55). According to Lommel, the connection between the cult of the dead and the Cargo cult rests on the fact that the natives do not know Europe, the place of origin of the cargo: they do not even know that it exists. ("Europa . . . das ihnen kein Begriff war und auch nicht sein konnte." Ibid.) However, in order fully to understand the attitude of the natives, so imbued with mythology in regard to the cargo, we feel that another "inexperience" of the natives is also important, one that is typical of native culture: their "inexperience" in the process of manufacturing the goods. The lack of such experience seems to us to be a determining factor in their attitude toward the cargo.

[1] For further details on funeral traditions connected with the concept of a dwelling place of the dead across the sea, see Lanternari: "Origini storiche dei culti profetici melanesiani," *S.M.S.R.*, XXVII (1956), pp. 77–82. With respect to the mythical-ritual theme of the ship of the dead, as related to fishing and seafaring populations, see Lanternari: *La grande festa*, pp. 413–28.

the spirit of every deceased person embarks on a ship as soon as it leave the body, and is thereby transported to its insular home. This conviction is reflected in a variety of burial rites practiced by the natives, which include burial at sea, encasement of the body in a canoe-shaped coffin, shipping the body to sea in a canoe, or weighting down the body to make it rest on the bed of the ocean. The belief in the island of the dead reflects the sea voyages undertaken by the natives in their past quest for a homeland, and is not found in the cults and myths of Africa or of the Americas, whose aborigines were not seafarers. On the other hand, however, these three continents share belief in the return of the dead, because their native cultures stem equally from agrarian economies.

SYNTHESIS

When the messianic cults of Melanesia are viewed in the light of their relationship both to the natives and to the West, it becomes apparent that they are a religious reflection of the sharp cultural antagonism engendered in part by the different significance which these two civilizations attribute to manufactured goods. For all Westerners, goods are the end product of a mechanical process of which they are the guiding power, whereas for the natives, Western goods are a new and foreign element that has no place in their collective memory or knowledge. The chaotic reactions of the aborigines to the arrival of Western goods are likewise a new and foreign element. These reactions are due to a historical fact which has not yet been fully evaluated, namely, that the natives had no experience in the manufacture of these goods but that they knew the whites to be very skilled, even as they knew themselves to be skilled in agriculture.[2] The arrival of Western

[2] See my essay, "Sulle origini dell'agricoltura" (On the Origins of Agriculture), in *Annali del Museo Pitré*, Palermo, V-VI, 1956. This historical explanation of the modern Melanesian cults also implies their efforts to

goods, therefore, constitutes the moment of impact between two types of civilization which, having developed on totally different terrains, have inevitably taken totally different courses. The clash occurs when the products of a civilization that has reached the peak of the machine age are suddenly placed before a civilization that has only reached a peak of agricultural development and is still unaware of the mechanical and industrial processes.[3]

The lack of personal experience in making Western goods caused the natives to believe that these items were of supernatural origin. Their traditional belief that the dead would

---

solve certain complex cultural problems which the cults reveal, and certain related political and administrative problems as well. In view of the fact that the chaotic religious and political conditions originate in the gap between native culture and the culture of the foreigners, one must arrive at the conclusion that the gap can only be filled by placing the natives within the pattern of production of European goods—on a free basis both as users and as producers—so that reasons for further and continued cultural clash may be eliminated. Up to what point this fundamental fact has been accepted by the Europeans remains to be seen. Ralph Piddington, in this regard, has underlined the limitation of the actions taken thus far to aid native progress. He points out that very few administrators or missionaries have taken steps to encourage the natives to move ahead. They insist, if anything, that "progress" shall come along European lines. The New Imperialism (which is an imperialism of ideas and values) demands that the political independence and economic progress of the natives remain within the limitations of European ideals, and only within such limitations can the natives be assisted (*Journal of Polynesian Society*, LXIV, 1 [1955], p. 173.) This looks very much like a game of politics, and it is being played in regard to cultural problems which it is the obligation of the Westerners to solve since they created them.

[3] Lommel has clearly seen this aspect of the cultural clash between native and Western society. The natives, he says, are "Menschen, die immer nur die fertigen technischen Produkte, das cargo sehen, niemals aber den Arbeitsvorgang, der zur Entstehung der technischen Produkt führt" (*Z.f.E.*, 1953, p. 58). Therefore, the marvels of European technique appear to the natives as the fruits of a "secret" knowledge, which they seek to attain by becoming Christians (Lommel: op. cit.). Local reaction to the encounter between native and Western techniques is to resort to a mythical explanation (Lommel: op. cit., p. 20).

return to earth endowed with supernatural powers to bring them riches made them view the new goods as these riches. Thus, they endowed Western man with the mantle of magic which is the attribute of the risen dead.

Chronologically, the development of the Melanesian cults occurred in several phases: the oldest, belonging in the pre-migratory era, is reflected in the belief in the resurrection of the dead; slightly less old is the belief in the ship of the dead, which stems from native experience in interisland travel; closer to our time is the prophetic element, reflecting experience gained from the Christian missions, grafted upon traditional belief in magic—the Christian message supporting the drive for liberty and independence as well as confirming the promise of the millennium.[4] The most recent phase, not yet reached by the Taro cult, for instance, has been stimulated by the arrival of Western goods, at which point the movement takes on very definite anti-Western implications.

The Melanesian movements are also important because they attest the dynamic quality of primitive[5] civilization, revealed in the restlessness of people seeking progress, often along tortuous and difficult paths, and often forced to pass through dramatic or even tragic experiences. In tracing the course of

[4] A. A. Koskinen, in his work, *Missionary Influence as a Political Factor in the Pacific Islands* (Helsinki, 1953), makes particular note of the relationship between "heresies" (the prophetic cults) and the work of the missions. He writes that prophetic movements in Oceania constitute a local reaction following immediately upon the mass conversions (of the past century). These movements indicate particularly the misunderstanding of Christianity on the part of the natives (ibid., p. 101). He underscores the antimissionary significance of these movements, which, nevertheless, claim for their own, as part of their traditional pagan heritage, certain Biblical elements (ibid., 102–4).

[5] The need for social advance geared toward liberation becomes more and more evident as the messianic movements develop. Other students of this problem have remarked that many of these cults, started at a mythical religious level, have tended to emphasize social and political elements (Lommel: op. cit., p. 57).

these movements, from their roots to their current flowering, through periods of depression and decline, of revival and expansion, one soon realizes that the old assumption, that immobility and cultural paralysis were characteristic features of this and other primitive societies, must now be discarded.

Two successive forms of motivation are evident in the Melanesian cults.[6] The first is antagonism and struggle against the white man and his culture; the second, brought on by the arrival of Western goods, is the awareness of the practical and economic significance of these goods, and a determination to find ways of coexisting with the whites in order to share the benefits they bring, although still clinging steadfastly to native cultural values. Struggle, thus, is followed by adjustment and the quest for peace.

The eagerness to advance and the vigorous native desire to find new means of mastering nature through indigenous skills, already proven in agriculture, lend momentum to the messianic movements. The Melanesians are gradually sorting out their heritage of traditions, while also, as Raymond Firth observes, striving to attain as rapidly as possible a new way of life better able to meet their needs, in the knowledge that the relinquishment of certain obsolete forms is the best means to the end they are pursuing. Last, it is evident that these movements reveal, beyond doubt, the outstanding role of religion in primitive cultures. At the same time, it is clear that their mythical and ritual content is historically determined by the actual needs of each particular society.

[6] Worsley: op. cit., p. 273.

CHAPTER

VI

MESSIANIC MOVEMENTS

IN POLYNESIA

IN THE EARLY PART of the nineteenth century, when the
leading missionary churches of England and France decided
to take Christianity to the aborigines of the Pacific, they were
unconsciously paving the way for the semi-pagan, semi-
Christian cults which shortly thereafter began to take shape.
A period of incubation seems to precede the rise of messianic
cults,[1] and it was only after the work of the missionaries had
been followed by territorial annexations and outright conquest
by the Western powers[2] that native resistance developed in
tangible religious and political ways. The prophetic movements
suddenly came to the fore, animating the political and military
actions of the Polynesians with religious fervor and giving
expression in a variety of traditional forms to the need for
freedom on the part of the indigenous populations.

[1] W. E. Mühlmann: *Arioi und Mamaia* (Wiesbaden, 1955), p. 243.
[2] See C. A. Julien: *Histoire de l'Océanie* (Paris, 1951), pp. 78 ff., 83 ff.;
A. A. Koskinen: op. cit., pp. 222-4.

A salient feature of most Polynesian cults is a strong political content. The highly developed warrior caste[3] in Polynesian society caused the religious movements to inspire, as well as to support, the bloody and unrelenting struggle of the natives against the whites who had seized their land, against the British forces, and against the native chiefs who went to the missions or to the colonial administration. The natives identified Christianity with the political power of the whites and were openly hostile to the missions and to every other aspect of Western civilization.

Although the Polynesian cults are molded upon local traditions, the significance of their rituals and their ideological content can only be properly evaluated in relation to the impact of the West upon native society, and to the effort suddenly made by the natives to inject Christianity into their own pagan beliefs. They replaced the names of their deities with Christian names, and took from Judaism and Christianity certain elements of doctrine and theology which seemed to fill vital gaps in their own culture.

The civilization of the Fiji Islands, which flourishes in an area bordering on Melanesia and Polynesia, where these cultures met and mingled, combines many elements of both, not only in the economic and social structure of society but also in the pattern of religious life. The Fiji system of agriculture, however, in which taro is grown on well-irrigated, neatly terraced land,[4] is strictly Polynesian, as is[5] also the social hierarchy

[3] The development of a warrior class coincides, as in the case of the Arioi of Tahiti, with the growth of an aristocracy. The Arioi are noble warriors (Mühlmann: op. cit., p. 139): here the warrior class is as one with the aristocracy.

[4] A. M. Hogart, cited in W. J. Perry: "The Geographical Distribution of Terraced Cultivation and Irrigation," *Mem. Proc. Manchester Lit. and Philos. Soc.*, LX (1915–16), pp. 16–17; Hogart, cited in W. H. Rivers: *Psychology and Ethnology* (London, 1926), pp. 282–3.

[5] Hogart: *Caste* (London, 1950), pp. 80 ff., 102. For the Polynesian in-

based on a powerful aristocracy and on a long-continuing monarchical rule.

The Tuka cult (or cult of immortality) was established around 1885 by the prophet Ndungumoi,[6] who had been taught, in revelation from an ancestor, how to endow his followers with immortality through the use of special water, which he always carried in a bottle.[7] The prophet's private life seems to have been as dissolute as possible, and while he preached against Christianity he also revived such practices as ritual cannibalism, which the natives had forgone many decades earlier. His cannibalistic rituals were performed upon enemies slain in the many violent clashes between the followers of his cult and the whites, such as the armed rebellion which broke out against the British after an intense period of evangelization during which the prophet had announced the imminent expulsion of the white rulers and the regeneration of the world.[8] Ndungumoi is identified with Ndegei, central deity of the ancient Fiji cults, as well as with Jehovah. The reasoning behind this is that Ndegei was the one true God of the natives, and Jehovah the one true God of the Bible; hence Jehovah and Ndegei were one and the same.[9] Ndegei, like Jehovah, had created the world, its vegetable and animal kingdoms, and its human beings. Like Jehovah, Ndegei had sent a deluge upon the earth and, having embodied himself in a snake, now lived in a mountain cave.[1] The traditional myth made it easier to identify the Fiji god with Jehovah than with Christ. Moreover,

---

flux in the Fijis, see Hogart: "Myths in the Making," *Folklore*, XXXIII (1922), p. 62.

[6] See chapter 5.

[7] B. Thomson: *The Fijians* (London, 1908), p. 141; A. B. Brewster: *The Hill Tribes of Fiji* (London, 1922), pp. 240–6.

[8] Thomson: op. cit., pp. 144–5.

[9] J. Waterhouse: *The King and People of Fiji* (London, 1866), p. 303.

[1] Ibid., p. 356.

the Polynesians, like many other aboriginal people, could accept the Old Testament, but were hostile to the New because Christianity was the religion of the ruling minority.

The twin sons of the god Ndegei, said the myth, had once traveled into the land of the white men, where, their true names being unknown, they had been called Jesus and Jehovah. The divine twins were now on their homeward journey, bringing with them all the dead and enough bounty to give eternal prosperity and happiness to the people of Fiji.[2] The ambivalence of the Tuka cult is shown in the combination of such elements as the return of the dead with that of Jehovah and Jesus, identified with the divine twins of paganism. Incidentally, the belief in the return of the dead is of Melanesian origin, and the belief in the one true God, of Polynesian origin. Another cult, similarly compounded of Melanesian and Polynesian elements touched by elements of Judeo-Christian belief, is known as the Nanga cult, which grew almost simultaneously with that of Ndegei.

One of the significant Polynesian cults which molds Christian elements into pagan forms is the Mamaia, in the Society Islands,[3] which was inspired by the discontent of the natives with mission policies. Although the missions opposed annexation of native land by the imperial powers, they threw their support to the native dynasties of rulers, on condition that these, in turn, embrace Christianity. When this occurred, the people found that they were ruled by theocratic dynasties which took orders from the white mission churches.[4] Also,

[2] Thomson: op. cit., pp. 141, 142.

[3] The name Mamaia, probably derived from *Mamoe* (sheep), means "Flock of God" (Mühlmann: op. cit., p. 246). The sect called Mamoe, found in the Tuamotu Islands, east of Tahiti, may have been a branch of this. A. C. E. Caillot: *Les Polynésiens orientaux au contact de la civilisation* (Paris, 1909), p. 38.

[4] Mühlmann: op. cit., p. 226.

239

the missions taxed the natives in order to finance both their evangelism and their ruthless drive to destroy paganism, and the dynastic rulers helped them to achieve these ends. All traditional customs, such as tattooing and painting the body, and all native dances were forbidden. Punishment for carrying on pagan usages was meted out mercilessly and ranged from death for conspiracy, rebellion, or homicide, to hard labor for minor transgressions.[5] As J. A. Moerenhout points out,[6] the cause of Christianity was not advanced by these policies; the Mamaia movement developed in protest against the missionaries as well as against local authority. Interestingly enough, the cult began within the Christian community.

The Mamaia cult was founded in 1828 by the prophet Teau, a Christian of Panavia, an island west of Tahiti,[7] who declared himself to be the true Christ and able to perform miracles. The seething discontent against the missions caused large numbers of converted natives to follow Teau's movement. The missionaries reacted by imposing bodily punishment on the "heretics," such as forcing them to swim around the island in shark-infested waters. But such persecution only strengthened the sect, which soon expanded far beyond Tahiti. In 1828, the destruction of the effigy and altar of the god Oro at the sanctuary of Opoa,[8] in Marae Taputapuatea, central shrine of worship of the Mamaia cult, set off a violent rebellion in which King Tamatoa IV played a major role by declaring war on all pagans on his island. The missionaries exiled all the Mamaia leaders, but these zealots gained a following not only at Raiatea, where they were imprisoned, but as far away as Bora Bora, Maupiti, and Tahaa.[9]

[5] J. A. Moerenhout: *Voyages aux îles du Grand Océan*, Vol. II (Paris, 1837), pp. 480–2, 513–14.
[6] Ibid., p. 481.
[7] Moerenhout: op. cit., p. 502.
[8] Mühlmann: op. cit., pp. 224–5.
[9] Moerenhout: op. cit., pp. 503, 515.

Queen Pomare and King Tapoa of Tahaa,[1] who sought the restoration of pagan traditions, gave full support to the march of the so-called "heretics" against the missions. As long as this struggle lasted, the cult remained vigorous and lively, but when France and England went to war against each other for control of the missions, the pagan-Christian conflict was relegated to a secondary role. The British emerged victorious, and all non-Protestant missions were expelled;[2] and the Mamaia cult, which had sided with the French Catholics, was abolished.

When one considers the repressive measures enforced by the Christian missions, day after day from 1797 to 1828, in an effort to erase paganism, and the brutal wiping out of the Arioi people, one realizes that the Mamaia cult was the welling up of frustrations and anger long repressed but not extinguished. The Mamaia cult has many elements in common with the messianic movements of Melanesia and other places: collective trances, prophetic messages heralding the expulsion of the whites, belief in the return of the dead and the coming of a new era.[3] It also has two specific aspects not found in Melanesia: a deep political bitterness against the whites almost inevitably bound to lead to strife; and the identification of pagan deities with God and the saints of Christianity. The cult's political bitterness and urge to fight are derived from the strong military structure of Polynesian society,[4] which is governed by a disciplined hierarchy always ready for action and in constant training and practice in the arts of war.

In the Mamaia cult, the identification of the god Oro with Christ and the revival of popular pagan practices fitted into a religious framework in which the priesthood played a leading

[1] Ibid., pp. 332–41. The prophet-chiefs of the Mamaia, in the war, were Tavarii, Tutuai, and Vaipai (p. 337).
[2] Mühlmann: op. cit., p. 235.
[3] Ibid., pp. 194, 213.
[4] Ibid., p. 242.

241

role. The structure of Polynesian theology, influenced by the secular caste system, had one deity ruling the others somewhat like a secular king, and so provided an ideal vehicle for carrying Judeo-Christian monotheistic concepts into the traditional religion. But the Christian elements became paganized, rather than the reverse. In Melanesia, on the other hand, the absence of a traditional religious hierarchy barred the acceptance of the Christian Trinity and of a hierarchy of angels and saints. These cults also looked to the returning dead for salvation, whereas the Polynesian cults turn to Christ as the Savior expected to return to earth to redeem them.

According to Dr. Moerenhout, the way of life and the behavior of the Mamaia followers were devoid of morality,[5] even though their prophets claimed to be guided by Jesus Christ, St. John, and St. Paul, and their prophetess by the Virgin Mary. Actually, the faithful considered themselves to be true Christians and were certain that paradise awaited them. They prayed as Christians and read the Bible,[6] and regarded Jesus as the Savior who would annihilate their enemies and chase the British from their land.[7] However, in the background of their Christian belief stood the pagan god, Oro, god of the Arioi people, who commanded licentious rituals. The paradise expected by the Mamaia was a replica of the Arioi paradise, replete with sensual and earthly rewards.[8] From the Old Testament the Mamaia drew elements useful to their own ends. Solomon's polygamy, for instance, justified their attachment to this practice despite the vehement ef-

[5] An example of dynastic conflict is furnished by the war waged by Tati, Christian king of Papara, against the Mamaia and the pagan supporters of the pagan Queen Pomare of Tahiti. Moerenhout: Vol I, pp. 332–41.
[6] Moerenhout: Vol. II, p. 504.
[7] Mühlmann: op. cit., p. 239.
[8] Moerenhout: op. cit.; Lanternari: La grande festa, chapter 5.

forts of the missions to put an end to it. The myth of the god Oro, divine son of Taaroa, who comes to earth and then returns to heaven to intercede for all men with his father, found its reflection in Jesus Christ, a fact which was so well exploited that the pagan element engulfed the Christian. W. E. Mühlmann describes Mamaia as a replica of the cult of Arioi, and as a final effort on the part of the natives to bring the power of their traditions to bear on the teachings of the missionaries with sufficient force to crush them.[9] The restoration of traditional religious rituals was ostensibly the purpose of the Mamaia cult, but its true objective was to expel the whites.[1] Its religious leaders, while preaching and making prophecies, were also instigating the war with the British which lasted from 1830 to 1836.

In Hawaii, American Protestantism had been very successful in introducing Christianity to the natives, largely because of the early conversion of such royal personages as Kaahumanu and Kinau, who belonged to the powerful Kamehameha dynasty.[2] In 1827, however, when the struggle between Britain and the United States became further embittered by the arrival of the Jesuit missionaries, the roots of paganism—which had not died out—suddenly produced new growth, in the form of native religious movements which combined paganism with Christianity.

Outstanding among them is the Hapu cult, founded in 1825 by a prophetess of that name. She announced that the end of the world would come for all who had not embraced her doctrine and who did not worship Jehovah and Jesus. At her death the natives canonized her and made her the third person

[9] Mühlmann: op. cit., pp. 238, 243.
[1] Ibid., p. 243.
[2] Koskinen: op. cit., p. 43.

of their trinity, composed of Jehovah, Jesus, and Hapu. Her relics were worshipped, and her body, dressed like a pagan idol, was laid in the House of Refuge,[3] which was a sanctuary and a place of refuge for all warriors, in accordance with Hawaiian tradition.[4] While awaiting the end of the world, Hapu's followers built her a temple and, giving up all other forms of work, gathered there to worship their new trinity. When the end of the world failed to occur, the cult declined and the temple was burned to the ground by the missionaries.[5] But the anti-Christian spirit which Hapu had inspired did not die, despite the outward conversion to Protestantism of many natives and their leaders.

The introduction of Roman Catholic liturgy and doctrine among the populations eventually stimulated a revival of interest in pagan rituals. The natives regarded fasting, the cult of images, the worship of relics, alimentary proscriptions, and other Jesuit commands as the continuation of traditional pagan practices to which they had long been accustomed.[6] At the same time, the efforts of the Protestant missions to discredit and ridicule Roman Catholicism[7] produced an alliance between pagans and Roman Catholics in opposition to the Protestants,[8] an alliance not unlike that formed in Tahiti between the Mamaia sect and the French missions to combat the English. This curious alignment came to light in 1827, when Boki, native governor of Cahu, pursuing his political ends, became the leader of a formidable anti-Protestant and antimonarchist conspiracy. Governor Boki, formerly a Protestant and now a

[3] J. J. Jarves: *History of the Hawaiian or Sandwich Islands* (London, 1843), p. 340.
[4] Ibid., p. 53.
[5] Ibid., p. 240.
[6] Ibid., pp. 255–6.
[7] Ibid., pp. 257–8.
[8] Koskinen: op. cit., pp. 257–8.

Papist, drew to his side the Roman Catholics and the pagan revivalists,[9] against Queen Kaahumanu of Hawaii and the young king, her son. A carefully planned uprising did not materialize, owing to the sudden death of Boki, but the revived paganism showed its strength whenever the antipagan laws were relaxed, as they were in 1833, by order of King Kauikeauli. Disorders broke out at that time which led to killings and to the destruction of churches.[1] The Roman Catholics rejoiced, reading into the riots an anti-Protestant attitude which was "flattering to them."[2]

It is interesting to note the importance attributed in the Hapu cult to Jehovah as well as to Jesus Christ. Local polytheism provided precedents for the joint worship of Jehovah and Jesus: the old beliefs gave equal status to Father Lono, the supreme being, creator of all things, and to Kane, or Tane, originator of all cultivated plants, including the invaluable taro roots.[3] The emphasis on Jehovah is also due in part to Protestant insistence on the use of the Old Testament, based on the assumption that much of the content of Christian doctrine was beyond the grasp of the natives. Mosaic law, the ten commandments, the theocratic pattern of the Judaic kingdom, and the battles waged against paganism by the faithful of Jehovah seemed more relevant to the native tradition than many ideas and facts found in the New Testament.[4] Eventually, however, the belief in Jehovah and in the "Chosen People" was used by the aborigines, not as part of a doctrine to which they had become converted, but as an

[9] Jarves: op. cit., pp. 248, 259.
[1] Ibid., pp. 272-5.
[2] Ibid., p. 276.
[3] Handy: "Polynesian religion," p. 303; "Perspectives in Polynesian religion," *J.P.S.*, XLIX, 3 (1940) p. 320.
[4] Koskinen: op. cit., p. 55.

instrument with which to defend their own right to freedom and self-determination.

In Samoa a pagan-Christian cult was established in 1863 by a local preacher named Sio-vili, who prophesied the end of the world and the advent of a Messiah called Sisu Alaisa, a native adaptation of the name of Jesus Christ.[5] Like the Christian missionaries, the promoters of this sect believed in a single God, Lord of the Universe, and in His Son (Sisu Alaisa); but they also restored polygamy and the ritual dances abolished by Christian rule, and established independent religious feasts of their own. A healing prophetess who worked with Sio-vili announced the coming of Sisu Alaisa on the crest of a wave, bringing from heaven all the food that the natives needed. Huge crowds of natives, having given up their jobs because the Messiah would take care of them, and feasting on roasted pig and taro root, rushed to the shore to see the event. Despite disillusionment, the cult survived.[6] Samoa's pagan tradition has a supreme deity named Tangaloa, creator of mankind and of all the world,[7] and also a god who died and was mourned with special rites.[8] As we have said, the pagan-Christian cult of Sio-vili is based on belief in God the Father and in His Son Sisu Alaisa, who died and was to be mourned and remembered with appropriate rituals. Thus two religious beliefs, separated by different ages of history, had merged to meet the challenge of a new age.

[5] W. T. Pritchard: *Polynesian Reminiscences* (London, 1866), p. 206.

[6] Pritchard: op. cit., pp. 205-7. The cult of Sio-vili is founded, like others of its kind, on the "possession" of the adepts, who, through the work of the spirit of Jehovah or of Jesus Christ, go into convulsions. The movement, through the past experience of its founder, is linked with the Mamaia cult. J. D. Freeman: "The Joe Gimlet, or Siovili cult," in *Anthropology in the South Seas*, ed. Freeman and Geddes (New Plymouth, 1959).

[7] Pritchard: op. cit., p. 112.

[8] G. Turner: *Samoa* (London, 1884), p. 21.

246

A considerable number of religious movements combining pagan and Christian elements developed in the Tuamotu Archipelago (French East Polynesia), largely as local reactions to both Roman Catholic and Protestant evangelism, as well as to American, British, and French missionaries. One such sect, known as Kanito or Sanito, emerged in 1884, inspired by the Latter-day Saints—the native words *kanito* or *sanito* are corruptions of the word "saint."[9] The sect appears to have brought about a great revival of paganism in many local forms.[1] Radiating widely into the Makatea, Ragiroa, and Anaa islands, and, in fact, throughout French Polynesia,[2] the Kanito followers spread many traditional pagan beliefs. To these they added two new tenets: *pahapa*, that the sins of the fathers are visited on their children; and *kaitipa*, that the spirits of the dead return to taunt the living.[3] The followers of Kanito led licentious lives and performed obscene dance rituals,[4] which they claimed were interpretations of the essential concepts of Judaism, Christianity, and paganism.[5] From the fragmentary information available about the many pagan Christian cults which developed in the Tuamotu Islands in the second half of the nineteenth century, it seems reasonable to assume that one of the most popular was the "Hissers," devoted almost exclusively to the evocation of the dead. During the rites the priest, who had magical powers, remained seated in silence until the worshippers chose to break into song and hiss loudly to call the departed. Soft hissing sounds responded from the roof of the place of worship, and were

[9] B. Danielsson: *Work and Life on Raroia* (Stockholm, 1955), p. 100. For the Kanito or Sanito cult in general, see Caillot: op. cit., pp. 33, 34, 35 ff.
[1] Caillot: op. cit., p. 53.
[2] Danielsson: op. cit., p. 100.
[3] Caillot: op. cit., p. 39.
[4] Ibid., pp. 33, 34, 40.
[5] Ibid., p. 38.

taken to be the voice of the dead, which the priests, now in a trance, interpreted for the faithful.[6]

Other Tuamotu cults were the Mamoe (which means sheep), similar to Mamaia on the nearby Society Islands, and the Israelites.[7] The Israelites is significant when related to the vast array of beliefs, stemming from the Old Testament and disregarding the New, which spread through Polynesia after the arrival of the missionaries. By emphasizing the theological and doctrinal concepts of the Old Testament, the Protestant missionaries enabled the natives to link their traditions with the Scriptures, and this fusion eventually resulted in the formation of a new cult.

Probably the most important religious movement in New Zealand is the Hau-hau, which sparked the Maori war against the missions. Heavily weighted with Hebrew elements, this cult contributed to the self-identification of the Polynesians with the "Chosen People of Israel."

Hau-hau was the name originally given by the white man to a cult founded in 1826 by Te-Ua, who called it Pai-marire, meaning "good and merciful."[8] *Rongo-pai-marire* means "the good news of peace"—proclaimed by the prophet, who stressed the peace-loving and internationalist character and purpose of the movement. In spite of his declarations, however, the cult had a history of violence, cruelty, and warfare. One of the worst phases of the British colonial war, which caused almost continuous bloodshed in this area from 1860 to 1870,

[6] R. L. Stevenson: *In the South Seas*, Vol. I (Leipzig, 1901), pp. 274-5.

[7] Caillot: op. cit., p. 38.

[8] The final line in the songs, *rire-rire, hau-hau*, was a supplication for mercy (*rire*) to God, in a form which might be a transliteration of *miserere mei*. For this, see R. W. Winks: "The Doctrine of Hauhauism," *J.P.S.*, LXII, 3 (1953), pp. 214, 218, 219. Hau signifies "wind" and refers to the use of the wind by Jehovah to send his messages to man from the sacred *niu* pole (ibid., pp. 200-2).

is linked to the growth of the Hau-hau, which emerged with full force around 1865.[9] For some time prior to 1860, the British had been giving increasing support to the demands of the white farmers for more and better land. Around 1860, therefore, the Maori concluded that the British had no intention of honoring their agreements and were about to seize all native property.[1]

Father Felice Vaggioli, an Italian historian who lived in New Zealand at the time, described the situation just before violence broke out between the British and the natives, as follows:

By 1860, the Maori had had to convince themselves that the colonial administration, now lined up against them, was backing the unjust demands of the white farmers with its guns, and was determined to have its way or destroy the native populations. In the face of this unexpected realization, the Maori developed a mortal hate of the British and took up arms to defend their rights. . . . After four years of

[9] The history of the Hau-hau movement is in F. Vaggioli: *Storia della Nuova Zelanda* (Parma, 1896), Vol. II, pp. 356–457. The religious aspects of the movement are considered in Winks: op. cit., pp. 199–236. A brief historical summary is found in W. Greenwood: "The Upraised Hand," *J.P.S.*, LI, 1 (1942), pp. 1–28. See also the preface by J. Andersen, pp. i–v. In this admirable work, light is shed, without prejudice and with great acumen, on the problems inherent in the cultural contact, on the need to justify in a positive way the aboriginal institutions, without bias or aspersions, while at the same time condemning British colonial policy (pp. 1–80). The Ringa-tu is presented here, for the first time firsthand, as a cult quite different and apart from the Hau-hau, although linked to it by historical circumstances. I have unfortunately not had access to the following works: S. B. Babbage: *Hauhauism* (Dunedin, New Zealand, 1938); F. M. Keesing: *Modern Samoa* (London, 1934), regarding a Mau cult in Samoa; I. L. G. Sutherland: *The Maori People Today* (Wellington, 1940); F. Keesing: *The South Seas in the Modern World* (New York, 1941).

[1] Vaggioli: Vol. II, pp. 310–11. The Treaty of Waitangi, up to that time, had regulated relations between the British and the natives.

fierce fighting, they were ejected by force from their own peaceful homes, while their forts, huts, and villages were burned to the ground, their cemeteries desecrated and thousands among them allowed to perish of starvation, cold, and hardships while the survivors were abandoned to their miserable fate. . . . The natives also saw that the British forces displayed no religion, no conscience, and no morals. For forty years, the Protestant teachers had been saying that Protestantism was a religion of love, that all those who professed it were loved and respected, that all who embraced it would be protected and their rights preserved inviolate forever, and that they would receive their share of prosperity and wealth.[2]

The Maoris, who had accepted Christianity in large numbers, repudiated the faith en masse in 1864, and geared themselves to take revenge on the British forces and on the missionaries. The new Hau-hau movement burst onto the scene at this point, going swiftly into action against certain British soldiers who, led by a Captain Lloyd, had raided a Maori cornfield in the area of Taranaki. The natives defeated the raiders, killed many, and forced the others to flee. The swiftness and violence of Hau-hau action had strong motivation. A month earlier, the body of a great Maori chief, killed by the British, had been mutilated with the consent of the authorities, to allow a British doctor to preserve certain tattooed portions of the skin. It was in the religious tradition of the Maoris that any offense perpetrated against a great chief called for a price of blood (*utu*).[3] The occasion for revenge was furnished by the soldiers' raid on the cornfield. The skulls of the British killed in the affray were made into ritual trophies and used in the native ceremonies. The skull of

[2] Vaggioli: op. cit., p. 357.
[3] J. Andersen, in Greenwood: op. cit., pp. 1–11.

Captain Lloyd was carried from tribe to tribe and became the symbol of a covenant between God and the Hau-hau sect, from which the prophet Te-Ua derived ever-increasing inspiration and prestige.[4] By their sudden return to ancient usages, the natives, though converted to Christianity, had made it clear that the purpose of the new cult, the Hau-hau, was the full restoration of their religious traditions.[5]

Te-Ua, once the priest of a native Maori cult, later a convert to the Anglican faith, and now the prophet and leader of Hau-hau, informed his followers that the angel Gabriel had taught him the rituals of the new religion and that they were now to be carried out. The Hau-hau ceremonies took place around a pole called *niu*, which was regarded as a divine symbol, a beacon to the faithful and an instrument of communication with God.[6] Sacred dances and special songs called *karakia* and *waiata* were created upon instructions from the prophet—the words used in the ritual singing being an extraordinary jumble of Hebrew, English, German, Greek, and Italian, the languages of Western culture. Rhythmic dancing in this, as in many native rituals in other parts of the world, was carried to a fever pitch, until the faithful fell prey to collective seizures and trances.[7] The *niu* ritual was performed each morning, every day, for the purpose of producing a state of ecstasy in the participants. Three long colorful banners, displaying white crosses similar to those on the British flag and on the mission banners, hung from the top of the sacred pole. The worshippers marched around the pole, with increasing speed, bending over as they paced, so that the edges of the banners might touch their heads and shoulders, for it

[4] Greenwood: op. cit., p. 8.
[5] Vaggioli: Vol. II, pp. 358–60, 363.
[6] Winks: op. cit., p. 211.
[7] Ibid.; Greenwood: op. cit., p. 13; Vaggioli: Vol. II, p. 360; P. H. Buck: *The Coming of the Maori* (Wellington, 1952), p. 223.

was from this contact that the emanation of the power of Jehovah reached them. The pole, or *niu*, and the wind spirits, *hau*, were the symbols of two pagan deities, Riki and Ruru, the god of war and the tutelar divinity of the founder, respectively; and their effigies were displayed high on the banner. During the initiation, the postulants sat at the foot of the pole, keeping their eyes fixed on the top of it, in a posture which demanded prolonged physical and mental effort. Because of the strain, combined with the heat of the day, the shouting of the worshippers, and the furious pace of the dancers going round and round, the candidates for initiation were hypnotized; their bodies were then seized by the others and tossed repeatedly into the air until they became unconscious. As soon as they recovered, they were considered initiated into the cult, and were pushed summarily into the march.[8]

The supreme deity of the cult, although called Jehovah, was a composite of Tane, a pagan deity, and the God of the Jews.[9] From the earliest times, the Maoris had worshipped a Great Creator, named Tane, who had assigned to the sun and to the stars their special places in the celestial orbit and, from the union of Earth and Sky, had made the first man, called Tiki. Tane had then created the first woman from a piece of clay, to which he had given life from his own divine breath.[1]

Jehovah represents the Maoris' belief that they are descended from the Tribes of Judah. Te-Ua, who regarded himself as the new Moses, was also called Tiu, meaning Jew.[2] He had declared that the Maoris were the new "Chosen People of God," that New Zealand was the new land of Canaan, and that Jehovah, the Supreme Being, would speak to them from

[8] Winks: op. cit., p. 209.
[9] Vaggioli: op. cit., pp. 361–2, 363.
[1] Buck (Te Rangi Hiroa): *Les migrations des Polynésiens* (Paris, 1952), pp. 243–5.
[2] Vaggioli: Vol. II, p. 360.

the top of the *niu* pole, as he had spoken to Moses on the Biblical Mount.[3] Maoris and Jews, said Te-Ua, were children of the same father; and just as the Jews were forbidden to communicate with the gentiles, so the Maoris could have no contact with the *paheka* (British) who had imposed their yoke on the native people, even as the Egyptians had made slaves of the Jews.[4] The day will come, said the prophet, when all the *paheka* will be cast out of New Zealand, thereby putting an end to the present world and ushering in the millennium. Then, he added, the Maori dead will rise again and the Jews will come to New Zealand to form with us a single people and to build a new life for all mankind.[5] The history of the Jewish people, taught by the missionaries as a model of religious strength and endurance, was learned by the natives as a model of political action for modern times. The connection was made even clearer when a missionary, the Reverend Thomas West, stated that certain somatic traits justified the assumption that Polynesians and Jews were of the same racial stock.[6] The identification of the Maoris with the Jews was accepted by the natives as an established fact, as is shown by the following tragic episode. In 1865 the Reverend C. S. Volkner, an Anglican priest, was sailing into the harbor on a British ship, when the rumor spread among the Hau-hau followers that he was a spy. The Hau-hau assaulted the vessel and captured the crew and the clergyman. Dr. Volkner was hanged and the crew imprisoned, with the sole exception of Captain Levy, who, being a Jew, was set free. "The God of the Hau-hau," said the followers of the cult, "protects his

[3] Ibid., pp. 360-1.
[4] Ibid., pp. 358, 363.
[5] Ibid., pp. 363, 365.
[6] Thomas West: *Ten Years in South Central Polynesia* (London, 1865), p. 253. See also, for the same prejudice, H. Nevermann: "Götter der Südsee," *Die Religion der Polynesier* (Stuttgart, 1947), p. 56.

Chosen People";[7] and whereas any white was regarded as an enemy, unlimited haven and hospitality were offered to a Jew. In the rituals, the Maori believed, the divine power of Jehovah was transmitted to them from the *niu* pole; and they exalted the Jewish God because they knew that He would protect the Hau-hau against the armies of the *paheka*.[8]

The Christian elements absorbed by the cult were the cross to symbolize the crucifixion of the natives[9] at the hands of the whites, and baptism, which was actually a purificatory bath traditionally used to consecrate warriors before they went into battle. Native warrior bands were called "the Twelve," regardless of their number, in deference to the Biblical significance of this number, Jacob having had twelve sons and the Apostles having been twelve. The first twelve men of each fighting unit were solemnly consecrated to God by placing one foot in the river while the priest sprinkled their body with water,[1] after which they were believed to be forever under divine protection.[2]

The Hau-hau is basically a combative, militant movement; each follower accepts the sacred duty of fighting the *paheka* unto death. The march and the rituals around the *niu* represent

[7] Vaggioli: Vol. II, pp. 372-3; Greenwood: op. cit., p. 14-15; Koskinen: op. cit., p. 101. The idea was widespread among the Maoris that they represented one of the Lost Tribes of Israel; the Mormons contributed to this notion. See Winks: op. cit., p. 231.

[8] Winks: op. cit., pp. 228, 232.

[9] Ibid., p. 207.

[1] Ibid., p. 212.

[2] The divining test of the "shield" was performed by the high priest. He stood motionless and erect in a state of trance in the center of a circle of adepts of the cult, balanced his shield horizontally between the thumbs and forefingers of both hands, and invoked Uenuko, god of war. While by mediumistic power the shield rotated very slowly, the adepts waited in complete silence. Wherever the point of the shield stopped, the person nearest to it was one of the chosen. This was repeated twelve times. (Winks: op. cit., pp. 211-12). Other warriors were then added to this select group without the shield test.

the holy war and assure the fighters of God's presence on the battlefield. When the prophet Te-Ua was informed of the defeat of the Maoris at Taranaki, where more than fifty men, including Chief Hepanaia, had been killed, he assured his followers that these men had been killed because their own faith in victory had not been strong enough.[3] And his followers believed him. When the faithful march around the pole they raise their arms to the sky, crying: *"Hapa-hapa, Pai-marire hau-hau,"* which means: "May they [the enemy bullets] pass us by, good and merciful lord." *Hapa-hapa!*[4] was the cry with which they went into battle, and their fighting spirit was so completely at one with their religious faith that they believed spiritual victory had been achieved even when the secular reality was a resounding military defeat. An episode which attests to this concerns the lone survivor of a defeated Maori regiment who walked toward the British encampment in order to reach the sacred *niu*, now in the white man's hands, and to perform his rituals at the foot of it. Caught by the British as he marched with eyes staring at the top of the pole, he surrendered to his captors, saying: "I have returned among you so that you may be turned to stone." While the commanding officer shouted "Fire!" to the squad, the Hau-hau yelled *"Hau-hau Pai-marire"* as he fell.[5] The sacrifice made by countless Maoris testifies not merely to their military valor but also, and above all else, to their religious fervor for a cause for which they were ready to give their life.

The only important element of Hau-hau belief unrelated to its pagan origin is the belief in the end of the world and in the regeneration of life, which, to the natives, signifies liberation from the rule of the white man. The end of the world, in Hau-

[3] Greenwood: op. cit., pp. 9–10.
[4] Winks: op. cit., p. 228.
[5] Ibid., p. 203.

hau terms, is not a terrifying and final cataclysm, but only the expulsion of the last Britisher—after which, in an atmosphere of peace, the dead will rise again and the prophet Te-Ua will appear in the guise of Moses[6] or of Jesus Christ.

By the year 1865 the British had organized themselves to fight the religious leaders and the fanatical followers of Hau-hau, laying traps for them or forcing them back into the jungle. Although often beaten, the natives always sprang back,[7] diminished in numbers but not in fanaticism. Finally, Te-Ua surrendered to the British, but under a succession of other leaders the cult continued until 1892. The last of the leaders was Te-Whiti,[8] a mystic who kept alive the native's hope of independence, and who guided their efforts despite the fact that he was arrested several times during the ten years of his leadership. Those who preceded him were Taikomako, Rua-Kenana, Te-Kooti—the founder of the Ringa-tu move-ment—and Kereopa. A price was put on Te-Kooti's head, but he was never captured; Kereopa was betrayed by one of his followers and executed by the British in 1872. With his death, the fight between the Hau-hau and the whites came to an end.

The new movement initiated by Te-Kooti was a Christian version of the Hau-hau. It was called Ringa-tu, which means "raised hands," from the traditional religious custom of the Maori, who always raise their hands in prayer. Te-Kooti sought to renovate the Hau-hau by giving it much higher religious and moral standards; and although he started the new cult in the thick of the fighting against the British, the movement did not attain full development until the war was over and the process of acculturation had begun to make

[6] Vaggioli: Vol. II, pp. 262; Winks: op. cit., p. 232.
[7] Vaggioli: op. cit., pp. 378 ff., 383, 390.
[8] Ibid., pp. 506–34; Greenwood: op. cit., p. 66.

headway.[9] Te-Kooti Rikirangi was an inconspicuous Maori who sided with the British in the battle of Waerenga-a-hika, in which Poverty Bay was wrested from the Hau-hau fighters. Then Te-Kooti found himself accused of collusion with Hau-hau followers, imprisoned, and deported to the remote Chatham Islands, without benefit of trial or proof of guilt. It was said at the time that the injustice of the British had created a leader[1] who otherwise might never have come to the fore. In prison Te-Kooti studied the Bible, read it aloud to his fellow prisoners who were Hau-hau followers, and eventually conceived a new religious movement based on ideas taken from the Scriptures. It was also during their imprisonment that the Hau-hau followers first identified themselves with the Jews of the Captivity and New Zealand with Zion. Shortly after Te-Kooti had predicted that an ark would be sent by God to liberate them, a British freighter, the *Rifleman*, came into the port of Wharekauri (1868), and the Hau-hau prisoners were put to work unloading the cargo. The prophet made a plan of escape, which succeeded without a hitch. The Hau-hau seized the ship and Te-Kooti piloted her into Poverty Bay.

Back among his people, Te-Kooti organized a new force and launched the victorious campaign against the British which became known as the "massacre of Poverty." Throughout the fighting he found time to instruct his followers in the meaning of the Bible, using his own translation of the texts.[2] The Ringa-tu cult is a native interpretation of Christianity inspired by Te-Kooti's personal experience in living through certain

[9] H. B. Hawthorn: "The Maori: a study in acculturation," *Amer. Anthr. Assoc. Memoirs*, XLVI, 2 (1944), pp. 16–20.

[1] Greenwood: op. cit., pp. 19–20.

[2] Greenwood: op. cit., pp. 21–5. A price was put on Te-Kooti's head, but it was discontinued in 1883, after fifteen years of struggle and the prophet's preaching. Relations with the government were normal after that, with one exception: he was arrested once because of a projected visit to Poverty Bay to commemorate the "massacre." Ibid., p. 74.

Biblical events. Both in trance and in a fully conscious state, the prophet claimed to have lived through the exile and captivity of the Jews in Egypt, their liberation and exodus under the leadership of Moses, and their return to the land of Canaan after fighting many enemies. Remembering how Moses, after crossing the Red Sea, had had to fight the inroads which paganism had made among his people, and how he revived their faith in the one God by prophesying the coming of the Messiah, Te-Kooti, as soon as he had escaped from prison, set about reforming the fanatical Hau-hau cult and turning it toward Christianity. He prophesied the coming of a second Messiah, who would perfect the cults he was then establishing.[3] At Te-Kooti's death in 1893, the faithful of Ringa-tu organized a regular church, which held its first general assembly in 1938 to elect a poutikanga (meaning "sustainer"), a general secretary, and an executive committee. From that time on, its officers have been elected regularly every two years.[4]

Members of the Ringa-tu meet for worship every Saturday, and on every twelfth day of the month. They venerate the number twelve, as did the Hau-hau. They hold a great religious festival to mark the two New Years of pagan origin, which fall, respectively, on the first of January and the first of July, and also celebrate the first day of June, preceding the planting of the crops, and the first of November at harvest time. The latter is a Thanksgiving festival, whereas in June the emphasis

[3] Greenwood: op. cit., pp. 59–60, 69–71.

[4] Greenwood: op. cit., pp. 49–52. The poutikanga in power in 1953 was Paora Taramea, elected in 1938 (Winks: op. cit., p. 235). The 1936 census showed 500 Ringa-tu as compared with 500 Hau-hau (Greenwood. op. cit., p. 78). Although Te-Kooti forbade his followers to have any contact with the missionaries (whether Anglican, Roman Catholic, or any other), he considered the Anglican church closely related to the Ringa-tu church and, in substance, believed that it was possible to move from one to the other (Greenwood: op. cit., p. 67). In fact, the Anglican church is the strongest denomination in New Zealand (ibid., p. 78).

is placed on invoking the blessings of God upon the new seed.[5]
Followers come from near and far to the traditional native
meeting house, for they do not have a special place of worship.
The ritual consists mainly in the responsive reading of passages from Scripture, the congregation being led by the
Tuhunga (priest), and in the recitation of prayers for the sick,
at the end of which the faithful partake of a ceremonial meal
together.[6] Most of the prayers are addressed to God the
Father, rather than to Jesus Christ, and the day of rest and
worship is Saturday rather than Sunday, because of Polynesian
attachment to Judaism rather than to Christian traditions.
Te-Kooti predicted a number of events which actually occurred during his lifetime or shortly thereafter, but he also
prophesied the coming of the Messiah, who would rise with
the Eastern Star and would complete the work which he
himself had started among the Maoris.[7] In one of Te-Kooti's
prophecies we find these words, which he claimed to have
learned in a trance: "This is my beloved Son, follow him!"[8]
This would indicate his acceptance of Christian belief, even
though his emphasis was on the Old Testament.

The messianic movements of Polynesia have many mythical
elements in common with cults flourishing in Melanesia, such
as the end of the world and its regeneration, and the resurrection of the dead, as well as the major objective, common to all
messianic movements among primitive peoples, which is
independence from foreign rule. Native resistance to the
cultural influence of the West is typical of agrarian populations
because their society is rooted in the place from which they
derive a livelihood. Despite the similarities, stemming chiefly

[5] Greenwood: op. cit., p. 61.
[6] Ibid., pp. 41–8, 56.
[7] Ibid., pp. 69–71, 74.
[8] Ibid., pp. 72, 75.

from the agrarian nature of both the Melanesian and the Polynesian economy, Polynesian cults contain elements which are exclusively their own. For instance, the Melanesian cults do not have a hierarchy of deities, because there is no ecclesiastical caste or hierarchy in their history. Polynesian cults, on the other hand, have a theological hierarchy leading to the Supreme Deity, which reflects the structure of the ecclesiastical hierarchy as well as the social and political aristocracy, which is both powerful and hereditary. The strength of the castes comes from the nature of Polynesian economy. Based on an annual excess of yield from the soil, it has tended to build up wealth, ownership of land, and power. The belligerent aspects often manifested in the Polynesian cults are absent in Melanesia, which does not possess the highly developed military class typical of Polynesian society. This military group was originally identified with the aristocracy and was active in countless feuds and rivalries between native dynasties and families.

A survey of religious movements in Polynesia reveals three clearly defined stages of development, as follows:

1. The first is based on belief in the regeneration of the world, the resurrection of the dead, and cultural resistance to the inroads of the West, all of which are common to most native religious movements in other parts of the world.

2. The second, and more recent, establishes new deities, part pagan and part Biblical; advocates organized military resistance; and, in the end, instigates total war against the churches and governments of the West. This stage is found only in Polynesia, which has a military class and a well-developed economy that provides security for the entire year.

3. The third, and most recent, stage dates back to the first contacts between natives and missionaries in the past century,

and to the seizure of land by the whites, which also occurred at that time. In this phase, religious movements tend to identify native society with the Israelites, but they also accept Christ as a member of the divine hierarchy.

Nearly all rituals used in the first and second phases of development are taken from the great Polynesian Feast of the New Year, including the worship of the dead, belief in their return, expectation of the millennium, and acceptance of military elements.[9] In the traditional Feast of the New Year, the participants engage in ritual combat to signify their readiness to protect the ancient customs, but in the new messianic cults this combative rite takes on a specific and timely significance: symbolically, or in actual fact, it is directed against the presence of the white man, whose intent, they know, is to destroy the native culture. When battle flares out, the religious forces, once quiet and introspective, become violent and throw themselves into the struggle for the protection of their cultural, religious, and political right to independence.

Polynesia, as well as Melanesia and Australia, is evidence that monotheism cannot be transplanted and naturalized in a primitive culture which lacks adequate economic and social development. Even when Jehovah and Jesus are accepted, we find them merged with mythical figures of pagan tradition, leading inevitably to a "paganization" of Judeo-Christian monotheism. Strong polytheism seems to prevail chiefly in societies that have a well-organized hierarchical structure, an advanced form of agriculture, and sound economic foundations.[1] But, whatever the society and whatever the original traditions, nowhere does one find a pagan religion suddenly

---

[9] For this section, see Lanternari: *La grande festa*, Part II.

[1] For the relation between polytheism and the hierarchical societies, see Lanternari: "Conclusions," in *La grande festa*.

yielding to the impact of the white man or supinely accepting his doctrines. On the contrary, what is evident everywhere is a chain of new cults and religious movements, developing one from the other, in reaction to the cultural impact of the West. Each of the "new" cults conveys, with greater or lesser effect, the concept of salvation and regeneration inherent in pagan tradition and now coupled with a modern, vigorous affirmation of the peoples' striving for independence and freedom.

CHAPTER

VII

MESSIANIC MOVEMENTS IN
ASIA AND INDONESIA

INDONESIA

D URING World War II Indonesia was shaken by a
series of political, military, and social upheavals which had a
profound effect on the native populations of the islands. The
capitulation of the Dutch, the Japanese occupation, the proclamation of the Indonesian Republic by the occupying power,
and the reoccupation of the country by the Dutch aroused
widespread ferment among the people. Long before any organized political or social movement had capitalized on these
conditions, the popular awareness of potential crises was manifested in the emergence of new religious cults, which paved
the way for forthcoming secular reforms.

Throughout the war years, the Indonesians had been subjected to the pressures of two opposing ideological drives:
one was fostered by a relatively small group of Indonesian
intellectuals, working toward national independence, who
promoted a plan for emancipation under cover of Japanese

occupation; the other was a campaign of antiwhite and anti-Dutch propaganda carried on by the Japanese, which actually strengthened Indonesian nationalism, even though this was not Japan's intent. The Japanese slogan "Asia for the Asians" was also immensely effective, although what the Japanese really meant was "Asia for Japan." Under the occupation, there had been considerable military training. The Indonesians had been comparing Oriental successes with Western failures, and a republic, fictitious though it may have been, had come into being, thus creating an illusion of Indonesian sovereignty. When the Japanese capitulated and the Dutch eventually returned, the Indonesians were dismayed. And they were soon confronted by a new problem. Their traditions had become a symbol of the independence they sought, but were no longer capable of meeting their needs: the pressure of outside events beyond their control was making it imperative that reforms and changes be instituted in order to permit Indonesia to borrow all it needed from the Western world. Neither Japanese nor Dutch rule had solved this problem, and many local attempts at reform degenerated into chaotic confusion, out of which there emerged several religious prophets whose messages combined native tradition with certain messianic ideas of Islam. The ensuing tensions and conflicts transformed popular sentiment into a tangle of uncertainties and frustrations.

In Sumatra and Java, for example, the population was in a strange state of anxious expectation. Yet nobody seemed to know what was expected,[1] and the situation was ripe for the acceptance of prophetic messages and messianic movements of every kind. Here and there groups of natives, spurred by their religious leaders, were seen racing through cities, towns, and villages—greatly agitated but without apparent purpose.

[1] P. M. van Wullften Palthe: *Psychological Aspects of the Indonesian Problem* (Leiden, 1949), pp. 1-2.

Many who saw them believed that the advent of the Mahdi, or Messiah, was at hand, because Islamic prophecy had foretold that the Mahdi would be preceded by mass movements and popular agitation.[2] Fed and crystallized by an ever-growing antipathy for the Dutch,[3] these movements finally assumed political form and served to bring about the revolution of 1945–49.

In Java, the messianic message of Islam came in the guise of two cults called Hizbul Waton and Sabillera. Both were taken up chiefly by fanatics under the guidance of mystics, who eventually cast in their lot with the armies of the Indonesian Republic, attacking European and Chinese minorities and waging "holy wars" full of violence and cruelty. Between 1949 and 1952, the government of the Republic was often forced to place restraints on the Darul Islam, a religious movement bent on bringing about the fulfillment of an ancient prophecy by establishing a Moslem theocracy based on ideas then being promoted by several Indonesian Mahdis.[4] These cults, rooted in local religious traditions, as their belief in the traditional Mahdi prophecy demonstrates, merely revived an early phase of Islamic messianism antedating all contact with the West.[5] They also revealed a religious and ideological connection between ancient prophecies, slightly reworded to meet new needs, and new prophecies recently launched.

A further illustration of this is provided by the revival of one of Java's oldest prophecies, the Prophecy of Prince Jayabhaya. At some time between 1130 and 1160 this scion

[2] Ibid., p. 6.

[3] Ibid., pp. 9–11.

[4] Van der Kroef: "The Messiah in Indonesia and Melanesia," *Scientific Monthly*, LXXV (1952), p. 162.

[5] For the stratification of cultures in Indonesia and the cultural policy of Holland and of the missions before World War II, see R. Kennedy: "Acculturation and Administration in Indonesia," *Am. Anthr.*, XLV, 2 (1943).

of the House of Kadiri predicted that all of Indonesia would fall under the rule of a yellow race, after which it would attain permanent independence and freedom. These events, he said, would be preceded by a huge crop of rice and wheat that would grow to inordinate height in the fields. When the Japanese occupied the islands, the prophecy was recalled, and the Indonesians looked for independence to follow upon the expulsion of the yellow rulers.[6] Under Dutch rule, an ideology called Ratu adil made headway (the name meant Just and Benevolent Prince) with the promise that the Just Prince would put an end to hard times by restoring the splendors of Indonesia's ancient past. Several prophets appeared thereafter. Calling themselves Ratu adil, they instigated riots and an uprising against the rule of the Netherlands.

In the nineteenth century Islam played a key role in the messianic movements of Java, inspired partly by Moslem mystics from India and partly by a Moslem revival which had occurred just after the Javanese war of 1825–30. The Indian mystics were Kjai Hasan Maulani and Mas Malangjoeda. The leader of the Moslem revival was a Javanese prophet named Prince Diponegoro. In 1842 Maulani founded a part-political, part-religious movement which gained a following in West Java; the population believed his prophecies and set out to await the universal catastrophes that were to precede the liberation of the faithful from foreign rule. The political ferment was such that the Dutch exiled the prophet. A similar fate befell Malangjoeda, whose inflammatory messages had spread rapidly in 1887. Prince Diponegoro, who instigated and led the rebellion known as the War of Java, used his personal prestige and power to restore the moral and religious values of traditional Javanese society. The veneration which grew up around him was such that his memory has

[6] Van der Kroef: op. cit., p. 161.

inspired several recent messianic movements in that area,[7] where he is still spoken of as the "Liberator Prince" and the "Hero of Liberty."

As the nineteenth century ended, the native reaction to changes forced upon village life by the Dutch expressed itself in support of the Saminist cult, a movement based on expectation of the millennium and fraught with social and political implications. Its founder was a peasant named Samin, from Blora, in central Java, who preached against capitalism and advocated an immediate return to rural economy. He also announced the imminent collapse of Dutch rule and the advent of an era of peace and prosperity for the Javanese. He did this with such persuasive arguments that his followers refused to recognize the administrative authority of the Dutch, occupied lands and woods controlled by the administration, and refused to pay taxes or stay on their jobs. Samin was captured and deported; this ended the movement in Java, but the cult survived and grew elsewhere, especially in Bantam.[8]

In Sumatra, several nativist movements were inspired by the activities of a strange group of nomads who raided the countryside, committing thefts of every kind and calling them "chivalry in defense of the people." They took orders from men who were wrapped in legend, two among them being Ronin and Ken Agrok. The Dutch were not able to wipe out this unusual form of banditry, even in the period of the Great Dutch Peace—between 1920 and 1940—when cannibalism, head-hunting, and tribal strife were brought almost completely under control. A study of these robber bands, made by van Wullften Palthe prior to 1940, shows that they

---

[7] Ibid., pp. 161-2.

[8] W. F. Wertheim: *Indonesian Society in Transition* (The Hague), pp. 311-12; Van der Kroef: op. cit., p. 162; G. M. Turnan Kahin: *Nationalism and Revolution in Indonesia* (Ithaca, 1952), pp. 43-4. As to the role of "modern" Islam in the revolution, see pp. 44-9.

were prompted by strong religious motivation. They operated under magical and mystical inspiration and gathered around a leader to stage periodical *rompoks*, or raids, in their neighborhood. According to the natives, these "chiefs," endowed with mysterious powers, were "inspired creatures," whose name, physical appearance, and date of birth had special occult meaning. The band accepted their leadership only after being told to do so by direct revelation when in trance. The members were pledged to certain rituals and to a code of honor; their most important bond consisted of the common possession of an *ilmoe* capable of performing miracles. An *ilmoe* could be an amulet, a formula, a password; but the knowledge of which specific item was an *ilmoe* came only after meditation (*tapa*) or in trance. An *ilmoe* could also be a gift or could be inherited at birth. Thanks to the *ilmoe*, members of the band became invisible and invulnerable during the *rompok*, while anyone who opposed them would be seized instantly with paralysis or catalepsy. The bands believed that if they suffered a loss or were arrested, or if their plans miscarried, this occurred because one among them had transgressed the rigid norms governing the use of the *ilmoe*, or had failed to perform with the utmost fidelity the instructions received during the religious rituals preceding the raid. In general, the population did not regard the bands as predatory, but rather as groups of men worthy of awe and respect, since their purpose was ostensibly to restore justice, social order, and the traditional customs which the whites were trying to destroy.[9] Their motivation was similar to that of the secret societies which raided the countryside to head-hunt, find new amulets, steal a magic formula, or learn a new divinatory ritual. From Hinduism and Buddhism the bands had borrowed the habit of *tapa*, or meditation, but the influence of Islam

[9] Van Wullften Palthe: op. cit., pp. 4, 27–9.

was present in their expectation of the millennium or of a Mahdi.

The Mahdist influence is likewise noticeable in certain religious movements that emerged a few years before World War II in the form of sudden outbursts of collective mysticism. Groups of fanatics would come together by inspiration, to perform ancient Hindu or Mohammedan rites or to try to restore the ways of the past. Many women would go into trance (*dikir*) and by direct revelation assure their followers that the millennium was at hand. Great crowds would then climb to the top of a mountain to meet the "gods" descending from their heavenly abodes. Although they were moved initially by a religious purpose, the ferment they produced was fraught with political significance and posed a major threat to the Dutch colonial government. Especially after 1945, more and more of these groups sprang up around the country, and they no longer concealed their intention of driving the Westerners out of the land.[1]

In Borneo the Njuli movement, which arose in the first decades of the present century, also preached expectation of the end of the world, to be followed by an era of freedom, equality, and prosperity for its followers. In Celebes the Mejapi cult came into being at about that time, and it was as strong politically as religiously. Similar to it was the Parhu Damdam, which caught the fancy of the Bataks in Sumatra. Both announced the coming of a Savior for the "Chosen People of God."[2] Varied as they are, the messianic cults of Indonesia have one distinctive trait in common which causes them to differ strikingly from cults of other regions. They do not include Christian elements, have no ecclesiastical organization behind them, and are, instead, influenced by Islam and

[1] Ibid., pp. 30–1, 33–4, 45, 53–4.
[2] Van der Kroef: op. cit., p. 162.

its Mahdi belief. In substance, they are composed of the following elements:

1. A nucleus of original pagan beliefs, going back as far as the Paleo-Malaysian period, with magico-mystical manifestations, numerous deities, and many secret societies with aggressive intentions.

2. A Hindu-Buddhist element, with traditional heroes and liberators who emerge victorious from combat and play a major role in the recent messianic cults, in which the Indian influence is very strong.

3. The Mahdi doctrine, an Islamic element of fairly recent growth.

4. The new messianic message, expressing popular reaction to the clash between native society and colonial rule. This element, which only emerged in recent times, is rooted in precolonial traditions but draws its power from events that occurred between the end of the nineteenth century, through World War II, to 1949, when national independence was attained.

VIETNAM

Vietnam is another Southeast Asian country where religious movements of a messianic character, filled with political implications, served to direct the people's struggle for independence. The principal movements were the Cao Dai and the Hoa Hao, both very much involved in the political history of what was then French Indochina. In 1954, when the Geneva agreement put an end to the long and bitter fight between the French and the forces of Vietminh, using the 17th parallel as the cease-fire line, two separate states were established, Vietminh in the north in the Communist sphere, and Vietnam in the south, with the proviso that unification would be negotiated in due course. Vietnam became a republic by referendum in 1955, when the Emperor Bao Dai was deposed, and now comprises territories formerly known as Annam and Cochin China. The decades preceding these events, when the country was under French colonial rule, were marked by a series of battles and reprisals against the two major religious movements, Cao Dai and Hoa Hao.[3]

The Cao Dai movement really started in 1925, although its first appearance dates from 1919. The founder was a mandarin named Nguyen Van Chieu, but it was Le Van Trung who spread the movement. In 1919 Van Chieu had a vision in which he saw the spirit of God (Cao Dai) and heard a divine voice bidding him go forth to proclaim a new doctrine to his people. The symbol of the new cult was the Eye of God surrounded by rays, signifying the omniscience and universality of the Almighty. In 1925 Van Chieu had a second vision, this time in the presence of several officials of the local government, including Le Van Trung, who, at that time, was a merchant on the brink of ruin because of his dishonest practices. Le Van Trung was so deeply moved by Van Chieu's vision that he changed his way of life and became one of the most zealous apostles of the cult. Shortly thereafter, Van Chieu retired to private life, leaving Van Trung as chief priest and promoter of Cao Dai. Gradually he built a powerful ecclesiastical organization, with churches, chapels, and a large cathedral, and also trained missionaries to preach the doctrine. The cult had its central seat at Go Ken, near Tay Ninh, but later moved to Long Thanh on the Cambodian border.

Cao Dai means High Place, or Reigning God, and its full

[3] Another political sect, which was not religiously motivated, operated in Cochin China at the same time. It was called the Binh Xuyen sect. B. B. Fall: "The Political-Religious Sects of Viet-Nam," *P. A.*, XXVIII, 3 (1955), pp. 235–53.

Vietnamese name, Dai Dao Tam Ky Pho Do, signifies the Third Pardon of God. The cult is both spiritualistic, because it is based on visions and trances, and syncretistic, because it includes elements from Buddhism, Taoism, and Christianity. According to Cao Dai doctrine, God has already remitted the sins of mankind in the West by sending Moses and Jesus, and in the East by sending Buddha Sakyamuni and Lao-tse. In granting these amnesties to humanity, God chose to become man, whereas in granting the Third Pardon he would remain pure spirit, having appeared in this form to Van Chieu and Van Trung. The prophets of Cao Dai proclaimed a message of "love, life, and truth" conceived in universal terms which recognize all religions and seek to cement them into a single entity. In the Cao Dai cathedral, the images of Confucius, Christ, Buddha, Lao-tse, and others are displayed side by side in the midst of images of divine eyes repeated ad infinitum.

The complex Cao Dai church organization is based on the Roman Catholic pattern, with administrative, legislative, executive, and controlling bodies, in addition to a welfare service for the sick and a military organization. Central authority is vested in the Cun Trung Dai, headed by the Giao Tong, or Supreme Pontiff, who is not a living person but the spirit of Ly Thai Bach, a Vietnamese philosopher and holy man of another age, who is represented temporarily on earth by the high priest Trung.

Although universal in a religious sense, the Cao Dai cult was in a sense the national church of Vietnam. As such, it was a very effective force working simultaneously toward emancipation and against colonialism, and promoting efforts to break away from the restraints of traditional culture. The anti-French libertarian tendencies of Cao Dai came strongly to the fore in 1934, after the death of Le Van Trung, when a group within the movement, called Tien Thien, began to emphasize the messianic meaning of the doctrine, inviting their followers to await patiently the repatriation of Prince Cuong De, a national hero exiled to Japan, who would lead them to victory. Thus, the Cao Dai movement took on more political significance against the French, who, in trying to eliminate the Tien Thien group, only succeeded in pushing it into the arms of Communism.

Prophecies heralding liberation and freedom multiplied at the outbreak of World War II, and the return of Cuong De was awaited with increasing eagerness. Tac, Grand Master of the cult, and his close associates were deported by the French to Madagascar; their followers appealed for Japanese intervention and formed military units of their own under such names as "The White Hats" and the "Voluntary Forces of the Interior." In 1945, exploiting the French defeat in Europe, these forces asserted themselves and formed a coalition with forces in Vietminh. They were then able to negotiate a truce and demand the return of their exiled leaders. Weakness in France had been so successfully exploited that by 1949 Vietnam had gained independence under the Emperor Bao Dai; between 1947 and 1953 there also arose a strong demand for emancipation from Vietminh, which had shown little favor toward the religious sects of Vietnam. Several times the Cao Dai followers gave strong support to the national movement led by the Emperor against Vietminh, but when the French were defeated by the Communists at Dien Bien Phu and the fighting was at an end, the leaders of Cao Dai appealed for moderation to the heads of both governments, Ho Chi Minh and Bao Dai. Later the Cao Dai was instrumental in bringing about the transformation of

Vietnam from a feudalistic society to a united independent state.[4]

The other major religious movement, known as Hoa Hao but more accurately called Phat Giao Hoa Hao, did not develop until 1939, and now has more than one million followers in the delta region of the Mekong River. The Hoa Hao doctrine stems from the evangelism of an earlier prophet, Phat Thay Tay An, who, in 1830, had already announced that the Vietnamese empire would collapse under the impact of the West. The prophecy survived the prophet and spread throughout Cochin China, fomenting the revolts of 1875 and 1913, which nearly overthrew the French in the Mien Tay region. But although the flames of revolution seemed extinguished, the embers were still hot, and the slightest movement among the natives could rekindle their fire. It was not difficult for Huynh Phy So, founder of Hoa Hao, to revive the spirit of rebellion all over the land. Born in 1919 in the village of Hoa Hoa (hence the name of the cult), he was a sick and melancholy child; when his elementary schooling was completed, he was sent to the Seven Mountains in the care of a medicine man, from whom he learned the arts of magic and healing as well as the doctrine of Phat Thay. Still sickly, he returned to his native village in 1939. One evening, while walking around the family altar, he suddenly felt that he had been healed and was to go forth to preach the creed of Phat Thay.

This gospel was a reformed Buddhism and commanded its followers to renounce all the costly religious rituals which

[4] For the Cao Dai movement, see Fall: op. cit., pp. 237–43; G. Gobron: *Historie et philosophie du Caodaïsme* (Paris, 1949); Pham C. Tac: *Le Caodaïsme-Phap-Chanh-Truyen* (Paris, 1953). From the government and landowning circles, the Cao Dai spread to the rural areas. In 1938 it had 300,000 adepts. Le Thanh Khoi: *Le Viet-Nam; histoire et civilisation* (Paris, 1955), pp. 449, 456–7. See also Nguyen Tran Huan: "Histoire d'une secte religieuse au Viet-Nam," *Revue de Synthèse*, 1959.

burdened the poor with debts. Huynh Phy So also sought a return to traditional simplicity in religious worship, without temples, pagodas, statues, or sacred objects and with all efforts centered in prayer. Hoa Hao followers made symbolic offerings of rain water, flowers, and incense to Buddha and to their national heroes, to express their cleanliness and purity of heart as well as to chase away the evil spirits. The prophet not only opposed the ceremonial forms of Buddhism and Taoism, but also forbade such old usages as the sale of child brides, wrestling, gambling, and the use of liquor and opiates. The four daily prayers of the Hoa Hao followers are addressed to Buddha, to the Kingdom of the Enlightened Lord, to relatives living and dead, and to all who are still shrouded in the darkness of ignorance. The second prayer, to the Kingdom of the Enlightened Lord, is related to the messianic Buddhist prophecy of Mahayana (the Enlightened), to which the influence of Christianity added the concept of a kingdom of universal peace.

The Hoa Hoa, rich in revolutionary significance and strong in the personality of the prophet, soon took on obvious social and political meaning. The prophet had foretold the Franco-Japanese War; and when the fighting broke out, his followers believed this to be the end of the world and the prelude to the New Kingdom. They abandoned the fields to await the millennium on a hilltop. The prophet was banished by the colonial government, but this only helped him to gain a wider following from his place of exile. Finally he was sent to an institution for the insane at Saigon, but he converted his doctor, who in 1949 lost his life fighting against Vietminh. Declared sound of mind, the prophet was released from the hospital and exiled to Bac Lieu; many of his followers were sent to a concentration camp at Niu Bara. What had happened at the Saigon hospital happened again, in even more dramatic manner, at Bac Lieu: the prophet's dwelling became the goal of pilgrimages, which the French were unable to prevent. As a final resort, they exiled him to Laos, and he was liberated by the Japanese in 1942.

In no way inclined to servility, Huynh Phy So remained true to the goal of emancipation which had originally sparked the Hoa Hao movement. He foretold the defeat of Japan, even though he had obtained weapons for his movement from them. And when their surrender came in 1945, the Hoa Hao movement was already well in control of the areas south and west of Saigon in South Vietnam. The Hoa Hao, like the Cao Dai, clashed with the French. Bloodshed ensued many times between 1945 and 1947, until the prophet, who by then had founded the Social-Democratic party of Vietnam (Dan Xa), was ambushed and killed by the agents of Vietminh. The death of the founder caused the Hoa Hao to shift policy and to collaborate with the French as the Cao Dai had done. Gradually the movement lost its centralized strength and was split by schisms and dissensions which hastened its decline.[5]

In conclusion, the sects of South Vietnam are strongly political. This is fostered by the nature of their organization, based on a powerful hierarchy with an armed force of its own. Once peace and national independence had been established, the armed bodies were absorbed by the national army and the religious drive lost momentum, chiefly because of rivalries between minor prophets and would-be leaders, often in conflict with the policies of the national government.

The following elements may be singled out in the Cao Dai and Hoa Hao cults:

1. The link with ancient traditions found in the healing

[5] For the Hoa Hao, the only source to which I had access was Fall: op. cit., pp. 243–9, 251–3.

and magical practices of the Hoa Hao and in the spiritualist trances of the Cao Dai, the founder of Hoa Hao having been a healer.

2. The messianic trait expressed in the expectation of a hero coming to liberate the land (Cao Dai) and in the belief in the Kingdom of Peace (Hoa Hao). These, in turn, were manifestations of native reaction to foreign rule and of the people's yearning to be free, as much from the formalism and rigidity of the ecclesiastical hierarchy as from the white man's colonial rule.

3. The pacifist and universalist beliefs drawn from Buddhism and Taoism, merged with Christian elements.

4. The ecclesiastical and secular organization combining Taoist and Buddhist tradition with Christian structural elements. The union of these elements eventually gave rise to active military formations which were nationalistic, conservative, and strongly opposed to all foreigners.

5. The new ritual forms into which these elements are merged, with both ancient and modern foundations. These are directed toward bringing about a total renovation of the religious and political life of the people.

PHILIPPINES

The Philippine Islands were under Spanish occupation from the early seventeenth century through 1898, during which time the Roman Catholic faith was widely introduced among the native populations. However, even under Spanish rule, there was a great deal of religious ferment which produced native movements of a so-called "heretical" nature, especially in the rural areas. On various occasions these movements had been headed by native-born former members of a Catholic religious order, who had become openly antagonistic to the Spanish hierarchy. In 1840 a priest named Apollinario de la

Cruz founded the Confraternity of St. Joseph among the Christian and Westernized Tagalogs of the Manila area; the true purpose of his religious body was to work for the political and religious autonomy of the natives. He was called "King of the Tagalogs."[6]

Allied with the anti-Spanish movements, a secret society called Katipunan, meaning the Very High and Very Respected Society of the Sons of the People, had come into being in 1892, and was militarily prepared to fight the Spaniards to the bitter end. Five years later another movement, called Colorum, came to support it. The Colorum started at Tayabas in southern Luzon, and spread rapidly to the provinces of Tarlac and Nueva Ecija as well as among the inhabitants of Mindanao. It was centered in the worship of the Sacred Heart, which the faithful believed would make them immune to Spanish weapons. Its followers awaited the return of Rizal, their national hero, shot by the imperialists during the 1896 battles for independence. The leaders of Colorum claimed to have received guidance from the spirit of Rizal: in his behalf they announced the approach of the millennium, bringing the abolition of taxes, the remission of all debts, and the end of Spanish rule. The cult takes its name from a native interpretation of the liturgical words "*saecula saeculorum*," which are repeated in unison during Roman Catholic services. The worship was held at the foot of Mount Cristobal, where the faithful could hear the "holy voice" giving them inspiration and instructions. On one occasion, when the Katipunan had scored a minor military success, the Colorum started a religious procession in which their "saint," Juan Magdalo, robed as John the Baptist, was borne aloft on a throne while the faithful marched in long white robes

[6] J. Chesneaux: "Les hérésies coloniales," *Rech. Int. Marx.*, VI (March-April, 1958).

like the Apostles. At first the Spanish authorities were taken aback by the unusual sight, but they soon overcame their surprise and opened fire on the procession, leaving the ground covered with dead and wounded. Only a handful of survivors, including Magdalo, managed to escape.[7]

When the United States gained control of the Philippines after the Spanish-American war of 1898, several religious sects asked for autonomy. They were the forerunners of the great surge toward independence which finally brought freedom to the islands in 1946. In 1902 two Filipino priests, Gregorio Aglipay and Isabelo de las Reyes, who had fought with Aguinaldo against the Spanish in 1896, founded the Christian Aglipay Church, while still prospers all over the islands. This church accepts both the Old and the New Testament, believes in the retribution of good and evil, and recognizes the divinity of Jesus Christ, but introduces Tagalog into the liturgy and gives considerable play to popular traditions both in the rituals and in the iconography. It worships not only the Roman Catholic saints but also such heroes of Filipino independence as Rizal, Burgos, Gomez, and Zamora.[8] It does not recognize the authority of the Pope, chiefly because it originated in the fight against the Roman Catholic Church's effort to destroy all forms of native worship and culture. It is not unlike the dissident Christian churches of Africa, Oceania, and the Americas, which also

---

[7] Ibid., pp. 176-7; T. A. Agoncillo: "The Revolt of the Masses. The Story of Bonifacio and the Katipunan," *Philippine Social Sciences and Humanities Review*, XXI (1956) (Quezon City), pp. 43-4 (Katipunan), p. 195 (Colorum).

[8] Chesneaux: pp. 176-8. He cites Alip: *Political and Cultural Study of the Philippines* (Manila, 1950-52); J. A. Robertson: "The Aglipay Schism in the Philippines," *Cath. Hist. Rev.*, IV, 3 (1918); G. F. Zaide: *History of the Filipino People* (Manila, 1958), pp. 218-19. On Christian-Filipino syncretism, see J. L. Phelan: *The Hispanization of the Philippines* (Madison, 1959), pp. 78-84.

sprang out of a colonial environment, demanding independence and religious freedom for the native populations.

The earliest phase of messianism in the Philippines was one of anti-European struggle, gradually followed by the establishment of an independent Native Church, with a doctrine consisting of pagan and Christian elements selected to serve the people's effort to achieve self-government. These messianic religions were often actively revolutionary, always separatist, and always opposed to Roman Catholicism. The messianic concept of salvation (as in the Colorum) was always tied in with certain historical experiences derived from the people's fight for freedom (of which Rizal is a heroic symbol).

JAPAN

Many messianic movements developed in Japan after World War II, to fill spiritual and ethical needs which the old religions could no longer satisfy in the face of radical changes brought on by the defeat. All these cults are founded on Shinto Buddhism and may best be described as "new growth from old roots." Nonetheless, since the traditional religion had failed to save the country from devastation and humiliation, it was natural that new religious doctrines promising security and salvation and an era of prosperity should be strongly identified with universal peace. These movements are opposed as vigorously by the official Japanese church as they are by the state; both bodies are primarily concerned with restoring Shinto to its erstwhile position of power and dominance. They also express the antagonism of the Japanese to centralized religion and reveal—once again, as always in the history of Japan as far back as the seventh century—the continuing struggle between the highly organized clergy of a state church, engaged in protecting itself, regardless of mass needs, and the religious vitality of people seeking a spiritual message of contemporary relevancy.

A survey made in 1950–52 shows that the Mioshi movement, also called the Divine Doctrine, or Tenshi-kodai-jingu-kyo (Religion of the Absolute Almighty God), spread and flourished among the people of Honshu, starting from Yamaguchi and reaching into Osaka, Yokohama, and Tokyo. The Mioshi doctrine was promoted by a prophetess named Kitmura Sayo, who later changed her name to Ogami-sama, meaning the Great Venerable Goddess; it proclaimed her to be the adopted daughter of the Absolute Almighty God, who had sent her to earth to redeem mankind before the world came to an end. Ogami-sama's mission was explained to her in the course of a great many revelations, which started when she was a child and continued with growing intensity as her own asceticism developed in accord with Buddhist tradition. She was a miracle worker, a healer, and a clairvoyant, who came as the awaited redeemer to fulfill the messianic promise of Mahayana Buddhism. Under the influence of messianic movements of Indian and Iranian origin, Mahayana Buddhism foretold the coming of a Matreya, or redeemer, who was to appear on earth at the close of a cycle, when evil had saturated the world and after which law and justice would be established.[9]

The Divine Doctrine opens a new road to salvation for all mankind by which every believer will communicate with God through the prophetess, as other believers, two thousand years earlier, had communicated with God through Buddha. The Mioshi religion borrows from Buddhism the doctrine of *karma* (the sum of a person's actions in one existence deciding his destiny in a subsequent existence) and of *samsara* (belief in cycles of existence); it declares that the catastrophe of war,

[9] G. Tucci: *Asia religiosa* (Rome, 1946), p. 139.

281

with its dire consequences, was brought upon mankind by man's own transgressions, which enslaved him to the evil spirits governing the world of darkness. Man, said the prophetess, beguiled by the pleasures of the senses, had departed from the way of spiritual perfection, but confession, prayer, meditation, and ecstasy were now being proffered by the new cult as a means of redemption in order to extirpate the six roots of evil: regrets, desires, covetousness, hate, passion, and lust.

The Buddhist heritage is evident in the doctrinal and ritual pattern of the Mioshi cult, which emphasizes inner purification from sin and error, and puts into Buddhist terms the need for regeneration expressed by other messianic cults. Mioshi is opposed to all traditional and hierarchical forms of religion which can no longer meet the demands of the people, but also bears the imprint of Shinto in the numerous deities recognized as surrounding the Almighty God, which are referred to in one of the principal Mioshi prayers as "the eight million Gods" from whom they implore peace.[1]

Unquestionably the strongest of several religious movements that grew out of Shinto in the past century and detached themselves from it in 1882 (Shuha Shinto) is the Tenrikyō cult,[2] started in 1838 by a peasant girl from Samaiden in the province of Yamato, whose name was Nakayama Miki. The girl, it is said, sought out an itinerant priest (Yamabushi) to assist a member of her family who was

[1] For the Mioshi cult in general, see R. Olson: "A New Messianic Cult in Japan," *Kroeber Anthropological Society Papers*, VIII, 9 (1953), pp. 78–81.

[2] In this regard, I would also refer to R. Pettazzoni's citations in *La confessione dei peccati*, Vol. I (Bologna, 1929), p. 202, note 63. Also H. Van Straelen: "Un messianisme japonais contemporain," *Arch. Soc. Rel.*, IV (1957), from which I have taken the most recent data on the Tenrikyō movement.

gravely ill. The priest put her in a trance, and used her as a medium to transmit the power to heal. During the trance, Nakayama Miki had a revelation, soon followed by others, in which she learned the truth about all deities and about the creation of the world. She was told that from original chaos Almighty God had created the ancestral couple, Izanagi and Izanami, endowed them with body, soul, and mind, and caused them to bring forth the first human generation. All this had been performed by the Creator through rituals and magical powers, even as he had separated the earth from the sky and the water, demarcated the continents, and made the world.

By including in its theology no less than ten other deities, Tenrikyō became a blend of Shinto and Christianity; it promised that when all mankind had been purified and had achieved redemption through a given cycle of lives, all human beings would live to be a hundred and fifteen years old. The rituals, prayers, and dances, performed in the great Temple of Tenri-Shi, the central and original seat of the cult, are believed to cleanse the soul from the dust of sin and the body from sickness, which is regarded as God's punishment for human failures. Once all mankind has attained this state of perfection, the blessed rain of Kanro will fall upon all creatures from the sacred pillar (Kanrodai)[3] in the Temple. Bliss will then reign upon the earth, and neither temples nor prayers will be needed.

From its inception, Tenrikyō was a redemptive religion: it offered healing and salvation, and its social, economic, and other secular aspects became more significant as the cult grew in power and in acceptance.[4] Rising as a popular reaction to

[3] The Kanrodai column in the temple of Tenri-Shi indicates the exact spot where the prophetess Miki had her first revelation. There are now about 14,000 Tenrikyō temples, with some 90,000 preachers. Van Straelen: op. cit., pp. 124, 127.

[4] Van Straelen: op. cit., p. 131.

the hegemony and institutionalism of Shinto, it matured in the suffering which Japan experienced during and after World War II. When the patriarch (Shimbashira) of the Tenrikyō cult speaks to the followers of what has now become the strongest and most widely diffused messianic movement in Japan, these are his words: "Everyone has a longing for peace and happiness. It is the most natural human desire. Then why is our life full of varied strifes and conflicts? our happy home life disturbed and our peaceful social life destroyed? . . . If we had mutual love among ourselves, this world of ours would be converted into a higher and happier world. The cause of all our troubles is our shortcomings in the love of humanity. Today we must love mankind as never before. This is our reason for introducing to the people of the world the teaching of Nakayama Miki, foundress of Tenrikyō, the Religion of the Heavenly Wisdom."[5]

These cults do not, of course, offer a complete picture of religious movements in modern Japan, for a great number of smaller groups have arisen all over the country, especially since the end of World War II. Mostly of Shinto derivation, although without its institutional limitations and its imperialistic overtones, these minor sects certainly do not have upon the masses the spiritual or social impact of the traditional Shinto faith from which they stem, especially since they emerge chiefly among the middle class and are often linked with powerful financial interests which use religion as a front for their own ends.[6] In a way, these minor cults may be looked upon as a negative side of the religious life of modern Japan, which is offset, at least in part, by such positive popular movements as Mioshi and Tenrikyō.

[5] Ibid., p. 124.
[6] Oguchi-Iichi: "Authoritarianism in Japanese Religion," *Religion East and West*, I (1955).

To conclude, one finds the most distinctive aspect of current religious movements in Japan in the variety of tendencies and traditions they have absorbed and reshaped, and also in their lack of a true messianic message. That there is no such message is not surprising when one considers that Japan had been seeking liberation, not from foreign rule but from forces within its own society. The promise of a heavenly kingdom or a holy city, found in many cults and in Christianity, is only necessary when the people are in desperate need of a refuge from oppression and foreign hegemony. In Japan, one class of the population was not struggling to escape from the grip of another, and the need for change and regeneration was felt equally by everyone in terms of finding protection from war and its consequences. This endows the Japanese cults with a broad universal outlook, expressed in the quest for universal peace and brotherhood. In Japan, the individual, as well as society, is very much aware of his relationship to the rest of the world; the Japanese have inherited this attitude from the speculative nature of Buddhism and Christianity (Brahma and the Vedas in one case, Judaism in the other), which is now coming to the fore to meet the broader challenge of the times. Lastly, it may be said that this insistence on universal peace and universal brotherhood is the typical expression of people profoundly hurt by war and deeply scarred by the destruction that it brought.

CONTINENTAL ASIA

The information available about modern messianic movements on the Asian mainland is rather limited. One cult called Burkhan, from the Mongolian word for Buddha, was established in the Altai mountain region in 1904 by a prophet named Chot Chelpan; its followers were mostly the huntsmen and shepherds of the great reindeer region. The area had been under the loose political control of Russia since the seventeenth century, although rivalry between Russia and China for control of the territory persisted for centuries, until 1866, when the Czars prevailed. For a long time the people had to pay taxes to both countries. The restoration of the ancient Mongolian Empire was the hope which the Burkhan cult held out in a doctrine compounded of elements from Lamaist teachings, from Buddhism, and from Christianity. According to legend, Chot Chelpan had had a revelation in which a white-clad horseman on a white steed had assured him that Oirot Khan, a mythical native hero and a descendant of Genghis Khan, would soon restore his own kingdom on this earth. The horseman also instructed Chot Chelpan to found a nativistic cult, aimed against the Westerners and dedicated to the restoration of traditional rites and the rejection of all religion and customs introduced by the Russians.

The Burkhan ritual includes a daily offering of milk made to heaven and to the cardinal points. The followers may never allow a drop of animal blood to pass their lips; they may not cut down living trees; they may not smoke a tobacco pipe as a token of friendship and peace but shall, instead, offer a twig of the juniper tree for burning. The faithful must place in front of their dwelling a censer and four altars made of birchwood; they must worship the sun and moon as their brothers; they may not partake of food in the company of Christians or of natives converted to Christianity; they must put an end to the pagan worship of the Great White Mountain and must burn the drums of the shamans as instruments of the Erlik (devil); they may not make friends with the Russians, who, says the prophet, are their enemies and will soon be swallowed up into the bowels of the earth; they may not touch or use Russian currency and must return it if it comes into their hands. As is evident, the cult is a combination of pagan elements, of other elements replacing the pagan, and of still others taken from Christianity. The messianic message is also probably of pagan origin,[7] adapted to meet popular aspirations, such as liberation from foreign rule.

An interesting episode in the history of relations between the Russians and peoples under their rule at the time of the great Russian expansion in the sixteenth and seventeenth centuries indicates that the contact between different cultures does not inevitably produce conflict or enmity. The case in point, which concerns the Cossacks and the Reindeer Tungus of northwestern Manchuria, also highlights the relationship of cause and effect as between messianic religious movements and the state of subjection of one people to another. In the year 1615 the Tungus fell under the rule of Cossacks, but it was not until 1870 that the latter came to settle on the western border of Manchuria and had their first encounter with the Tungus. Far from viewing each other with antagonism, they quickly established excellent relations: these remained unchanged and were not allowed to deteriorate. The reason for this rather unusual reaction is that both peoples were more or less at the same level of social and religious development and that their respective economies were complementary rather than competitive. The Reindeer Tungus were herdsmen and hunters and the Cossacks were farmers, and exchanges between them were profitable to both. From the religious standpoint, the Cossacks, more closely bound to Christian

[7] For the Burkhan movement, see L. Krader: "A Nativistic Movement in Western Siberia," *Am. Anthr.*, LVIII, 2 (1956). R. H. Lowie ("Le messianisme primitif," *Diogène*, XIX [1957], p. 89), citing O. Manchen-Helfen (*Reise ins asiatische Tuwa* [Berlin, 1931], p. 96), mentions a similar movement in the Tanna Tuva region in Outer Mongolia. A prophet appeared who cursed the Russian invaders while at the same time commanding his followers to set fire to the drums of the shamans.

doctrine than the Tungus, who were also Christian, discovered in the beliefs of the latter certain pagan elements, also found in Cossack tradition, which the Tungus had preserved to offset the aspects of Christian teaching which they had not accepted.[8] At the same time, the Tungus learned from their neighbors much which they had never understood about Christianity, and the religious exchange further improved their relations.

The Cheremis, a people of Finnish stock who inhabited the Upper Volga and Kama regions, developed an interesting religious movement of their own during the latter part of the nineteenth century. The cult was called Kugu Sorta, meaning Great Candle;[9] it emerged quite suddenly around 1870, with a strong anti-Czarist emphasis, under the leadership of the Jakmanov brothers, in the district of Jaransk. Those who have made a study of this movement describe it as a preparation for the popular uprisings against the Russian missionaries who had begun to penetrate the area at that time. The Cheremis, after a violent and determined resistance, had been conquered by Ivan the Terrible, and had been "collectively" converted to Christianity, the conversion having been nominal and expedient, as later developments proved.[1] The Kugu Sorta, which later gained a large following in the regions of Urzum and Kazan, called itself a Christian cult, but it soon became apparent that it opposed Christianity and was mercilessly persecuted by order of the Czar. The leaders were deported to Siberia, their property was seized, and the followers were compelled to practice Christianity. Although the sect went underground, it was not destroyed and eventually rose again.

[8] E. J. Lindgren: "An Example of Culture Contact without Conflict," *Am. Anthr.*, XL, 4 (1938).

[9] T. A. Sebeok and F. J. Ingemann: *Studies in Cheremis*, V. F. P. A., XXII (1956) pp. 320–7.

[1] Ibid., pp. 26–8, 316–19.

The name Great Candle came from the ritual, which required large candles of beeswax to be lighted during outdoor ceremonies. The cult had neither a place of worship nor a priesthood and was dedicated to a Supreme Being called Jume, creator of all things and benevolent judge of men, as well as to several lesser gods. Prayers were said in front of tables placed under linden or cedar trees and furnished with vessels containing seeds of such food plants as wheat, rye, and oats and also of hemp. One candle stood in the center of the prayer table and others were placed in holes inside the vessels. Three candles were dedicated to the three co-creators (*puirešo*), who acted as intermediaries between the Supreme Being and man; and six to the guardian angels (*šukše*), who watched over the individual lives of the faithful. Other candles were dedicated to the Mother of Life (a pagan deity) and to her six angels. Prayer ceremonies were held every Friday; family rituals were presided over by the head of the family and community rituals by the elders of the sect. Ceremonies were held on a larger scale on certain special occasions throughout the year, including the winter solstice, when the herds were let out to pasture, when they returned to shelter in the autumn, at seeding and at harvest time, and when the animals were sent to slaughter. The prayers were offered in thanksgiving and in repentance of sins. Food and beverages were placed on the tables, and the great ceremonies ended with a banquet. The cult forbade the worship of icons or effigies of any kind, and many taboos governed the eating habits and sex relations of the followers. The use of any medicine was forbidden, and prayer was the only form of treatment for the sick.

Many pagan elements are embodied in Kugu Sorta, such as the Mother of Life, the spirits called *keremet*, the animal sacrifices, the sacred numbers 7, 3, and 9, the cult of "sacred trees," and the choice of feast days coinciding with agricultural events.[2] Mingled with them are such Christian elements as the worship of angels and baptism. Christ is regarded as a prophet like Mohammed, and neither is considered divine.[3] The concept of universal brotherhood, too, is of Christian inspiration. Marriage is prohibited with persons outside the sect, but aside from this restriction Kugu Sorta is not exclusive or intolerant of other beliefs, differing in this respect from Christianity. The purpose of such ancient practices as the sacrifice of animals,[4] traditionally offered in petition for prosperity and riches, is now a plea for the remission of sins.[5] The doctrine declares that God, having created the world from the Pleiades, will cause it to return to this source after the Day of Judgment, when all sinners will be destroyed and all believers saved by climbing to the top of the sacred prayer trees, where they will abide forever in happiness. The Day of Judgment will occur during the Tenth Era, the Ninth being then in progress and the full cycle of the world consisting of seventeen eras in all.

The doctrine of brotherhod binds the followers within a religious pattern not governed by priests or by any individual of high rank. The Great Candle, around which the prayers are said, represents the solidarity and oneness of the faithful and, because it is made of beeswax collected by the followers of the cult, it becomes the symbol of collective work done for a common purpose.[6] The strength of the movement is derived from the fact that the people, oppressed by Russian rule and living in poor conditions, their society threatened with

[2] Ibid., pp. 313–19.

[3] The Cheremis for a long time suffered the influence of the Moslem Tatars, who had subjugated them in 1236. Subsequently, the Cheremis joined the Tatars in the struggle against the Russians.

[4] With regard to the relations between animal sacrifices and pastoral civilizations, see Lanternari: *La grande festa*, Part III.

[5] Sebeok and Ingemann: op. cit., pp. 322–3.

[6] Ibid., p. 336.

disintegration and their natural resources exhausted by ever-increasing taxation, sought spiritual support for their determination to resist and survive. Even after their uprising had been repressed without mercy and their property seized, the Kugu Sorta followers bravely refused to be impressed into military service by the Russians, and proceeded to set fire to all the weapons they could find. They did this while praying loudly to God that He might destroy the arms they had not found. They boycotted Russian goods and stood up to Czarist rule.[7]

In view of all this, it is interesting to note that when the Russian Revolution of 1917 brought the Bolsheviks to power, the Kugu Sorta, although opposed to capitalism, resisted the new Russian regime as strenuously as it had resisted the old, chiefly because the true purpose of the Cheremis was to restore their ancient traditionalist way of life and also because they paid little heed to economic and political facts. In 1930 Kugu Sorta was known to be still in existence and still trying to build a religious bulwark against Communism, but since then it has not been possible to learn what has become of it.[8] In any event, the ideas of unity promoted by the cult imparted great vigor to the striving for unity of the people of Finnish stock who later came together under the aegis of Finland.[9] This development demonstrates, once again, that any power which keeps a people in subjection bears within itself the seeds of another power that may rise to oppose it.

The religious history of mainland China also offers an example of a prophetic cult deeply imbued with political and social meaning, which led to a revolutionary uprising: the Taiping movement. Its rise occurred in the middle of the past

[7] Ibid., pp. 320–50.
[8] Ibid., pp. 321–2.
[9] Ibid., p. 337.

century, at a critical period in Chinese history, when the feudal aristocracy was oppressing the rural populations supported by the Manchu Dynasty under the despotic and capricious rule of the Empress Yehonala. Traditional loyalty to the church and to the empire, coupled with the rigid formalism of the Confucian religion, had been creating an ever-widening gap between the official religion and the people's striving for religious expression and solace. Religious cults had emerged from time to time, and attempted to breach the gap, but all of them had been systematically crushed.[1] The situation came

[1] At various times there had appeared in China certain groups of popular origin which sought to satisfy an inner urge for salvation which the Confucian religion, with its formalism and bureaucracy, was unable to comprehend. In Confucian terms, salvation meant total subservience to the sovereign and total adherence to the worship of the ancestors. Nonetheless, the appearance of religious groups of a popular and "heretical" character goes back to the ancient eras of Chinese history. These groups, of course, were always viewed as unorthodox and contrary therefore to the traditional religious principles embodied in the state religion. The motives for the conflict between official religion and these popular movements may be classified as follows, according to M. Weber: (1) The heretics used to come together to practice a way of life in accordance with their own principles and in so doing established associations which were not recognized by the state and therefore ran afoul of the existing laws. (2) The leaders of the heresies preached the salvation of the soul and rewards in the afterlife and in so doing were defrauding the believers; Confucian doctrine does not hold with rewards in the afterlife or with the salvation of the individual soul, other than those achieved by adhering rigidly to the codes and canons of civic and moral conduct. (3) The heretics refused to worship the ancestors, and even removed the tablets bearing the names of the dead which were preserved in special niches or chapels. See H. Maspero: *Les religions chinoises* (Paris, 1950), Vol. I, p. 123. In certain cases, the heretical leaders abandoned their families in order to dedicate their lives to monastic seclusion. In the Confucian faith, ancestor worship is the focal point of religious life in the community. Monastic seclusion is viewed as a form of social parasitism, and the quest for solitude and contemplation is regarded as an excuse to escape from the responsibilities of secular life and society. For these reasons, therefore, Confucianism persecuted these sects through-

suddenly to a head with the appearance of the Europeans in China.

Chinese isolation, which had lasted thousands of years, was quickly ended by the treaty of Nanking, signed in 1842, which enabled the commercial and military powers of Europe to force their way into the Asian continent under English leadership. China's five main ports were opened to British trade by the treaty, and Hong Kong was ceded to Britain outright. In 1844 similar concessions were gained by the United States and France, initiating a sad phase of commercial imperialism and exploitation for the Chinese. In the world's most heavily populated nation, England had found virgin territory for its trade as well as for the sale of the opium brought in from India. The successful aggression and penetration by the West had bared the weakness of the Manchu Dynasty, which gradually took the side of the whites and opposed the efforts of its own people to resist foreign inroads. The presence of for-

---

out Chinese history (M. Weber: *The Religion of China* [Glencoe, 1951], pp. 213–19). To cite an example of this persecution, in 1672 a "holy edict" was promulgated which suppressed all "false doctrines" (ibid., p. 215). For thousands of years Confucianism had fought without respite against Taoism because it was an antitraditional, anti-intellectual, mystical religion of spiritual salvation, usually originating in rural areas (G. Tucci: *Storia della filosofia cinese antica* [Bologna, 1922], p. 46); and against the Buddhist influence which entered from India in the first century and diffused itself gradually in every direction, carrying a message of salvation among the masses. See Weber: op. cit., pp. 216 ff.; Maspero: op. cit., Vol. II, pp. 65–83, 195–211. The early patrons of Buddhism in China were the priests of the Tao religion; see Maspero: op. cit., p. 204. A most enlightening study of the politico-religious movements with revolutionary implications and aiming at the expulsion of the ruling dynasties has been made by V. Y. C. Shih: "Some Chinese Rebel Ideologies," *Touang Pao,* XLIV, 1–3, pp. 150–226. See a review of it in G. G. H. Dunstheimer: "Deux études sur les religions chinoises," *Arch. Soc. Rel.,* IV (1957), pp. 133–6.

eigners became even more odious to them when special privileges were given to Christian missions.[2]

The Taiping movement began to take shape in 1850, and its great, though temporary, success is chiefly due to that fact that it opposed Manchu despotism, mandarin feudalism, and foreign rule in China. For fourteen years the Taipings kept the Manchu Dynasty at bay, opposing imperial rule with a rule of their own, which advanced rapidly through central and south China and eventually confronted the dynasty with the greatest threat it had ever known. The Heavenly Kingdom of Peace (Tai-ping Tien Kuo) was founded by Hung Hsiu Ch'üan, a prophet of noble lineage who lived among the rural population. Educated at a Protestant mission, he came into contact with Christianity at an early age and was strongly influenced by it in his later religious activities. Hung, linking his message to the popular traditional cult of the Heavenly God, announced that he was the Heavenly King, son of God, younger brother of Jesus Christ, come to earth to represent the Father, and claimed for himself and for his son the right to govern the entire world. Hung opposed traditional magic and idolatry, and replaced them with the Christian doctrine of a single universal God; he used the Old and New Testaments as well as the Shih Ching and other Confucian texts. The ritual Taiping bath was derived from baptism, even as the sacramental drinking of tea was an imitation of the Christian rite of Holy Communion. The faithful began their worship by singing the Doxology, heard readings from Scripture, recited the Ten Commandments, and heard Hung make proclamations such as the following: "The Father and the Elder Brother [Jesus] have descended upon earth and established the

[2] With regard to the connection between the Taiping movement and the socio-political crisis in China, and with reference to the missions, see K. M. Panikkar: *L'Asie et la domination occidentale du XV siècle à nos jours* (Paris, 1953), pp. 126-9, 157-61.

Heavenly Kingdom and taken me and the Junior Lord to regulate affairs pertaining to this world. Father, Son, Royal Grandson are together, the Lords of the New Heaven on Earth."[3]

Pagan and Christian elements are combined in Taiping ritual and doctrine, which ban the worship of images of the Virgin Mary or of Christian Saints but observe Christmas and keep Saturday as their Holy Day. The acceptance of polygamy was one of Taiping's major ties with Chinese tradition, but tobacco, liquor, and opium were prohibited, thus helping to implement the boycott of all European goods. Taiping's fight against opium had considerable effect on the shameful Opium War started by the British.[4] Worship of the Dead and of their graves is borrowed from Confucianism; the concept of a Heavenly King to govern the empire, who is also the high priest, is of pagan origin. The Taiping Kingdom developed its own hierarchy and had recruiting centers to train warrior priests and administrative districts, which were also church parishes. The Heavenly Ruler, assisted by a deputy King and by Kings of the North, East, South, and West, constituted a hierarchy copied from the Chinese state.

Particular stress was placed on military skill and valor, regarded as the most important virtues, an emphasis which indicates the revolutionary and martial nature of the cult. Taiping departed from Confuciansim by insisting on prayer and penance as necessary instruments to enable the faithful to observe the commandments, which, it was claimed, human nature alone was not sufficiently strong to do. The cult opposed the magical rites of Taoism, the idol worship of Buddhism, and the saint worship of the Roman Catholic Church;

[3] Panikkar: op. cit., p. 159. He cites Hall: "Tseng-kuo-fan and the Taiping Rebellion," *Yale Historical Publications*, XVIIII.

[4] Panikkar: op. cit., pp. 120–6, especially pp. 129–31.

in this it agreed with Judaism on the one hand and with Protestantism on the other. Thus, Taiping made it possible for the Chinese to absorb certain elements of Christianity, such as monotheism and universalism, both of which the missions had vainly tried to promote,[5] and it also interpreted Christianity to suit native traditions and used it to strengthen its own political antifeudal and anti-Western goals. Originating in the province of Kwangtung and Kwangsi, the movement spread through Honan and into south and central China, until the capital of the Heavenly Kingdom was established at Nanking in 1853; the Chung-Wang, or Faithful Prince, was the prophet's chief collaborator in organizing the Kingdom.[6] The threat to the Empire had now grown so strong that the Emperor marched his forces against the Taipings and after a long struggle captured Nanking in 1864. The Heavenly King took his own life. His son, who had been proclaimed King by the Chung-Wang, was imprisoned and then put to death; and the revolution was suppressed. But the iconoclastic zeal of the Taipings left indelible traces on the land: great imperial libraries had been destroyed, famous universities wrecked, and the pagoda of Nanking sacked, in the frenzy to cleanse the country of idolatry and of orthodox Confucianism.[7] The Manchu Dynasty was restored and remained securely in power until 1911, when it was overthrown by the revolution of Sun Yat Sen, which had its roots in the Taiping movement.[8]

[5] Weber: op. cit., pp. 160–1.

[6] The autobiography of Chung-Wang, paradoxically enough published by the bitterest enemy of Taiping, Tseng-kuo-fan, is an important document. It was rendered in English by W. T. Lay.

[7] Panikkar: op. cit., pp. 160–1.

[8] For the Taiping movement in general, see Weber: op. cit., pp. 219–24; Panikkar: op. cit., pp. 158–61; E. P. Boardman: *Christian Influence upon the Ideology of the Taiping Rebellion* (Univ. of Wisconsin Press, 1952), which was not available to me; Chesneaux: op. cit., pp. 172–4.

The three groups of component elements in the Taiping cult reflect the three phases of its historical and cultural development. The first embodies the myths and rituals of rural Chinese religion and covers the period of the cult's spread among the people.[9] The second is strongly Confucian in the use of texts and canons, in the creation of a hierarchy of royal personages, in its cult of the dead, and above all in its political and immanent interpretation of the Christian promise of a Kingdom of Heaven. Taiping identifies the Christian paradise with its own Heavenly Kingdom in Nanking and stands for the historical phase of the movement which struck out for secular goals. The third and most recent phase is fortified by the addition of such broader Christian elements as monotheism and universality.

When viewed in the light of China's history, Taiping appears as a powerful focal point of innovations in which ancient and modern factors—tradition and change—have all become merged to meet the needs of a people of great ancient culture, who are striving to achieve progress and independence.

In countries such as Burma and Siam (Thailand) the nationalist movements which brought about independence are allied with the prevailing traditional religion, which is Hinayana Buddhism, or "Little Vehicle." Religious experience, even in these notably advanced countries, was interlaced with political and social events during the crucial period when the forces of progress and renewal were rising to the peak of their power.

Burma, which had been part of India under British rule, was granted semi-autonomous government in 1937, and attained full independence in 1948. The influence of India's movements for freedom was strongly felt by the Burmese,

[9] Maspero: op. cit., Vol. I, chapter on "La religion populaire."

THE RELIGIONS OF THE OPPRESSED

who imitated them, but endowed them with deep religious meaning. The Council of Buddhism, founded at the end of World War I, made Buddhism the symbol of Burmese nationalism and an active anti-Western religious force; the leaders of Burma's nationalist movement all made a profession of Buddhist faith.[1]

The same general trend developed in Thailand, where the kings who led the movement for progress and emancipation were also the Defenders of the Faith; although here Buddhism, on the whole, underwent considerable changes (Hinayana). King Rama IV (1917–21) spearheaded a Buddhist renascence by ordering the publication of the *Tripitaka*. Spurred by the Buddhist revival, Thailand achieved political independence in fact as well as name at the end of World War I and abolished all extraterritorial rights. In 1932 the absolute monarchy was replaced by a constitutional monarchy.[2]

In Thailand, as in Burma, Buddhism, which is a religion of salvation, was the vehicle in which the political and social demands of a new age found expression and fulfillment. In Indonesia, by contrast, it was Islam which played this important role: the religious-oriented nationalist movement Sarekat Islam emerged as early as 1908.[3]

An interesting difference between the messianic movements of Asia and Indonesia, as compared with those of Oceania, Africa, or the Americas, is found in the lack of uniformity in the former and the striking display of uniformity in the latter. In each area of the Asian world the messianic cults emerged in a form which was typical only of the culture from which they stemmed. The course they followed was influenced by existing conditions and requirements. In the Philippines, for

[1] Panikkar: op. cit., pp. 328–9.
[2] Ibid., pp. 329–31.
[3] Ibid., p. 332.

298

example, the Colorum, after several evolutionary phases, became an independent church and took a road not unlike that of the prophetic movements of Africa, North America, or New Zealand, which moved from a stage of active striving for liberation to a second one of adjustment. The Kugu Sorta of the Cheremis was wholly a movement of adjustment and did not go through an active phase as did the Colorum; its objective was religious, rather than political or military, independence. Certain movements with strong political and military implications, on the other hand, made no initial effort to organize a church[4]—as in the case of the Cao Dai in Vietnam and of Taiping in China. Asia also produced a variety of somewhat primitive cults based on a belief in the millennium—which indicates cultural affinities among the populations of Indonesia and Oceania.[5] Lastly, there are some highly evolved cults, as in Japan, where Buddhist beliefs have been transformed to meet the challenges of the aftermath of World War II.

As a general statement, by way of conclusion, it may be said that the differences of form and development in the messianic movements of Asia and Indonesia stem from the differences in the cultures which produced them. In turn, these differences were influenced by the nature and vehemence of the impact between aboriginal and Western civilizations and by the attitudes of the native people to the foreigners in their midst. Although many factors and circumstances have prevented the development of a Pan-Asian drive, uniting all re-

[4] For the recent development of Christianity in China and the National Association of Chinese Christians, see Pettazzoni: "La libertà religiosa della nuova Cina, *Atti del Convegno sugli Scambi con la Cina* (Milan, 1957).

[5] For reasons of expediency and because of their genetical relationship to the Melanesian movements, the prophetic cults of Dutch New Guinea are dealt with in the chapter on Melanesian movements.

ligious movements in Asia, nonetheless all these movements have arisen from a spiritual and historical crisis fraught with political and social implications. This state of affairs has impelled the populations to search for ways to change conditions and to overcome the crisis.

CHAPTER

VIII

CONCLUSIONS

THE MESSIANIC MOVEMENTS of modern times constitute one of the most interesting and astonishing results of the cultural clash between populations in very different stages of development. Indeed, not only do these movements reveal the reactions of people affected by this clash; they also serve the interests of the more advanced civilizations by tearing down barriers erected by Western colonialism and ethnocentrism. Moreover, they call for a reappraisal and updating of Western values within a human framework much broader than that provided by the nationalism of the nineteenth century.

Although these movements are primarily religious in character, they also demand and strive to secure for their followers certain riches without which life itself is scarcely worth living. These riches are freedom and salvation:[1] freedom from sub-

---

[1] The prophetic and nativistic movements are defined as movements of salvation (*Heilserwartungsbewegungen*), by G. Guariglia (1958, p. 184), who commits himself to this definition especially with reference to the "historical" prophetic movements of the modern West, seeing in them a central aim which is salvation.

301

jection and servitude to foreign powers as well as from adversity, and salvation from the possibility of having the traditional culture destroyed and the native society wiped out as a historical entity.

These movements may be studied from a variety of angles; in the past these were usually typological or sociohistorical. The typological approach seeks to identify a "type" within each movement, a "type" being the sum total of certain common factors which remain constant regardless of the varying manifestations of the movements themselves, and therefore constitute their basic structure. This approach fits into the requirements of *phenomenalism*, which regards phenomena as the only objects of knowledge. Religious phenomenalism in particular is concerned with finding a "type" structure within the multiform expressions of religious life, and may therefore be called *typological phenomenalism.*[2] In studies and interpretations of "types," the emphasis sometimes is placed on the point at which types become unified. In this case the categories and subcategories of types become established. This is *classified typology*, based on differences in patterns,[3] whereas *phenomenological typology* is based on differences in phenomena.

In judging the messianic movements from this latter point of view, one finds in every cult such phenomena as a prophet or guide who founds his movement on traditional myths which coincide with the substance of the revelations he had received. Revelations may come from a Supreme Being, as in

[2] The phenomenological approach prevails in Wallace, 1956; Inglis, 1957; Voget, 1956, and others. However, even within the work of these authors it is easy to find sociological concern and some classification.

[3] The classifying approach prevails in Linton, 1943; M. Smith, 1959; Wallace, 1959; Guiart-Worsley, 1958; De Queiroz, 1958, and so on. Guariglia has attempted classified typology (seven types) (1958, pp. 183 ff.; also 1959) in a general study—this being the first such effort made after the older work of Wallis—to embrace in one over-all view the most disparate movements at the ethnological level.

Africa; from the Great Spirit, as in North America; from the Spirit of the Dead, as in Melanesia and also, to some extent, in Africa and America; or from national heroes who inspired such cults as Koréri in Melanesia, Apapocuva in Brazil, the Dream Dance and the Peyote cult in North America. Messianic cults all involve a belief in society's return to its source, usually expressed in terms of the expectation of the millennium and the cataclysms and catastrophes that are to precede it, and also embody a belief in the rising of the dead, in the reversal of the existing social order, in the ejection of the white man, in the end of the world, and in its regeneration in an age of abundance and happiness.

Often the chiliastic myth, or myth of the millennium, involves the coming of a Messiah in human form, whose redemptive action is to be the fulfillment of society's hope that the traditional ways of life can be restored. The Messiah, regarded as the re-creator of the world, is usually the personification of some national hero whose return has been long awaited, or of the ancestor who founded the cultural lineage, that is, either Adam or Jesus Christ. Sometimes the Messiah is identified with the Europeans, taken as a collective entity and representing the risen dead.

These salient features and others found in the messianic movements may be viewed in the light of a study of phenomena in general, or may be analyzed as strictly religious developments. Neither of these two approaches, however, explains the cults as historical facts, for neither examines their genesis or their function in relation to the society in which they grew. The method which classifies types by placing them in certain given categories merely fulfills a preliminary and structural purpose, which, if taken as an end in itself, would make it impossible to evaluate these movements as a part of human history, which they are. Classification has its place, but

303

not in the abstract. It is a factor in the comparative study of these movements as history, and a factor in the analysis of them as a dynamic force.

In using the sociohistorical approach,[4] which can be well served by both forms of typological investigation, we find the proper framework in which to see the internal force binding two such otherwise unequal factors as the personality of the prophets and founders and the religious mass function of these cults. There is probably no known religious phenomenon in which the dialectical interpretation of relationships between personality (the individual personality of the prophet) and culture (the social personality of the group) becomes more convincing than it does in regard to messianic cults. More than forty years ago, W. D. Wallis gave a brilliant description of this relationship:

> A survey of messianic movements and a correlation of the Messiah's initiative with the prevailing social atmosphere, seems to indicate that the individual is member of a class and the vehicle of a higher purpose which envelops his individual and unique efforts. Whether this purpose is imparted to him by the group of which he is a part or for whose salvation he strives, is another question. The individual is reacting to his environment and that environment may be different from the environment of the group. How, then, shall we answer that much asked question, Is this individual initiative or social compulsion?[5]

[4] The sociohistorical method has a tradition which includes such names as Max Weber, 1924; Mooney, 1891; Wallis, 1918, 1943; Barber, 1941; Slotkin, 1956; Balandier, 1953, 1955, 1957; Worsley, 1957; De Queiroz, 1958.

[5] Wallis uses such terms as "messianic" and "messiah" in place of others which seem to me more comprehensive, such as "prophetic" and "prophet." In my view, the "messiah" is the awaited savior, whereas the "prophet" is he who announces the arrival of one who is to come. The prophet himself can be the "messiah" after he has died (for example, Kimbangu,

We create an unreal difficulty when we consider individual initiative and social law as mutually exclusive or as,
when referred to the same act, incompatible concepts. Both
concepts are referable to the same act, just as the genius in
his accomplishment may be both the most indebted man and
the greatest contributor of his age. In fact, one might almost
say that he is the one because he is the other. Individual initiative may properly describe an act which is, at the same
time, the forwarding of a group purpose. The same act may
be designed to serve both the individual and his group: both
aims may be co-ordinated in the individual. . . . Man is part
of the gravitational, part of the biological and no less a part
of the social system. But he not only is a part of them, he
has a part in them.[6]

Thus, as to the relationship between the individual initiative
of the prophet and his social environment, it may well be
stated that above all in the person of the prophet does the individual become the point at which the past and the future
converge. He gives a creative impulse to a prospective "moment" of history, and into him, in turn, flows the tradition
which is history's moment of retrospection.[7]

The increasingly close contacts between whites and natives
that have developed in the course of the last hundred years,
especially under the stress of two world wars, have given
rise to nativistic religious movements in almost every part of
the globe. Two factors have contributed most substantially to
this: the intensified efforts of imperialism to bring the
aborigines under control, and the growing awareness on the

Matswa, etc.) and his return is expected as a redeemer, or when the
prophet himself, leaning upon an earlier messianic myth, declares himself
to be the prophet-messiah (the Negro Christ, or Jesus himself).

[6] Wallis: op. cit., pp. 255-7.

[7] Lanternari: *La grande festa*, p. 463.

part of the native peoples of the economic and cultural lags in their own societies as compared to the civilization of the West. Therefore, it is the impact made upon the so-called "primitive" societies by the colonial powers that has brought about conditions favoring the rise of messianic movements. One must also note, however, that a few such movements have emerged in reaction to oppression of another kind, as, for instance, in contemporary Japan, where they have been motivated by political, social, and cultural problems generated by the war and its aftermath in the context of a deeply religious society. In colonial areas, especially in Asia, prophetic movements have arisen chiefly within well-established religions, such as Islam, Buddhism, Taoism, or Confucianism; others stem from class or institutional conflict and other internal struggles. Illustrations of the latter are the Burkhan and Kugu Sorta, in reaction to Czarist rule, and the Taiping movement, which strives to overcome both Chinese feudalism and missionary Christianity. Lastly, certain messianic cults are found in primitive societies totally divorced from foreign influences; their origins and motivations have not been ascertained for lack of data and the difficulty of gathering it. For example, it is virtually impossible to document the early phase of the Koréri cult in New Guinea or the sixteenth-century cults in Brazil, which predate any contact with the West.

Most of the messianic movements dealt with here involve native societies which have experienced the impact of Western Christian civilization and find themselves in religious opposition to it. In this respect, and on the basis of considerable documentary evidence, it may be said that "primitive" societies have borrowed from the evangelism of the missionaries a great many elements in which they saw a reflection of their own experiences of life, even though portrayed in Western Christian terms. This has occurred among such widely separated peoples as the Maoris of New Zealand and the Kikuyus of Kenya, the Bantus of South Africa, the Negroes of Jamaica, and the Ghost Dance followers of North America. Here an indigenous population persecuted by its European rulers and familiar with the Bible has found in the ever-persecuted Jews a Biblical counterpart of its own plight and because of this identification has felt entitled to claim direct descent from the tribes of Israel.[8] The polygamy practiced by David, Jacob, and Solomon offered religious justification for the polygamy of the natives, which the misionaries had so violently condemned. The messianic quest for escape from servitude took Moses for its model, and arrest, capture, and death of a native prophet sought its inspiring precedent in the passion of Jesus Christ. Certain aboriginal groups have found a validation of their traditional beliefs in such Western messianic movements of Judeo-Christian derivation as Jehovah's Witnesses. In some instances, it is an African Messiah who recognizes a kinship with the white man's prophetic movement; in others, the reverse occurs, as when the Mormons recognized the Ghost Dance followers as brothers. This intertwining of facts and processes makes it impossible to establish a clear-cut distinction between the so-called "primitive world" and the so-called "highly developed" modern world—because of their historical relationship, the study of one often sheds new light upon the other. The existence of such interconnection and the similari-

---

[8] Vaggioli: Vol. II, pp. 372-3; Sundkler: op. cit., p. 72 (sect of the Israelites). The identification with the persecuted people of Israel is common to all the prophetic cults of Polynesia. See Lanternari: "Culti profetici polinesiani," *S.M.S.R.*, XXVIII, 2 (1957), pp. 70, 77-8. For the independence of various prophetic and messianic cults, viewed as "converging" phenomena at different cultural levels and in disparate areas, see Lowie: op. cit., pp. 48, 59 *passim* (Zionist "churches"). For the Tafari cult and its identification with the Hebrews, see chapter 4, Central America; for the relationship between the Ghost Dance and the Mormons, see chapter 3, North America.

ties in the historical experience of otherwise very different groups make it clear why a "primitive" society would find confirmation and support for its own religious movements in a prophetic cult of Western origin.

The people of Africa and the aboriginal populations of Oceania and America are undergoing religious experiences similar to those of Christianity at its inception, when its martyrs gave their lives not merely in witness to their individual faith but as militant members of the Christian vanguard, fully aware of the revolutionary impetus which their sacrifice would impart to those who carried on. These similarities are in no way accidental, for the prophetic mission of Moses, the hope of salvation of the exiled Jews, and the teachings of Jesus all have their roots in human crises and dilemmas. Christianity was born at a time of acute tension between the state and the people, when the vested interests of the priesthood and the spiritual needs of the masses were at odds; these conditions provided a core from which the messianic message of Christ took its first growth, to blossom into a doctrine of redemption, and salvation for all. In turn, the Christian message had its roots in the messianism of Moses handed down by the prophets. Looking back even further, we see how Moses himself was brought forth by the cultural impact between a pastoral population whose religion was based on the worship of a single God, and a settled agrarian society with strong polytheistic beliefs.[9] In this setting, the prophetic message of the Promised Land became the only hope of salvation for the Jews, whose very survival had been placed in serious jeopardy by the shattering experience of exile.

Whether it be an internal conflict, as in the case of Chris-

[9] The interpretation of the prophetic movement of Moses as the outcome of the clash between a religious culture involving pastoral populations and an agricultural civilization was already set forth in the conclusion of my work, La grande festa, pp. 450-1.

tianity, or the clash between different cultures, as in the age of the Jewish prophets, and whether the Messiah promises salvation in the hereafter or upon earth, the fact remains that the origins of the messianic movements now identified with the religion of the West provide historical antecedents for the nativistic messianic movements of people under colonial rule. This is so for two reasons: all of them have arisen equally from crisis and dilemmas, and they all convey a message of salvation and hope. It may well be said that many "primitive" peoples are now on the same religious path followed by Western civilization at the birth of Christianity, even though the West has relegated the memory of that experience to very ancient history. But history cannot be erased, nor have cultural and religious conflicts ceased to occur in our time. The messianic message of old appears now in a new garb. This is true of the Latter-day Saints, or Jehovah's Witnesses, of the movement of Saint Simon, or, going further back into the past, of the "heresies" of the Middle Ages,[1] and of many movements of religious and social revival scattered throughout history. Everywhere, in primitive as in highly developed societies, the messianic movement emerges from a crisis, to offer spiritual redemption.

Beyond the similarities, it is also important to see the differences between movements generated by a conflict between societies or by the clash with an external force, and those generated by dissensions[2] within the pattern of one society—even though we should view the distinction between external and internal motivation in a dialectical sense and not as a static condition. Indeed, there is no messianic movement of external origin which does not also have certain internal motivations, since all of them are linked with one another within

[1] N. Cohn: *The Pursuit of Millennium* (London, 1957).
[2] R. Bastide: "La causalité externe . . . ," *Cah. Int. Soc.*, XXI, 3 (1956).

309

the historic process, even as there are no prophetic movements engendered by internal conditions which do not also have external repercussions. The impact from outside which produces a crisis within society compels the internal forces of that society to make a choice between clinging to traditions rendered obsolete by events, or developing new patterns of culture better able to meet the new challenge. Although the messianic cults arising from conflict with Western culture are by far the most numerous, primitive societies have also produced movements to meet critical conditions of purely internal origin. To these we apply the term *endogenous*. Some examples are the anti-sorcery societies of Africa; the sixteenth-century cults of the Tupi-Guarani tribes in Brazil, which either preceded or were immediately subsequent to Portuguese occupation;[3] the pre-Western phase of the Koréri movements in New Guinea;[4] the messianic Taro cult of the Orokaivas in New Guinea.[5] Even in movements directly consequent upon the impact of the white man, it is not uncommon to find that a first phase of active irredentism (the Ghost Dance of the Plains Indians, the Hau-hau of the Maoris) is followed by another which brings about contemplative religion (the Peyote cult, the Ringa-tu of the Maoris, the native African churches). Cultural conflict with the whites is by no means the only motivation behind the messianic movements, but it is by far the most prevalent because of its disconcerting effects upon native society, culture, and religion.

Although one should bear in mind the dialectical meaning applied here to such terms as "internal" and "external," it is

---

[3] Métraux, in *Handbook of South American Indians*, pp. 97–8; Pereira de Queiroz: "Autour du messianisme," pp. 3–30, 111–112. See chapter 4.

[4] Kamma: op. cit. See Chapter 5.

[5] Lanternari: "Origini storiche . . . ," pp. 33–42; Williams: *Orokaiva Magic*, pp. 12 ff.; Chinnery and Haddon: op. cit. See chapter 5.

significant that the factors which precipitate movements derived from intercultural clash are external, whereas in movements sparked by other causes the precipitating factors are internal. The messianic pattern of Judaism, from Moses through the Prophets of the Exile, contains both external and internal motivations. The impact between a pastoral and an agrarian society being external, the clash between monotheism and polytheism has left a mark on the entire history of the religion of Israel. It later found its way into the Christian Church: the clerical hierarchy is patterned on the priesthood of the Hebrews, and institutional demands are often at issue with the spiritual needs of the faithful and of society as a whole. The conflict between "popular" and "official" religion is evident in the early prophetic movements, from the Essenes to the Sect of Qumran, and continued to affect the course of Christianity from the Middle Ages through the Reformation to the messianic movements of our day. In all of them the contrast is clear between the demands of the people and the needs of their society on the one hand, and action determined from "above" by the clerical hierarchy on the other.[6] The rise of the Mormons and of the Watch Tower movement illustrates this point. The understanding spontaneously developed between these two movements and certain indigenous groups further illustrates the conflict between missionary churches and modern powers on one side and "primitive" cultures on the other; or, to put it differently, the inbalance between such overpowering institutions as church and state and the unanswered needs of society.

Religious movements motivated by intercultural clash usually have a different orientation from those arising from

[6] For the conflict between the "official" and the "popular" moment, in religious life, see Lanternari: "Religione popolare e storicismo," *Belfagor,* VI (1954).

within the society. The former tend to seek salvation by immediate action through militant struggle or through direct and determined opposition to the foreign forces which beset them: we see "primitive" societies turning against Europeans, the Jews under Moses turning against the Egyptians and Canaanites, the Prophets of the Exile turning against Babylon.

Endogenous movements, on the other hand, look for salvation through spiritual, cultural, or ethical channels, as illustrated by the Apostles and by other forms of Christian action in more recent times. For these salvation implies a methodical advance toward life in the hereafter, where the individual may truly attain liberation. The hope of salvation is focused on the eschaton, or end of the world, which takes on a positive meaning through the renunciation of worldly goods, whereas in the aboriginal movements it is the earthly goods which carry the greatest weight. The transcendental nature of Christianity sets it historically apart both from the messianic movements that preceded it and from those arising among primitive peoples which strive equally for human salvation on earth.

One may wonder what caused Christianity so to transform the values inherent in the earlier prophetic messages. A determining factor is the endogenous nature of the Christian movement, which developed from an urban society overburdened by hierarchical structures. Christianity arose and grew as a "popular" manifestation in reaction to the presence within its society of two oppressive forces, the Jewish priesthood and the Roman Empire, which could be fought on religious grounds only if the existing values of that society were rejected and others of purely spiritual and nonworldly significance were adopted in their stead. The redemptive message of Christianity—opposing the form and nature of both church and state at that time—was obliged to offer, as it did, a total escape from reality by holding out the promise of a kingdom able to overthrow all the worthless institutions which sustained society.

A similar and equally radical escape from reality is offered, although in different form, by the messianic cults rising from within the society of primitive peoples. For instance, the Tupi cults of precolonial Brazil are based on the promise of mass escape from the homeland into a mythical "Land without Evil" to be found—according to tradition—on the seacoast or across the ocean. Here, as in the case of early Christianity, the oppression from which escape was sought was within the native society, not bearing down upon it from without. The establishment of a new society in a new place seemed the answer; this was also the essence of the Christian message. The same is true of the Mormons, who sought to found a "new city" away from their secular environment, to be reserved exclusively for the members of the cult. The Tafari movement in Jamaica is also "escapist," fostering the Negroes' dream of returning to a long-abandoned homeland in Africa as the only possible salvation from their current conditions of life. Many movements seek to attain the heavenly abode by founding a "holy city," which, in most cases, is regarded as the "new Jerusalem." Such are the recent messianic cults of Brazil at Canudos, Joazeiro, and Contestado; the sect of Lazzaretti, which built a church on Mount Labro to be its "Holy City"; the Taiping movement in China, whose founder created a "Heavenly Kingdom" in opposition to the empire which he tried to overthrow by force of arms.

A "holy war" is sometimes unleashed from a "holy city" against the evil powers operating within the society but regarded by the faithful of the cult as an external force because, in following their prophet, they have become isolated from that society. This was the course taken by the prophetic cults

313

of Brazil,[7] by the Taiping in China, and by the movement of Lazzaretti.[8]

In the final analysis, all the endogenous messianic movements, regardless of their cultural level, are impelled by their nature to escape from society and from the world in order to establish a society and a world of their own beyond history, beyond reality, and beyond the necessity of fighting to bring about change and improvement. These movements only engage in social or political struggle when they can do so as a force having become external to their own society and to the hostile powers within that society from which they had originally sought to escape. In these particular conditions, the endogenous movements take on the characteristics of the messianic movements of external origin, as well as their purpose, which is to defeat the enemy rather than to escape from him.

The religious escapism typical of the endogenous movements, to which Christianity offered a transcendental answer, is not confined to them alone. The quest for a way out of the earthly confines and a belief in the regeneration of the world are present, to some extent, in all prophetic cults. Were this not so, these movements would not be religious; it is inherent in the nature of religious experience that temporary evasion from the world can be achieved while awaiting the final hour of redemption. Even the establishment of "churches" by some of the messianic movements, after they have reached the phase of adjustment, expresses the desire of the faithful to "separate" themselves from secular society and to establish another beyond its reach. The rituals common to most messianic movements, with such supernormal manifestations as col-

[7] Pereira de Queiroz: "Autour du messianisme," pp. 11–16; "Die Fanatiker des 'Contestado'" (nineteenth-century movements in Brazil); T. H. O'Dea: *The Mormons* (Mormons); Métraux: *La Religion des Tupinamba* (messianic migratory movements among the Brazilian Tupi).

[8] J. Seguy: "David Lazzaretti . . . ," *Arch. Soc. Rel.*, V (1958), pp. 74–5.

lective possessions, incantation, trances, and visions, are a means of evasion in an atmosphere of exaltation and collective mystical uplift.

However, when one analyzes the collective psychoses, the rituals, and all the other forms of escapism found in most prophetic cults in primitive societies, it is soon apparent that they perform a special function which is not completed once the desire of the faithful for evasion has been fulfilled. Their purpose is to make a positive contribution to the regeneration of society as a whole, and the faithful may obtain a foretaste in terms of the sense of liberation experienced by these means.

The dynamic force within the native movements is revealed in the various phases of their development. The early phase of antagonism or open attack upon the church of the white man as well as upon his government is usually followed by another in which the elements of Christianity become acceptable even though outbursts of xenophobia and anticolonialism continue. In this phase, the Bible comes into use and the so-called Christian native churches are established (and may even gain recognition) to speak for a pattern of Christianity which, in native eyes, is far more authentic than that promoted by the missionaries. There is no passive acceptance in this phase but, rather, a continuing quest for new religious values to meet popular needs; and the native churches tend to remain strongly opposed to the missions. Nevertheless, the transcendental quality of the Judeo-Christian faith is present in them through belief in the afterlife and in the justice of God.

The acceptance of Christian values, regardless of the natives' dislike of the missions, is easy to understand; once the early phase of conflict between whites and natives has quieted down, the whites are able to penetrate more and more deeply into native society, until they begin to pose from within the

315

grave threat they had previously represented from without. In such circumstances, the natives can no longer think of liberation in terms of actual combat but must devise other means of attaining independence; they resort to the establishment of independent churches, to escapist techniques such as the use of peyote, or to the acceptance of a transcendental doctrine. As the Zulu once said to the whites: "At first we had the land and you had the Bible. Now we have the Bible and you have the land"—and it is the Bible that becomes the refuge and the hope of salvation. When the pressure of the white man makes itself felt from within a society, the natives reach for the Bible, which they had refused to accept from the missionaries during centuries of evangelism. This "self-Christianization" of many native groups came about when the whites, having forced their way into the native environment, created conditions similar to those which fostered the growth of early Christianity. As it was for the first Christians of the Middle East and of ancient Rome, so it was for the native peoples of Africa, Asia, Oceania, and the Americas: pressures and oppression came upon them simultaneously from two sides, the militant hierarchy of the church and the authoritarian power of the state.

One fact of considerable importance emerges clearly from a general review of these religious movements among the aboriginal populations: religious growth has inescapable requirements of its own, which no ruling power or institution can afford to ignore or expect to destroy. The requirements exist whether the native cult leads into active struggle for independence or seeks gradual emancipation by establishing independent religious bodies to facilitate coexistence with the whites. The growth of religion among the natives allows no place for passivity or acquiescence; hence, the so-called "conversions" are more apparent than real, touching only the

316

surface of native belief and never reaching into their true religious life. These are facts which many enlightened missionaries willingly admit.

Bengt Sundkler, commenting on this situation, maintains that it can be demonstrated that groups as well as individuals (in South Africa) have gone from the mission church to the Ethiopian, from this to the Zionist, and finally, crossing the bridge of native Zionism, have returned to African animism, whence they had started out.[9] Referring to Melanesia and therefore to an altogether different cultural environment, other anthropologists and missionaries have arrived at identical conclusions. Peter Elkin, for instance, remarks that the work of the missionaries is for the most part superficial as far as native life is concerned. With few exceptions, most of the natives preserve their fundamental beliefs and their traditional religions; their ancient rituals are performed or remembered in hiding, ready to be resumed in the open as soon as the opportunity arises, or, in times of psychological crisis, they bring forth the Cargo cults.[1] Dr. Elkin's observation concurs with statements made by clergymen several decades earlier. The Reverend Lorimer Fison, a missionary in the Fiji Islands in 1884, said that when he spoke of the nominal acceptance of Christianity by the native he did so, not in a derogatory sense with regard to the work of the missionaries, but merely because this was the truth. The passing of the Wainimala tribe from paganism to Christianity, he felt, had been a nominal conversion, and only a few charlatans could describe it as the "conversion of a people" in the theological sense; the missionaries in the field certainly did not use such terms.[2] Dr. Fison's statement retained its validity for a long time; in 1895 there

[9] Sundkler: op. cit., p. 297.
[1] Elkin, op. cit., p. 7.
[2] L. Fison: "The Nanga," *J.R.A.I.*, XIV (1884), p. 37.

was documented evidence of new prophetic cults arising on Fiji,[3] as well as syncretic movements,[4] and in recent times the situation of Christianity on the island is still such as to make it most improper to speak of the "conversion of native communities." The survival of so much of ancient paganism is due largely to the medicine men, who are the carriers and custodians of its rituals. Moreover, one finds that the natives have identified Jesus Christ with their national heroes and that Christian doctrine has been accepted only to the extent that the natives believe it to be an instrument of magical power or *mana*. They believe European civilization has prevailed only because of its secret powers of magic and because of the greater amount of *mana* the white man is endowed with.[5] The fact is that Christianity is being translated into pagan terms, instead of paganism being raised to the level of Christian values, for what appeals to the natives is not the spiritual significance of the doctrine, but the magical power which they attribute to it.

The failure of the missionaries, taking their own word for it, as well as that of the anthropologists, shows that there are problems of cultural policy which the Christian church has been unable to solve with the religious means at its disposal. What occurred among the New Guinea tribes of Markham Valley in 1941, at the outbreak of World War II, offers a striking example of how artificial and devoid of roots the effects of missionary propaganda often are. The missions in this area, being German Lutheran, were closed down when hostilities broke out, and their members were interned in Australia as Nazis. No sooner had this occurred than pagan

[3] Cato: op. cit., pp. 146 ff.
[4] Ibid.
[5] Cato: "Disintegration, Syncretization and Change in Fijian Religion," *Mankind*, V, 3 (1956), pp. 101–6.

religious life sprang into the open, revealing a tremendous vitality clandestinely nurtured for many a long year. This is what a native had to say about his own religious convictions: "If the missionaries asked us who made our crops grow, we told them it was as they said: God, who lived above, made them come up. But we knew it was not God. It was the magic we had performed that made the yams grow big. Food does not come up on its own, and if we stopped these things we would have nothing. We hid them and knew our gardens would be well."[6]

No amount of outside propaganda or prohibitions from above can hope to prevent history from running its course. History obeys its own law, which is that the road to the future upon which it travels cannot be short-cut by any outside force striving to lead it back onto the road of the past. History must inevitably travel forward. Religious tradition may transform itself, correct itself, and overcome itself by spontaneous inner processes, but it will not deny itself under any sort of compulsion from the outside, for the simple reason that history cannot be arrested or eradicated.

The distinctions made here between religious movements generated from within society and those originating under pressures from without, between those which have an obviously revolutionary character and those which seek adjustment[7] or reform, are not intended to establish a framework

[6] K. E. Read: "Effects of the War in the Markham Valley, New Guinea," *Oceania*, XVIII, 2 (1947), p. 114.

[7] Slotkin: *The Peyote Religion*. Other writers single out three types of "nativism": revival movements, dynamic in character; movements of passive nativism; reform movements (Voget, 1956). The systematic and antidialectical division of movements as laid out by Linton (1943) appears to me to have become obsolete. In his classification he recognized two major types (revivalist nativism and perpetuator nativism) and four minor (magical revivalism, rational revivalism, magical perpetuation, and rational

within which these cults may be classified. Their purpose is to single out the various phases, or "moments," which occur in the tangible historical process of development and which are often so interlaced or dovetailed as to seem undistinguishable. For instance, certain of these movements (in Polynesia, in Melanesia, in America) pass gradually from the revolutionary phase to that of adjustment, whereas others, as in Africa, attain adjustment with Christanity only by establishing nativistic churches and do not thereby cease to be antagonistic to the colonial administration, for these churches have been known to instigate uprisings and other such actions. These distinctions and others, made by students in this field, become obliterated in the dynamic power of the movements which transport them from a position of hostile opposition, inclined to fall back on native traditions for an acceptable scale of values which can be modernized, to the attainment of full religious autonomy. Religious autonomy resolves the conflict between an outside power striving to destroy native culture and the culture's own power to resist and survive, between willful opposition to an alien culture and supine acquiescence in the demands of an alien ruling minority.

It is also worth noting that a great many religious movements, especially those arising in continental areas where communication is possible, have little difficulty in establishing intertribal co-operation and are often able to bring about a form of unity on a wider national scale. For instance, the

---

perpetuation). Even the principle of "nativistic" as defined by Linton has become obsolete. According to Linton (1943, p. 230), "a nativistic movement is any conscious organized attempt on the part of a society's members, to revive or perpetuate selected aspects of its culture." In our view, nativism should not be seen in this unilateral and conservative aspect, but rather in its broader, over-all aspect. Seen thus, it is turned against Western culture, and aims to establish an exclusive cult for the natives, a "new cult." For a similar critical view of Linton, and for this concept of "newness" inherent in the nativistic movements, see Worsley: op. cit.

Indians practice and celebrate Pan-Indian unity in the Peyote cult and the Dream Dance, to the rhythm of tom-toms or around the Peyote altar; the native tribes of South Africa or of the former French and Belgian Congo accept a Pan-African religion; the Cheremis developed a Pan-Finnish movement through the cult of the Great Candle.

All messianic or prophetic movements express a "moment" in history in which the forces of innovation, anticonservatism, and antitraditionalism come together to make a final break with tradition itself. They represent a revolutionary phase in the religious life of the native people, closely bound to the "popular" nature of the movements. Even as in the religious life of the modern civilized world[8] there is an "official moment" and a "popular moment" of "hierarchical Christianity" and "rural Christianity" which still bears a trace of paganism, so can similar "movements" be singled out in the development of religious movements in primitive societies everywhere. They, too, have their "moment" of conservative attachment to official tradition; and their "moment" of popular renewal, when the past finally is let go; and their "moment" of confrontation between ancient and modern, conservatism and revolution.

The "official" and the "popular" moments are linked to each other by the dynamic force, inherent in every religious culture, which moves ahead with the growth and development of the culture as a whole. The nativistic movements reveal that the point of exhaustion has been reached by traditional religion in its effort to procure salvation (salvation being the purpose of all religions); and by imparting new impulses to spiritual life in the masses they are able to meet the challenge of renovation thrown up by the drastic experiences to which their society has been subjected. All messianic movements, in this

[8] Lanternari: "Religione popolare e storicismo."

revolutionary phase as in their phase of adjustment, serve to implement the popular awareness of the need for change in the religious life and, in so doing, pave the way for reform in the cultural, political, and social structure of secular society.

The messianic movements are movements of the people as well as movements of innovation. Within the religious dynamics of their society they highlight the critical "moment" at which tensions and differences have reached a climax—the moment between traditional forms too static to move ahead and the new challenge to religious life. Because these movements are both popular and revolutionary, new and able to renew, because they are spurred by the urgent and vital needs of oppressed people and societies caught in a dilemma, they look to the future and to the regeneration of the world.

BIBLIOGRAPHY

GENERAL

Barber, B.: "Acculturation and Messianic Movements," *Am. Soc. Rev.* VI,5 (October 1941), pp. 663–9. Reprinted in *Reader in Comparative Religion: an Anthropological Approach* (Evanston, 1958), pp. 474–8.

Bastide, R.: "La causalité externe et la causalité interne dans l'explication sociologique," *Cah. Int. Soc.*, XXI,3 (1956).

Bateson, G.: "Culture-contact and Schismogenesis," *Man*, CLXXXVIII (1935).

Bram, J.: "Jehovah's Witnesses and the Values of American Culture," *Trans. N. Y. Acad.*, XIX,1 (1956), pp. 47–54.

Buonaiuti, E.: *Saggi di storia del Cristianesimo*, edited by A. Donini (Vicenza, 1957), pp. 327–98.

Buonaiuti, E.: *Gioacchino da Fiore, i tempi, la vita, il messaggio* (Roma, 1931).

Cassin, H.: *San Nicandro, histoire d'une conversion* (Paris, 1957).

Cassin, H.: "Quelques facteurs historiques et sociaux de la diffusion du Protestantisme en Italie Méridionale," *Arch. Soc. Rel.*, II (1956), pp. 55–72.

Chesneaux, J.: "Les hérésies coloniales," *Rech. Int. Marx.*, VI (March-April 1958).

Cohn, N.: "Réflexions sur le Millénarisme," *Arch. Soc. Rel.*, V (1958), pp. 103–7.

Cohn, N.: *The Pursuit of Millennium* (London, 1957).

Desroche, H.: "Micromillénarismes et communautarisme utopique en Amérique du Nord du XVII au XIX siècle," *Arch. Soc. Rel.*, IV (1957), pp. 57–92.

Desroche, H.: *Les Shakers Américains. Néochristianisme ou Présocialisme?* (Paris, 1955).

Donini, A.: "Chiese dissidenti e moti ereticali," *Rinascita*, XI-XII (1958), pp. 741–5.

Elkin, A. P.: "The Reaction of the Primitive Races to the White Man's Culture: a Study in Culture-Contact," *Hibbert Journal*, XXXV,4 (1937), pp. 537–45.

Bibliography

Emmet, D.: "Prophets and Their Societies," *J.R.A.I.*, LXXXVI (1956), pp. 13-24.

G. S. R.: "Questionnaire sur les Messianismes et Millénarismes," *Arch. Soc. Rel.*, V (1958), pp. 88-90.

Guariglia, G.: *Prophetismus und Heilserwartungsbewegungen als völkerkundliches and religionsgeschichtliches Problem* (Horn-Wien, 1959).

Guariglia, G.: "Prophetismus und Heilserwartungsbewegungen in niederen Kulturen," *Numen*, V,3 (1958), pp. 180-98.

Heberle, R.: *Social Movements: an Introduction to Political Sociology* (New York, 1951).

Hobsbawm, E. J.: *Primitive Rebels* (Manchester, 1959).

Isambert, F.: "Fondateurs, Papes, Messies," *Arch. Soc. Rel.*, V (1958), pp. 96-8.

Kovalevsky, P.: "Millénarisme et Parousie, Messianisme et Missions Chrétiennes," *Arch. Soc. Rel.*, V (1958), pp. 108-10.

Lanternari, V.: "Scienze religiose e storicismo: note e riflessioni," *Nuovi Argomenti*, XLII-XLIII (1960), pp. 93-113.

Lanternari, V.: *La grande festa: storia del Capodanno nelle civiltà primitive* (Milan, 1959).

Lanternari, V.: "Fermenti religiosi e profezie di libertà dei popoli coloniali," *Nuovi Argomenti*, XXXVII (1959), pp. 54-92.

Lanternari, V.: "Religione popolare e storicismo," *Belfagor*, VI (1954).

Lowe, W. L.: "Psychodynamics in Religious Delusions and Hallucinations," *American Journal of Psychotherapy*, VII (1953), pp. 454-62.

McNiff, W. J.: *Heaven on Earth: a Planned Mormon Society* (Oxford, 1940).

Mair, L. P.: "Independent Religious Movements in Three Continents," *Comparative Studies in Society and History*, I,2 (1959), pp. 113-35.

Manuel, F. E.: *The New World of Henri Saint Simon* (Cambridge, 1956).

O'Dea, T. F.: *The Mormons* (Chicago, 1957).

Pezzella, S.: "Davide Lazzaretti," *Ricerche Religiose*, XX,1-4 (1950), pp. 181 ff.

Price, A. G.: *White Settlers and Native Peoples* (Melbourne-Cambridge, 1950).

Schlosser, K.: "Prophetismus in niederen Kulturen," *Z.f.E.*, LXXV (1950), pp. 60-72.

Seguy, J.: "David Lazzaretti et la secte des Giurisdavidici," *Arch. Soc. Rel.*, V (1958), pp. 71-87.

Smith, M. W.: "Towards a Classification of Cult Movements," *Man*, LIX (1959), p. 2.

Stroup, H. H.: *The Jehovah's Witnesses* (New York, 1945).

Volpe, G.: *Movimenti religiosi e sette ereticali nella società medievale italiana* (Florence, 1926).

Wallace, F. C., Voget, F. W., Smith, M. W.: "Towards a Classification of Cult Movements: Some Further Contributions," *Man*, LIX (1959), pp. 25-8.

Wallis, W. D.: "Quelques aspects du messianisme," *Arch. Soc. Rel.*, V (1958), pp. 99-100.

Wallis, W. D.: *Messiahs: Their Role in Civilization* (Washington, 1943).

Wallis, W. D.: *Messiahs: Christian and Pagan* (Boston, 1918).

Weber, M.: *The Theory of Social and Economic Organization* (London, 1947).

Weber, M.: *Carismatica e i tipi del potere*, in *politica ed economia*, edited by R. Michels (Torino, 1934), pp. 179-262.

Weber, M.: *Sozial- und Wirtschaftsgeschichte* (Tübingen, 1924).

AFRICA

Africa To-day, ed., C. G. Haynes (Baltimore, 1955; 3rd ed., 1959).

Andersson, E.: *Messianic Popular Movements in the Lower Congo* (Uppsala, 1958).

Balandier, G.: "Brèves remarques sur les messianismes de l'Afrique Congolaise," *Arch. Soc. Rel.*, V (1958), pp. 91-5.

Balandier, G.: *Afrique ambiguë* (Paris, 1957).

Balandier, G.: *Sociologie de l'Afrique Noire* (Paris, 1955).

Balandier, G.: "Messianismes et nationalismes en Afrique Noire," *Cah. Int. Soc.*, XIV (1953), pp. 41-65.

Banton, M.: *West African City: Study of Tribal Life in Freetown* (London, 1957).

Banton, M.: "An Independent African Church in Sierra Leone," *Hibbert Journal*, LV,216 (1956), pp. 57-63.

Bartolucci, E.: "Problemi religiosi dell'Africa d'oggi," *La Scuola Cattolica*, II (1958), pp. 116-35.

Biebuyck, D.: "La société Kumu face au Kitawala," *Zaïre*, XI,1 (1957), pp. 7-40.

Bibliography

Bissainthe, G.: "Catholicisme et indigénisme religieux," in *Des Prêtres Noirs s'interrogent* (Paris, 1957), pp. 111–36.

Cardaire, M.: "L'Islam et le terroir africain," *Études Soudaniennes IFAN*, 1954, pp. 30–46.

Carpenter, G. W.: "The Role of Christianity and Islam in Contemporary Africa," in *Africa To-day* (1959), pp. 90–113.

Cavicchi, E.: "I Mau-Mau," *Missioni Consolata*, LIV,17 (1952) pp. 198–208.

"Cherubim and Seraphim," *Nigeria*, LIII (1957), pp. 119–34.

Coleman, J. S.: "Current Political Movements in Africa," *Ann. Amer. Acad.*, CCXCVIII (1955), pp. 95–108.

Continuity and Change in African Cultures, ed., M. J. Herskovits (Chicago, 1959).

Delord, R.: "Messianisme à Madagascar," *Le Monde Nonchrétien* (1948), pp. 975 ff.

Des Prêtres Noirs s'interrogent (Paris, 1957).

Dougall, J. W. C.: "African Separatist Churches," *Int. Rev. Miss.*, XLV (1956), pp. 257–66.

Eberhardt, J. "Messianisme en Afrique du Sud," *Arch. Soc. Rel.*, IV (1957), pp. 31–56.

Fermi, E.: "La chiesa in Africa," *Comunità*, XI,48 (1957), pp. 37–61.

Field, M. J.: *Akim-Kotoku, an Oman of the Gold Coast* (London, 1948).

Franza, A.: "Il risveglio dell'Africa," *Società*, IV (1956), pp. 715–37.

Herskovits, M. J.: "Anthropology and Africa, a Wider Perspective," *Africa*, XXXIX,3 (1959), pp. 225–37.

Herskovits, M. J.: "The African Cultural Background in the Modern Scene," in *Africa To-day*, 3rd ed. (Baltimore, 1959), pp. 30–49.

Hodgkin, T.: *Nationalism in Colonial Africa* (London, 1956).

Holas, B.: "Bref aperçu sur les principaux cultes syncrétiques de la Basse Côte d'Ivoire," *Africa*, XXIV,1 (1954), pp. 55–60.

Holas, B.: "Le culte de Zié: éléments de la religion Kono (Haute Guinée Française)," *Mémoires IFAN*, Dakar, XXXIX (1954), pp. 217–21.

Kuper, H.: "The Swazi Reaction to Missions," *African Studies*, V,3 (1946), pp. 177–89.

Leakey, L. S. B.: *Mau-Mau and the Kikuyu* (London, 1952).

Leenhardt, M.: *Le mouvement Ethiopien au sud de l'Afrique de 1896 à 1899* (Cahors, 1902).

Le Grip, A.: "Le Mahdisme en Afrique Noire," *L'Afrique et l'Asie*, XVIII (1952), pp. 3-16.

Marquard, L.: *Peoples and Policies of South Africa* (London, 1952).

Mendes Correa, A. A.: "Sociedades secretas africanas e ciência social," *Boletim Sociedad Geografica*, Lisbon, IV,6 (1954), pp. 219-34.

Messenger, J. C.: "Religious Acculturation among the Anang Ibibio," in *Continuity and Change in African Cultures*.

Mootsi, L. and Mkele, N.: "A Separatist Church: Ibandla-lika-Krestu," *African Studies*, V,2 (1946), pp. 106-25.

Mulago, V.: "Nécessité de l'adaptation missionnaire chez les Bantou du Congo," in *Des Prêtres Noirs s'interrogent*, pp. 19-40.

Parrinder, G.: "Les sociétés religieuses en Afrique Occidentale," *Prés. Afr.*, (February-March 1958), pp. 17-22.

Parrinder, G.: *Religion in an African City*, (London, 1953).

Parsons, R. T.: "Missionary-African Relations," *Civilizations*, III,4 (1953), pp. 505-18.

Paulus, J. P.: "Le Kitawala au Congo Belge," *Rev. Inst. Soc.*, II,3 (1956), pp. 256-70.

Raymaekers, P.: "L'Eglise de Jésus-Christ sur la terre par le prophète Simon Kimbangu," *Zaïre*, XIII,7 (1959), pp. 675-756.

Ross, E.: "The Impact of Christianity in Africa," *Ann. Amer. Acad.*, CCXCVIII (1955), pp. 161-9.

Schapera, I.: "Christianity and the Tswana," *J. Anthr. Soc.*, I (1958), pp. 1-9.

Schlosser, K.: *Propheten in Afrika* (Braunschweig, 1949).

Shepperson, G., and Price, T.: *Independent Africa: John Chilembwe and the Nyasaland Rising of 1915* (Edinburgh, 1958).

Shepperson, G.: "The Politics of African Church Separatist Movements in British Central Africa," *Africa*, XXIV,3 (1954), pp. 233-46.

Sundkler, B. G. M.: *Bantu Prophets in South Africa* (London, 1948).

Tastevin, R. P.: "Nouvelles manifestations du prophétisme en Afrique Equatoriale et en Angola," *C. R. Acad.*, XVI,3 (February 1956), pp. 149-54.

Tracey, H.: "Zulus Find the Middle Road," *Natural History*, LXIV,8 (1955), pp. 400-6.

Vilaldach, A. de V.: *La Secta Bwiti en la Guinea Española* (Instituto de estudios africanos, Madrid, 1958).

Watson, W.: *Tribal Cohesion in a Money Economy: a Study of the Mambwe People of Northern Rhodesia* (Manchester, 1958).

327

Bibliography

Westermann, D.: *The African To-day and To-morrow* (London-New York-Toronto, 1949), 3rd ed.

Willoughby, S. C.: *The Soul of the Bantu* (New York, 1928).

Wilson, M.: *Communal Rituals of the Nyakyusa* (London, 1959).

Wing, J. van: "Le Kibangisme vu par un témoin," *Zaïre*, XII (1958), pp. 563–618.

AMERICA

Angelo, J. de, and Freeland, L. S.: "A New Religious Cult in North Central California," *Am. Anthr.*, XXXI,2 (1929), pp. 265–70.

Barber, B.: "A Socio-cultural Interpretation of the Peyote Cult," *Am. Anthr.*, XLIII,4 (1941), pp. 673–5.

Barber, C. G.: "Peyote and the Definition of Narcotic," *Am. Anthr.*, LXI,4 (1959), pp. 641–6.

Barnett, H. G.: *Indian Shakers: a Messianic Cult of the Pacific Northwest* (Carbondale, 1957).

Barnett, H. G.: *Innovation: the Basis of Cultural Change* (New York, 1953).

Barrett, S. A.: "The Dream Dance of the Chippewa and Menominee Indians of Northern Wisconsin, *Bull. Milw.*, I,4 (1911).

Bastide, R.: "Le messianisme raté," *Arch. Soc. Rel.*, V (1958), pp. 31–7.

Bastide, R.: "Le messianisme chez les Noirs du Brésil," *Le Monde nonchrétien* (July-September 1950), pp. 301–8.

Brant, C. S.: "Peyotism among the Kiowa-Apache and Neighbouring Tribes," *South. J.*, VI (1950), pp. 212–21.

Collier, J.: "The Peyote Cult," *Science*, CXV (1952), pp. 503–4.

Collier, D.: "Peyote: a General Study of the Plant, the Cult and the Drug," *Survey of Conditions of Indians in U. S.*, XXXIV (Washington, 1937).

Collier, J.: *The Indians of the Americas* (New York, 1947).

Collins, J.: "The Indian Shaker Church: a Study of Continuity and Change in Religion," *South. J.*, VI (1950), pp. 399–411.

Comhaire, J.: "Religious Trends in African and Afro-American Urban Societies," *Anthr. Q.*, XXVI (n. s. 1), 4 (1953), pp. 95–108.

Daniels, W. M.: *American Indians* (New York, 1957).

Deardorff, M. H.: "The Religion of Handsome Lake: its Origin and Development," in "Symposium on Local Diversity in Iroquois Culture," edited by W. N. Fenton, *B. B. Amer. Ethn.*, CXLIX (1951), pp. 79–197.

Dittman, A. T., and Moore, H. C.: "Disturbance in Dreams as Related to Peyotism among the Navaho," *Am. Anthr.*, LIX,4 (1957), pp. 642–9.

Du Bois, C.: "The 1870 Ghost Dance," *U. C. R.*, III,1 (1939).

Eckert, G.: "Zum Kult des Buciraco in Cartagena," *Z. f. E.*, LXXIX,1 (1954), pp. 118–20.

Eckert, G.: "Prophetentum und Freiheitsbewegungen im Caucatal," *Z. f. E.*, LXXVI (1951), pp. 115–25.

Fletcher, A. C.: "The Indian Messiah," *J. A. F.*, IV (1891), pp. 57–60.

Gayton, A. H.: "The Ghost Dance of 1870 in South-Central California," *U. C. P. A. E.*, XXVIII (1930), pp. 57–82.

Gunther, E.: "The Shaker Religion of the Northwest," in *Indians of the Urban Northwest*, edited by M. W. Smith (New York, 1949), pp. 37–76.

Gusinde, M.: "Der Peyote Kult, Entstehung und Verbreitung," in *Festschrift zum 50 Jahrigen Bestandsjubiläum des Missionshauses S. Gabriel* (Wien Mödling, 1939), pp. 401–99.

Heizer, R. F.: "A California Messianic Movement of 1801 among the Chumash," *Am. Anthr.*, XLIII,1 (1914), pp. 128–9.

Hill, W.: "The Navaho Indians and the Ghost Dance of 1890," *Am. Anthr.*, XLVI (1944), pp. 523 ff.

Hoebel, E. A.: "The Comanche Sun Dance and Messianic Outbreak of 1873," *Am. Anthr.*, XLIII,2 (1941), pp. 301–3.

Howard, J. A.: "The Mescal-Bean Cult of the Central and Southern Plains: an Ancestor of the Peyote Cult?" *Am. Anthr.*, LIX,1 (1957), pp. 75–87.

Kroeber, A. L.: *Anthropology* (London, 1948).

Kroeber, A. L.: "The Arapaho," *B. Nat. Hist.*, XVIII,4 (1907), pp. 398–410.

Kroeber, A. L.: "A Ghost Dance in California," *J. A. F.*, XVII (1904), pp. 32–5.

La Barre, W.: "Twenty Years of Peyote Studies," *Current Anthropology*, I,1 (1960), pp. 45–60.

La Barre, W., McAllester, D. P., Slotkin, J. S., Stewart, O. C., Tax, S.: "Statement on Peyote," *Science*, CXIV (1951), pp. 582–3.

La Barre, W.: "The Peyote-Cult," *Y. P. A.*, XIX (1938).

Lanternari, V.: "Nota su alcuni profetismi americani," *Riv. Antr.*, LXV (1958), pp. 242–8.

Lasswell, H. D.: "Collective Autism as a Consequence of Culture Contact: Notes on Religious Training and the Peyote Cult at Taos," *Z. f. S.*, IV (1935), pp. 232–47.

329

Bibliography

Lesser, A.: "Cultural Significance of the Ghost Dance," *Am. Anthr.*, XXXV (1933), pp. 108–15.

Lesser, A.: *The Pawnee Ghost Dance Hand Game* (New York, 1933).

Linton, R.: "Nativistic Movements," *Am. Anthr.*, XLV (1943), pp. 230–40.

Linton, R., ed.: *Acculturation in Seven American Indian Tribes* (New York, 1940).

Lowie, R. H.: "Le Messianisme primitif: contribution à un problème d'ethnologie," *Diogène*, XIX (1957), pp. 80–94.

Lowie, R. H.: *Primitive Religion* (New York, 1924).

Lowie, R. H.: "Peyote Rite," *Hasting's Encyclopaedia of Religions and Ethics* (Edinburgh, 1908-27), IV, pp. 735–6; IX, p. 815.

McGregor, G.: *Warriors without Weapons* (Chicago, 1946).

McLeod, W. C.: *The American Indian Frontier* (London, 1928).

Malouf, C.: "Gosiute Peyotism," *Am. Anthr.*, XLIV (1942), pp. 93–103.

Mason, B. S.: *Dances and Stories of the American Indian* (New York, 1944).

Merriam, A. P., and D'Azevedo, W. L.: "Washo Peyote Songs," *Am. Anthr.*, LIX,4 (1957), pp. 615–41.

Métraux, A.: "Les Messies de l'Amérique du Sud," *Arch. Soc. Rel.*, IV (1957), pp. 108–12.

Métraux, A.: "The Guarani," in *Handbook of South American Indians*, edited by J. H. Steward, Vol. III (Washington, 1948), pp. 69–94.

Métraux, A.: "The Tupinamba," in *Handbook of South American Indians*, pp. 95–133.

Métraux, A.: "A Quechua Messiah in Eastern Peru," *Am. Anthr.*, XLIV,1 (1942), pp. 721–5.

Métraux, A.: "Migrations historiques des Tupi-Guarani," *J. S. Am.*, XIX (1931), pp. 1–45.

Métraux, A.: *La religion des Tupinamba* (Paris, 1928).

Métraux, A.: "Les Hommes-Dieux chez les Chiriguano et dans l'Amérique du Sud," *Rev. Tucuman*, II (1913), pp. 61–91.

Mooney, J.: "The Ghost Dance and the Sioux Outbreak of 1890," *Rep. B. A. E.*, XIV (1892–93), 1896, Part II.

Morgan, Lewis H.: *League of the Ho-de-No Sau-Nee or Iroquois*, I–II (New York, 1901; New Haven, 1954).

Nash, P.: "The Place of Religious Revivalism in the Formation of the Intercultural Community on Klamath Reservation," in

Social Anthropology of North American Tribes (Chicago, 1955), pp. 377-444.

Nettl, B.: "Observations on Meaningless Peyote Song Texts," *J. A. F.*, LXVI (1953), pp. 161-4.

Newberne, R. E. L.: *Peyote* (Lawrence, 1955).

Newcomb, W. W., Jr.: *The Culture and Acculturation of the Delaware Indians* (Ann Arbor, 1956), pp. 113-15.

Newcomb, W. W., Jr.: "A Note on Cherokee-Delaware Pan-Indianism," *Am. Anthr.*, LVII (1955), pp. 104-45.

Nimuendajú, C.: *The Tukuna* (Berkeley, 1952).

Nimuendajú, C.: *Leyenda de la creación y juicio final del mundo como fundamento de la religión de los Apapokuva-Guarani* (São Paulo, 1944).

Nimuendajú, C.: "Die Sagen von der Erschaffung und Vernichtung der Welt als Grundlagen der Religion des Apapokuva-Guarani," *Z. f. E.*, XLVI (1914), pp. 287-399.

Opler, M. K.: "Fact and Fancy in Ute Peyotism," *Am. Anthr.*, XLIV (1942), 151-9.

Opler, M. K.: "The Character and History of the Southern Ute Peyote Rite," *Am. Anthr.*, XLII (1940), pp. 463-78.

Opler, M. K.: "The Southern Ute of Colorado," in *Acculturation in Seven American Indian Tribes*, edited by R. Linton (New York, 1940), pp. 119-203.

Opler, M. K.: "The Use of Peyote by the Carrizo and Lipan Apache Tribes," *Am. Anthr.*, XL,2 (1938), pp. 271-85.

Opler, M. K.: "The Influence of Aboriginal Pattern and White Contact on a Recently Introduced Ceremony, the Mescalero Peyote Cult," *J. A. F.*, XLIX (1936), pp. 143-66.

Parker, A.: "The Code of Handsome Lake, the Seneca prophet," *N. Y. Bull.*, CLXIII (1913).

Pereira de Queiroz, M. I.: "Autour du messianisme," *Prés. Afr.* (June-July 1958), pp. 72-6.

Pereira de Queiroz, M. I.: "Classification des messianismes brésiliens," *Arch. Soc. Rel.*, V (1958), pp. 111-20.

Pereira de Queiroz, M. I.: "Die Fanatiker des 'Contestado,' " *S. Jahrb.*, V (1957), pp. 213-15.

Pereira de Queiroz, M. I.: *La guerre sainte au Brésil: le mouvement messianique du "Conquestado"* (São Paulo, 1957).

Pereira de Queiroz, M. I.: "Messiasbewegungen in Brasilien," *S. Jahrb.*, IV (1956), pp. 133-44.

Bibliography

Petrullo, V.: "Peyotism as an Emergent Indian Culture," *Indians at Work*, VII,8 (1940), pp. 51–60.

Petrullo, V.: *The Diabolic Root: a Study of Peyotism, the New Indian Religion, among the Delawares* (Philadelphia, 1934).

Provinse, J.: "American Indian in Transition," *Am. Anthr.*, LVI (1954), pp. 387–94. Reprinted in Daniels: *American Indians* (1957), pp. 82–8.

Radin, P.: "The Religious Experiences of an American Indian (John Rave)," *E. Jahrb.*, XVIII (1950), pp. 249–90.

Radin, P.: *The Road of life and Death: a Ritual Drama of the American Indians*, Bollingen Series V (New York, 1945).

Radin, P.: *The Story of the American Indian* (New York, 1927; 3rd ed., 1944).

Radin, P.: "The Winnebago Tribe," *Rep. B. A. E.*, XXXVII (1915–16), 1923.

Radin, P.: *Crashing Thunder: the Autobiography of an American Indian* (New York, 1926); *U. C. P. A. E.*, XVI, 7 (1920).

Radin, P.: "A Sketch of the Peyote Cult of the Winnebago: a Study in Borrowing," *J. Rel. Psy.*, VII (1914), pp. 1–22.

Radin, P.: "Personal Reminiscences of a Winnebago Indian," *J. A. F.*, XXVI (1913).

Raroport, R. N.: "Changing Navaho Religious Values: a Study of Christian Missions to the Rimrock Navahos," *Pap. Peab.*, XLI, 2 (1954).

Ray, V.: "The Kolaskin Cult," *Am. Anthr.*, XXXVIII (1936), pp. 67–75.

Redfield, R.: *The Primitive World and Its Transformations* (Ithaca, 1953).

Richardson, R. N.: *The Comanche Barrier to South Plains Settlement* (Glendale, 1933).

Rigaud, A. M.: "Le Rôle du Vaudou dans l'indépendance d'Haïti," *Prés. Afr.* (February–March 1958), pp. 43–67.

Schaden, E.: *Ensaio etno-sociológico sóbre a mitología heroica de algumas tribos indigenas do Brasil*, LXI (1946).

Shonle, R.: "Peyote: the Giver of Visions," *Am Anthr.*, XXVII (1925), pp. 53–76.

Skinner, A.: Review of A. C. Parker's *The Code of Handsome Lake*, in *Am. Anthr.*, XVII (1915), pp. 180–4.

Simpson, G. E.: "Jamaican Revivalist Cults," *Soc. Ec. St.*, V,4 (1956), pp. 321–442.

Simpson, G. E.: "Political Cultism in West Kingston, Jamaica," *Soc. Ec. St.*, IV,2 (1955), pp. 133–49.

Slotkin, J. S.: "The Menomini Powwow," *Milw. Anthr.*, IV (1957).

Slotkin, J. S.: *The Peyote Religion: a Study in Indian-White Relations* (Glencoe, 1956).

Slotkin, J. S., "Peyotism 1521–1891," *Am. Anthr.*, LVII,2 (1955), pp. 202–30.

Smith, M.: "Shamanism in the Shaker Religion of Northwest America," *Man*, CLXXXI (1954).

Speck, F. G.: "Notes on the Life of John Wilson, the Revealer of Peyote, as Recalled by His Nephew, George Anderson," *G.M.H. Ch.*, XXXV (1933), pp. 539–56.

Spier, L.: "The Prophet Dance of the Northwest and Its Derivatives," *Gen. Ser. Anthr.*, I (1935).

Steward, J. H.: "Acculturation Studies in Latin America: Some Needs and Problems," *Am. Anthr.*, XLV,2 (1943), pp. 189–206.

Stewart, O. C.: "Southern Ute Adjustment to Modern Living," in *Acculturation in the Americas*, edited by S. Tax (Chicago, 1952), pp. 80–7.

Stewart, O. C.: "Washo-Northern Paiute Peyotism: a Study in Acculturation," *U.C.P.A.E.*, XL,3 (1944).

Stewart, O. C.: "The Southern Ute Peyote Cult," *Am. Anthr.*, XLIII,2 (1941), pp. 303–8.

Tentori, T., in R. Biasutti: *Razze e popoli della terra*, IV (Turin, 1957), p. 731.

Voget, F. W.: "The American Indian in Transition: Reformation and Accommodation," *Am. Anthr.*, LVIII,2 (1956), pp. 249–63.

Wagner, G.: "Entwicklung und Verbreitung des Peyote-Kultes," *Baessler Archiv*, XV (1932), pp. 59–141.

Wallace, A. F. C.: "Revitalization Movements," *Am. Anthr.*, LVIII,2 (1956), pp. 264–81.

Wallace, A. F. C.: "Handsome Lake and the Great Revival in the West," *Am. Q.* (Summer, 1952), pp. 149–65.

Wallis, W. D.: *Messiahs: Their Role in Civilization* (Washington, 1943).

Wax, M: "Les Pawnees à la recherche du paradis perdu," *Arch. Soc. Rel.*, IV (1957) pp. 113–22.

Zaehner, R. C.: *Mysticism* (Oxford, 1956).

Bibliography

MELANESIA

Abel, C. W.: *Savage Life in New Guinea* (London, 1902).

Belshaw, C. S.: "Recent History of Mekeo Society," *Oceania*, XX,1 (1951), pp. 4 ff.

Belshaw, C. S.: "The Significance of Modern Cults in Melanesian Development," *Austr. Outl.*, IV (1950), pp. 116–25.

Berndt, R. M.: "Reaction to Contact in the Eastern Highlands of New Guinea," *Oceania*, XXIV,3 (1954), pp. 190–228; XXIV,4 (1954), pp. 255–74.

Berndt, R. M.: "A Cargo Movement in the Eastern Central Highlands of New Guinea", *Oceania*, XXIII,1 (1952), pp. 40–65; 2 (1952), pp. 137–58; 3 (1953), pp. 202–34.

Bodrogi, T.: "Colonization and Religious Movements in Melanesia," *A.E.A. Sc. Hung.*, II (1951), pp. 259–90.

Bureau for Native Affairs, Netherlands New Guinea: "Anthropological Research in Netherlands New Guinea since 1950," *Oceania*, XXIX,2 (1958), pp. 132–63, especially p. 143.

Burridge, K. O.: "Cargo Activity in Tangu," *Oceania*, XXIV,4 (1954), pp. 241–54.

Cato, A. C.: "Disintegration, Syncretization and Change in Fijian Religion," *Mankind*, V,3 (1956), pp. 101–6.

Cato, A. C.: "A New Religious Cult in Fiji," *Oceania*, XVII,2 (1947), pp. 146 ff.

Chinnery, E. W. F., and Haddon, A. C.: "Five New Religious Cults in British New Guinea," *Hibbert Journal* (1917), pp. 458–60.

De Bruyn, J. V.: "De Mansren cultus der Biakkers," *T.T.L.V.K.*, LXXXIII,4 (1949), pp. 313–31; *South Pacific*, V,1, pp. 1–10.

Dupeyrat, A.: *Papouasie: histoire de la mission, 1885–1935* (Paris, 1935).

Eckert, G. "Prophetentum und Kulturwandel in Melanesien," *Baessler Archiv*, XXIII,1 (1940), pp. 26–41.

Eckert, G.: "Prophetentum in Melanesien," *Z.f.E.*, LXIX (1937), pp. 135–40.

Elkin, A. P.: *Social Anthropology in Melanesia* (London, 1953).

Firth, R.: "The Theory of Cargo Cult: a Note on Tikopia," *Man* (September 1955), p. 152.

Firth, R.: "Social Change in Western Pacific," *J. of the Royal Soc. of Arts*, CI, 1909 (October 1953), pp. 803–19.

334

Fison, L.: "The Nanga," *J.R.A.I.*, XIV (1884).

Fortune, R. F.: *Sorcerers of Dobu* (London, 1932).

Guiart, J.: *Grands et petits hommes de la montagne. Espiritu Sancto, Nouvelles Hébrides* (Paris, 1958), 2nd ed.

Guiart, J., and Worsley, P.: "La répartition des mouvements millénaristes en Mélanésie," *Arch. Soc. Rel.*, V (1958), pp. 38–46.

Guiart, J.: "Institutions religieuses traditionnelles et messianismes modernes à Fiji," *Arch. Soc. Rel.*, IV (1957), pp. 3–30.

Guiart, J.: *Un siècle et demi de contacts culturels à Tanna, Nouvelles Hébrides* (Paris, 1956).

Guiart, J.: "John Frum Movement in Tanna," *Oceania*, XXII,3 (1952), pp. 165–77.

Guiart, J.: "Forerunners of Melanesian nationalism," *Oceania*, XXII,2 (1951), pp. 81–90.

Guiart, J.: "Cargo Cult and Political Evolution in Melanesia," *Mankind*, IV,6 (1951), pp. 227–9.

Held, G. J.: *The Papuas of Waropen* (The Hague, 1957), pp. 317–21.

Höltker, G.: "Die Mambu Bewegung in Neu Guinea. Ein Beitrag zum Prophetentum in Melanesien," *Ann. Lat.*, V (1941), pp. 181–219.

Hogbin, H. I.: *Transformation Scene* (London, 1951).

Hogbin, H. I.: "Native Christianity in a New Guinea Village," *Oceania*, XVIII,1 (1947), pp. 1 ff.

Hogbin, H. I.: *Experiments in Civilization* (London, 1939).

Inglis, J.: "Cargo Cults: the Problem of Explanation," *Oceania*, XXVII,4 (1957), pp. 249–63.

Kamma, F. C.: "Messianic Movements in Western New Guinea," *Int. Rev. Miss.*, XVI (1952), pp. 148–60.

Kamma, F. C.: *De messiaanse Koréri-bewegingen in het Biaks-Noemfoorse cultuurgebied* (The Hague).

Kroef, J. M. van der: "Culture Contact and Culture Change in Western New Guinea," *Anthr. Q.*, XXXII,3 (1959), pp. 134–60.

Kroef, J. M. van der: "Racial Messiahs," in *Race, Individual and Collective Behavior*, edited by E. T. Thompson and E. C. Hughes (Glencoe, 1958), pp. 357–64.

Lanternari, V.: "Origini storiche dei culti profetici melanesiani," *S.M.S.R.*, XXVII (1956), pp. 31–86.

Lawrence, P.: "Cargo-Cult and Religious Beliefs among the Garia," *Int. A.E.* (1954), pp. 1–20.

Leeson, I.: "Bibliography of Cargo Cults and Other Nativistic Movements in the South Pacific," *South Pacific Commission Paper* (Sydney, 1952).

Lehmann, F. R.: "Prophetentum in der Südsee," Z.f.E., LXVI (1935), pp. 261 ff.

Lehmann, F. R.: *Prophetismus in der Südsee* (Christentum und Wissenschaft, 1934), pp. 68 ff.

Lewis, A. B.: *The Melanesians* (Chicago, 1945).

Lommel, A.: "Der 'Cargo-Cult' in Melanesien: ein Beitrag zur Problem der Europäisierung der Primitiven," Z.f.E., LXXVIII,1 (1953), pp. 17–63.

Mair, L. P.: *Australia in New Guinea* (London, 1949).

Mead, M.: *New Lives for Old: Cultural Transformation, Manus 1928–1953* (London, 1956).

Murray, G. H.: "The Vailala Madness," *Papua Report* 1919–20, pp. 116–18.

Nilles, J.: "The Kuman of the Chimbu Region, Central Highlands, New Guinea," *Oceania*, XXI,1 (1950), pp. 64–5.

O'Reilly, R. P. P.: "Prophétisme aux Nouvelles Hébrides: le mouvement Jonfrum à Tanna (1940–1947)," *Le Monde nonchrétien* (1949), pp. 192–208.

Poirier, J.: "Les mouvements de libération mythique aux Nouvelles Hébrides," *J. S. Oc.*, V,5 (1949).

Pos, H.: "The revolt of 'Manseren,'" *Am. Anthr.*, LII,4 (1950), pp. 561–4.

Raff, E.: Appendix, in F. E. Williams: *Orokaiva Magic*, pp. 100 ff.

Reay, M.: *The Kuma: Freedom and Conformity in the New Guinea Highlands* (London, 1959), pp. 194–207.

Rosenstiel, A.: "Long-term Planning: Its Importance in the Effective Administration of Social Change," *H.O.* (1954), pp. 5–10.

Stanner, W. E. H.: "On the Interpretation of Cargo-Cults," *Oceania*, XXIX,1 (1958), pp. 1–25.

Thomson, B. H.: *The Fijians* (London, 1908), pp. 140 ff.

Williams, F. E.: "Mission Influence in the Keveri District of Southeast Papua," *Oceania*, XV, 2 (1944), pp. 89 ff.

Williams, F. E.: "The Vailala Madness in Retrospect," in *Essays Presented to C. G. Seligman* (London, 1934), pp. 369–79.

Williams, F. E.: *Orokaiva Society* (Oxford, 1930).

Williams, F. E.: *Orokaiva Magic* (London, 1928).

Williams, F. E.: "The Vailala Madness and the Destruction of Native Ceremonies in the Gulf Division," *Anthr. Report*, IV (1923), pp. 1–72.

Worsley, P.: *The Trumpet Shall Sound: a Study of 'Cargo' Cults in Melanesia* (London, 1957).

POLYNESIA

Babbage, S. B.: *Hauhauism* (Dunedin, New Zealand, 1938).
Best, E.: *Tuhoe, the Children of the Mist*, I-II (New Plymouth, 1925).
Brewster, A. B.: *The Hill Tribes of Fiji* (London, 1922).
Brown, J. Macmillan: *Maori and Polynesian* (London, 1907).
Caillot, A. C. E.: *Les Polynésiens orientaux au contact de la civilisation* (Paris, 1909).
Freeman, J. D.: "The Joe Gimlet, or Siovili Cult: an Episode in the Religious History of Early Samoa," in *Anthropology in the South Seas*, edited by J. D. Freeman and W. R. Geddes (New Plymouth, 1959), pp. 185-98.
Greenwood, W.: "The Upraised Hand, or the Spiritual Significance of the Rise of the Ringatu Faith," *J.P.S.*, LI,1 (1942), pp. 1-81.
Jarves, J. J.: *History of the Hawaiian or Sandwich Islands* (London, 1843).
Keesing, F.: *The South Seas in the Modern World* (New York, 1941).
Keesing, F.: *Modern Samoa* (London, 1934).
Keesing, F.: "The Changing Maori," *Memoirs of the Board of Maori Ethnol. Research*, IV (1928).
Koskinen, A. A.: *Missionary Influence as a Political Factor in the Pacific Islands* (Helsinki, 1953).
Lanternari, V.: "Culti profetici polinesiani, *S.M.S.R.*, XXVIII,2 (1957), pp. 55-78.
Moerenhout, J. A.: *Voyages aux îles du Grand Océan*, I-II (Paris, 1837).
Mühlmann, W. E.: *Arioi und Mamaia* (Wiesbaden, 1955).
Pritchard, W. T.: *Polynesian Reminiscences, or Life in the South Pacific Islands* (London, 1866).
Sutherland, I. L. G.: *The Maori People To-day* (New York, 1940).
Te Rangi Hiroa (P. Buck): *The Coming of the Maori* (Wellington, 1952).
Thomson, B.: *The Fijians* (London, 1908).
Vaggioli, F.: *Storia della Nuova Zelanda*, I-II (Parma, 1896).
Waterhouse, J.: *The King and People of Fiji* (London, 1866).

337

Bibliography

Winks, R. W.: "The Doctrine of Hauhauism," *J.P.S.*, LXII,3 (1953), pp. 199–236.

ASIA AND INDONESIA

Abegg, E.: *Der Messiasglauben in Indien und Iran* (Berlin-Leipzig, 1928).

Berger, P. L.: "Motif messianique et processus social dans la Bahaïsme," *Arch. Soc. Rel.*, IV (1957), pp. 93–107.

Boardman, E. P.: *Christian Influence upon the Ideology of Taiping Rebellion* (Madison, 1952).

Darmesteter, J.: *Le Mahdi depuis les origines de l'Islam jusqu'à nos jours* (Paris, 1885).

Dunstheimer, G. G. H.: "Deux études sur les religions chinoises," *Arch. Soc. Rel.*, IV (1957), pp. 133–42.

Fall, B. B.: "The Political-Religious Sects of Viet-Nam," *P.A.*, XXVIII,3 (1955), pp. 235–53.

Gobineau, Comte de: *Religions et philosophies dans l'Asie Centrale* (Paris, 1st ed., 1865; 10th ed., 1957).

Gobron, G.: *Histoire et philosophie du Caodaïsme* (Paris, 1949).

Guariglia, G.: *Il messianismo russo* (Roma, 1956).

Kamma, F. C.: *De messiaanse Koréri-bewegingen in het Biaks-Noemfoorse cultuurgebied* (The Hague).

Kennedy, R.: "Acculturation and Administration in Indonesia," *Am. Anthr.*, XLV,2 (1943), pp. 185–92.

Kovalevsky, P.: "Messianisme et millénarisme russe?" *Arch. Soc. Rel.*, V (1958), pp. 47–70.

Krader, L.: "A Nativistic Movement in Western Siberia," *Am. Anthr.*, LVIII,2 (1956), pp. 282–92.

Kroef, J. van der: "Culture Contact and Culture Conflict in Western New Guinea," *Anthr. Q.*, XXXII,3 (1959), pp. 134–60.

Kroef, J. van der: "The Messiah in Indonesia and Melanesia," *Scientific Monthly*, LXXV (1952), pp. 161–65.

Lindgren, E. J.: "An Example of Culture Contact without Conflict: Reindeer Tungus and Cossacks of Northwestern Manchuria," *Am. Anthr.*, XL,4 (1938), pp. 605–21.

Nguyen Tran Huan: "Histoire d'une secte religieuse au Viet-Nam: le Caodaïsme," *Revue de synthèse*, July-December 1958 (1959), pp. 265–81.

Oguchi, I.: "Authoritarianism in Japanese Religion," *Religion East and West* (Tokyo), I (1955), pp. 10–15.

Olson, R.: "A New Messianic Cult in Japan," *Kroeber Anthropological Society Papers* (Berkeley), VIII,9 (1953), pp. 78–81.

Phelan, J. L.: *The Hispanization of the Philippines* (Madison, 1959).

Robertson, J. A.: "The Aglipay Schism in the Philippines," *Cath. Hist. Rev.*, IV,3 (1918), pp. 315–44.

Rowley, H. H.: *Prophecy and Religion in Ancient China and Israel* (London, 1956).

Sebeok, T. A., and Ingemann, F. J.: "Studies in Cheremis: the Supernatural," *Viking Fund Publications in Anthropology* (New York), XXII (1956).

Smith, M. W.: "Synthesis and Other Processes in Sikhism," *Am. Anthr.*, L,1 (1948), pp. 457–62.

Straelen, H. van: *The Religion of the Divine Wisdom: Japan's Most Powerful Religious Movement (Tenrikyō)* (Kyoto, 1957).

Straelen, H. van: "Un messianisme japonais contemporain," *Arch. Soc. Rel.*, IV (1957), pp. 123–32.

Tac Pham, C.: *Le Caodaïsme-Phap-Chanh-Truyen* (Paris, 1953).

Wertheim, W. F.: *Indonesian Society in Transition* (The Hague, 1956).

Wulfften, Palthe P. M. van: *Psychological Aspects of the Indonesian Problem* (Leiden, 1949).

ABBREVIATIONS

A.E.A. Sc. Hung.	= Acta Ethnographica Academiae Scientiarum Hungaricae (Budapest)
Am. Anthr.	= American Anthropologist (Menasha)
Am. Soc. Rev.	= American Sociological Review (New York)
Am. Q.	= American Quarterly (Philadelphia)
Ann. Amer. Acad.	= Annals of the American Academy of Political and Social Sciences (Philadelphia)
Ann. Lat.	= Annali Lateranensi (Vatican City)
Anthr. Pap.	= Anthropological Papers, Museum of Anthropology, University of Michigan (Ann Arbor)
Anthr. Pap. Amer. Mus. Nat. Hist.	= Anthropological Papers, American Museum of Natural History
Anthr. Q.	= Anthropological Quarterly (Washington)
Anthr. Ser.	= Anthropological Series
Arch. Soc. Rel.	= Archives de Sociologie des Religions (Paris)
Austr. Outl.	= Australian Outlook (Melbourne)
B. B. Amer. Ethn.	= Bulletin, Bureau of American Ethnology (Washington)
B. Nat. Hist.	= Bulletin, American Museum of Natural History (New York)
Bol. C. L.	= Boletim, Facultade de Filosofia, Ciencias e Letras, Univ. São Paulo (São Paulo)
Bull. Milw.	= Bulletin of the Public Museum of the City of Milwaukee (Milwaukee)
Cah. Int. Soc.	= Cahiers Internationaux de Sociologie (Paris)
Cath. Hist. Rev.	= Catholic Historical Review (Washington)
C. R. Acad.	= Comptes Rendus, Académie des Sciences Coloniales (Paris)
E. Jahrb.	= Eranos Jahrbuch (Zurich)
Gen. Ser. Anthr.	= General Series of Anthropology (Menasha)

Abbreviations

H.O.	= Human Organization (New York)
Int. A. E.	= International Archives of Ethnography (Leiden)
Int. Rev. Miss.	= International Review of Missions (London)
J.A.F.	= Journal of American Folklore (Philadelphia)
J. Anthr. Soc.	= Journal of the Anthropological Society (London)
J.P.S.	= Journal of the Polynesian Society (Wellington)
J.R.A.I.	= Journal of the Royal Anthropological Institute of Great Britain and Ireland (London)
J. S. Am.	= Journal de la Société des Américanistes (Paris)
J. S. Oc.	= Journal de la Société des Océanistes (Paris)
Milw. Anthr.	= Public Museum of Milwaukee, Publications in Anthropology (Milwaukee)
N. Y. Bull.	= New York State Museum Bulletin (Albany)
P.A.	= Pacific Affairs (New York)
Pap. Peab.	= Papers, Peabody Museum of American Archaeology and Ethnology (Cambridge, Mass.)
Prés. Afr.	= Présence Africaine (Paris)
Rech. Int. Marx.	= Recherches Internationales à la lumière du Marxisme (Paris)
Rep. B.A.E.	= Annual Report, Bureau of American Ethnology (Washington)
Rev. Inst. Soc.	= Revue de l'Institut de Sociologie (Brussels)
Rev. Tucumán	= Revista, Instituto de Etnología, Universidad Nacional Tucumán (Tucumán)
Riv. Antr.	= Rivista di Antropologia (Rome)
S. Jahrb.	= Staden Jahrbuch (São Paulo)
S.M.S.R.	= Studi e Materiali di Storia delle Religioni (Rome)
Soc. Ec. St.	= Social and Economic Studies (Kingston, Jamaica)

South. J.	= Southwestern Journal of Anthropology (Albuquerque)
Trans. N. Y. Acad.	= Transactions of the New York Academy of Sciences (New York)
T.T.L.V.K.	= Tijdschrift voor Ind. Taal-, Land- en Volkenkunde (Djakarta)
U.C.P.A.E.	= University of California Publications in American Archaeology and Ethnology (Berkeley)
U.C.R.	= University of California Anthropological Records (Berkeley)
V.F.P.A.	= Viking Fund Publications in Anthropology (New York)
Y.P.A.	= Yale University Publications in Anthropology (New Haven)
Z.f.E.	= Zeitschrift für Ethnologie (Braunschweig)

343

INDEX

i

Index

Beyioku, A. E., 50

Bible, 5, 13, 26, 29, 51, 57, 118, 165, 307, 315, 316; and Ethiopian Church, 32, 42; and African messianic cults, 42–3; in Peyote cult, 71, 73, 78, 92; Shakers' rejection of, 147; and Tafarism, 162, 163; read by Te-Kooti, 257; *see also* New Testament, Old Testament

Bible Students (Jamaica), 164

Big Bill, 148

Big Moon Peyote cult, 71–3, 80, 93

Black Buffalo (Indian), 155

Black Wolf (Indian), 72

Boki, Governor, 244–5

Bole Maru cult, 114, 136, 137

Bonzo, Zaccharias, 23

Booth, Joseph, 44

Borneo, 269

Brant, Joseph, 116

Brazil: Candomblé in, 164, 185, 186; Takunas in, 169–71; Tupi-Guarani in, 171–81, 310, 313; Negroes in, 185, 186; new messianic movements in, 185–95; *beatos* in, 190, 191, 192

Buciraco (god), 182

Buddha, 272, 275, 281

Buddhism, 268, 270, 272, 276, 285, 286, 295, 306; and Phat Thay Tay An, 274–5; Shinto, 280; in Japan, 280, 281, 282; Mahayana, 281; in China, 293n.; Hinayana, 297, 298; in Burma and Thailand, 297, 298

Buka (Solomon Islands), 206

Bullboek massacre, 35

Buninia, 199, 201

Bureau of Indian Affairs, United States, 105, 107

Burkhan cult, 285, 286–7

Burma, 297, 298

Bushir, 30

Bwanga, 9

Bwiti cult, 54

Caddoan Indians, 68, 70, 141

Camargo, João de, 185

Cameroons, 52, 56

Campa Indians, 182, 183, 184

Candomblé cult, 164, 185, 186

cannibalism, ritual, 238

Canudos movement, 188, 190, 193, 313

Cao Dai movement, 270, 271–3, 276, 277, 299

Cape Possession, 208

Cargo cult, 202–13, 216–17, 229, 230, 317

Cayuga Indians, 115, 120

Celebes, 269

Celestial Christians (West Africa), 45–6

Central Africa, 9, 29, 44

Central America, 158

Chehali Indians, 149

Cheremis, 288, 291, 299, 321

Cherokee Indians, 112

Cheyenne Indians, 92, 151, 153, 155

Chichimeca Indians, 67

Chieu, Nguyen Van, 271, 272

Chilembwe, John, 35, 44–5

chiliastic myth, 303

China, 291–7, 299, 313

Chinnery, E. W. P., 199

Chippewa Indians, 142, 144

Chiriguano Indians, 178

Chot Chelpan, 285, 286

Christ, Jesus, 13, 29–30, 42, 45, 50, 51, 147, 190, 229, 272, 307, 308; Kimbangu as, 13; Matswa as, 15; Shembe as, 41; and Peyote cult, 69, 70, 71, 78, 87, 89, 91, 112, 113; as Fatherless Boy, among Cayuga, 120; in Polynesian cults, 241, 242, 243; in Hapu cult, 245; and Great Candle cult, 290

Christian Aglipay Church, 279

Christian Catholic Apostolic Church, 36–7

iii

Index

de las Reyes, Isabelo, 279
Delaware Indians, 72, 79, 80, 95, 98, 112, 124
Dieudonné movement, 23, 24
Diponegoro, Prince, 266
Divine Doctrine (Mioshi movement), 281-2, 284
Dowie, John Alexander, 37
Dream Dance, 130, 136, 142-5, 303, 321
Dreamers, cult of, 114, 128-31, 133, 138
Durban (South Africa), 7
Dwane, M., 33
Dyei (Creator), 170

Earth Lodge cult, 114, 134-8
Église, doctrine of, 25-8
Egypt, 33
Ekklesia, defined, 43
Ekuphakameni, Nazarene church at, 40
Elk Hair (Indian), 79-80, 81, 82, 84, 96
Elkin, A. P., 212, 226, 317
endogenous messianic movements, 310, 312, 314
Epikilipikili, 9
Equatorial Africa, 3, 7-8, 10, 28
Erlik (devil), 286
escapism, religious, 314-5, 316
Espíritu Santo (New Hebrides), 205
Essenes, 311
Ethiopia, 32, 161, 162
Ethiopian Church, 31, 32, 33, 39, 42
Ethiopian Order, 33
Eucharist, 41, 73, 88, 119
Exile, Prophets of the, 311, 312

Fatherless Boy, 120
Feast of the Harvest and of the Dead, 214

Febronio, 195
Federation of Northwestern Indian Tribes, 126
Federation of the Indians of America, 105
Festival of the Green Corn, 119
fetishism: defined, 8-9; in Africa, 9, 13, 21, 52, 61; in Haiti, 166
Fiji Islands, 211, 216, 237-8, 317, 318
Firth, Raymond, 209, 235
Fison, Lorimer, 317
Five Nations, 115; see also Iroquois
Frum, John, 209, 210

Gai'wiio, 115-23
Garvey, Marcus, 30, 160, 161
George, Doctor (shaman), 136
Ghana, 52
Ghost Dance, 63, 69, 70, 82, 86, 110, 114, 135, 307, 310; rebellion inspired by, 87, 108, 109; forerunners of, 123-7; early (1870), 131-134; Earth Lodge cult derived from, 134; hand game introduced into, 137-8; of 1890, 151-7
Ghost Shirt, 153
God: Judeo-Christian, 61, 113; in Peyote theology, 89, 90, 113; Polynesian belief in one true, 239, 260; see also Supreme Being
Gold Coast, 52, 60
"Good Message," 115-23
Great Awakening (Jamaica), 159
Great Candle (Kugu Sorta) cult, 288-91, 299, 306, 321
Great Spirit, 77, 90, 91, 96, 99, 109, 117-20 *pass.*, 124-28 *pass.*, 132, 141, 143, 144, 154, 303
Griffin, Victor, 72
Guarani Indians, 178-9
Guiravera, 179-80
Gusinde, Martin, 104

v

Index

Index

Index

Index

A Note about the Author

Vittorio Lanternari is professor of the History of Religions at the University of Bari and a lecturer in Ethnology at the University of Rome. He was born in 1918 and received his degree in History of Religions from the University of Rome.

Professor Lanternari belongs to an increasingly prominent group of Italian scholars in the field of religious science who represent the historical approach established by Benedetto Croce and Raffaele Pettazzoni. In their study of religious events, Lanternari and other scholars chiefly attached to the Universities of Rome, Cagliari, and Bari tend to find a synthesis between the historical and the phenomenological aspects of religion. In this light, they view religious life as one particular facet of civilization rather than as an independent and self-sufficient manifestation of life.

Professor Lanternari's published works include a historical monograph entitled *La grande festa: storia del Capodanno nelle civiltà primitive* and several essays in various Italian scholarly journals. This book is his first work to appear in English translation.

January 1963

A Note on the Type

THE TEXT of this book was set on the Linotype in JANSON, a recutting made direct from type cast from matrices long thought to have been made by the Dutchman Anton Janson, who was a practicing type founder in Leipzig during the years 1668–87. However, it has been conclusively demonstrated that these types are actually the work of Nicholas Kis (1650–1702), a Hungarian, who most probably learned his trade from the master Dutch type founder Dirk Voskens. The type is an excellent example of the influential and sturdy Dutch types that prevailed in England up to the time William Caslon developed his own incomparable designs from these Dutch faces.

Composed, printed, and bound by
The Haddon Craftsmen, Inc., Scranton, Pa.
Typography and binding design by
VINCENT TORRE